NARRATIVE
AFTER
DECONSTRUCTION

daniel punday

STATE UNIVERSITY OF NEW YORK PRESS

Published by
State University of New York Press, Albany

For information, address State University of New York Press,
90 State Street, Suite 700, Albany, NY 12207

Production by Judith Block
Marketing by Patrick Durocher
Composition by Doric Lay Publishers

Library of Congress Cataloging-in-Publication Data

Punday, Daniel.
    Narrative after deconstruction / Daniel Punday.
        p. cm.
    Includes bibliographical references and index.
    ISBN 0-7914-5571-8 (HC : alk. paper) — ISBN 0-7914-5572-6 (PB : alk. paper)
        1. Narration (Rhetoric). 2. Deconstruction. 3. Postmodernism (Literature).
    I. Title.

PN212 .P86 2002
808—dc21

                                    2002017744

10 9 8 7 6 5 4 3 2 1

NARRATIVE
AFTER
DECONSTRUCTION

contents

———◆———

preface

Narrative after Deconstruction. How should we understand the word *after* in this title? Narrative as informed by deconstruction? *In the wake of* deconstruction? Or is it rather narrative as an alternative to deconstruction? Narrative *instead of* deconstruction? Or, perhaps, narrative in the style of deconstruction? Narrative *as* deconstruction?

To narrate the movement from deconstruction to narrative is to adopt the very style that this book will analyze. But more than this, such a narration raises the question of temporality that is central to the deconstructive project from the outset. Most American critics were introduced to deconstruction through Jacques Derrida's book *Of Grammatology* (trans. 1976), a work that puzzled novices and confounded critics with the apparently contradictory temporality of "writing before the letter." Derrida's own intellectual roots are firmly embedded in phenomenology and in the interest in time consciousness, a concern that is manifest in his first work on Edmund Husserl. A penchant for perverse temporality is one of the things that the frequently divergent Derridian and de Manian camps of deconstruction always shared.[1]

So to suggest that critics have simply moved "beyond" deconstruction to narrative, or to speak even about narrative as constructed "after" the popularity of deconstruction, seems fundamentally unfair to deconstruction's own rich understanding of time. And yet to examine Derrida's own writing over the last decade is to be struck by precisely some sort of change in style and emphasis. His work has moved away from an early concern with semiotics and language and a later commitment to developing a formally experimental writing style, toward a type of writing that can only be described as narrative in its basic concerns.[2] Derrida's most recent work—books on Marxism, mourning and death, and the archive all come to mind—has circulated around issues of futurity and responsibility to the past. A recent collection of essays by and about Derrida entitled *Futures: Of Jacques Derrida* edited by Richard Rand nicely encapsulates the emphasis of this newer work. This interest in the relation between past, present, and future may have been implicit within Derrida's earlier writing, but the concern has come to dominate his recent work. Whether Derrida's recent writing is consistent with his earlier work or not, it is difficult to argue that there has not been some kind of shift in emphasis in his style of inquiry and in the types of concerns that provide the occasion for his writing.

And yet, to suggest that Derrida is no longer doing deconstruction, that the movement from deconstruction as it has been conceived in the past toward something that is more narrative means that he has rejected deconstruction is likewise wrong. Indeed, the complex transformation from one thing into another that may have "always already" been implicit within the former is both inherent to the deconstructive project from the outset, and the particular subject of Derrida's recent work. The clearest articulation of Derrida's recent interest in a kind of narrative of change is, I think, his book on the future of Europe, *The Other Heading* (1991). Derrida's discussion is occasioned by a colloquium on "European Cultural Identity" in 1990, but more broadly reflects a concern at the beginning of the 1990s about the breakup of cold-war animosities and alliances, and the ethnic nationalism that seemed to replace them. The question that faces Derrida is the future of European identity: "Must they [Europeans] re-begin? Or must they *depart* from Europe, separate themselves from an old Europe? Or else depart again, set out toward a Europe that does not yet exist? Or else re-embark in order to return to a Europe of origins that would then need to be restored, rediscovered, or reconstituted, during a great celebration of 'reunion'" (8). The question that most strongly confronts Derrida is the question of newness and its relation to the past. To describe the "new Europe" is in part to describe something implicit within European cultural traditions, which was always part of its "heading," the direction of its development. At the same time, however, Derrida is interested in the other potentials that are contained within that tradition, the possibilities of newness and of some "other heading." As Derrida writes, "But history also presupposes that the heading not be *given*, that it not be identifiable in advance and once and for all. The irruption of the new, the unicity of the other *today* should be awaited *as such* . . . it should be anticipated as the unforeseeable, the *unanticipatable*, the non-identifiable, in short, as that of which one does not yet have a memory" (18).

It is easy to see in *The Other Heading* how much Derrida's own recent work anticipates the question of narrative after deconstruction. In asking how the new Europe can be both part of a cultural tradition and "unanticipatable," Derrida invokes the question suspended within the title of this book: how can narrative come out of and also break from deconstruction? The mechanism of this complex temporality is more explicit within another of Derrida's recent books, *Archive Fever* (1995). Like *The Other Heading*, this book examines the relationship between futurity and a sense of past or tradition. Here this tradition is formulated more explicitly and in greater detail as the archive, the collection of materials and texts that have a special relationship to future scholarship. Derrida writes, "The archive has always been a *pledge*, and like every pledge, a token of the future. To put it more trivially: what is no longer archived in the same way is no longer lived in the same way" (18). For Derrida the founding of an archive is both this sort of pledge and at the same time an act of violence necessary to mark off the newness of an "unanticipatable" future. Specifically, this means the death of the individual whose materials furnish the archive: "the archive is made possible by the death, aggression, and destruction drive, that is to say also by originary finitude and expropriation" (94). Death provides the archive, and the founding of the archive in turn involves killing its source. Drawing on the Freudian context of the archive he is discussing, Derrida formulates this violence in terms of patricide discussed in *Totem and Taboo:* "It amounts to a repressed or suppressed parricide, in the name of the father as dead father. The archontic is at best the takeover of the archive by the brothers. The equality and the liberty of brothers. A certain, still vivacious idea of democracy" (95).

As Derrida's discussion of the archive makes clear, defining "another heading," a departure from the past, involves projecting back, into the past, a sense of origin that kills the object that is taken to authorize it. And this is true even when the spirit that results is "democratic" and institutionalized around a shared interest in the archival source. The same may well be said of what I will describe in this book as "post-deconstructive" criticism and its use of narrative. It is a mode of writing that takes its "heading" from deconstruction and that develops naturally out of the traditions and assumptions contained within that mode of thought. At the same time, however, this criticism marks itself off from deconstruction by projecting back into that "earlier" movement qualities that effectively kill it, defining it as past and as an origin from which a new mode of thinking can depart. To understand this "new" writing, this narrative after deconstruction, we need both to appreciate its continuities with deconstruction and to recognize the effort that it exerts to create the discontinuities that constitute it as a mode of thinking in its own right. To ask, ultimately, whether narrative after deconstruction isn't really simply more deconstruction is to miss the point. We must not allow ourselves to essentialize deconstruction into a theory that can never be archived; we must not be blind to the paradoxical working of deconstructive temporality even within the narratives that we construct about deconstruction itself.

Narrative after Deconstruction attempts, then, to walk a careful path between wholeheartedly embracing the rhetoric that defines deconstruction as a movement past and rejected, and a critical appraisal that insists that all criticism that follows from, and attempts to be true to, deconstruction must in turn itself be deconstruction. Chapter 1 begins with the voice of the former, as I summarize and discuss claims by critics who turn to narrative as a way of rejecting or moving beyond deconstruction. Chapter 2 turns back to deconstruction in general and to Derrida's writing in particular, as I search for the seeds of post-deconstructive criticism within deconstruction itself. Having established this complex relationship between deconstruction and post-deconstructive narrative, the remainder of the book examines the particular modes of textual construction that result from this "new" form of criticism and writing. Postmodernist fiction, with its commitment to self-reflexivity in the context of storytelling (introduced in chapter 3) provides examples throughout of how the abstract claims about interpretation after deconstruction translate into ways of constructing texts. Discussions of narrative space (chapter 4) and time (chapter 6) are interspersed with reflections on the limits of the textual model that I develop (chapters 5 and 7), and with consideration of the implications of this model for subjectivity and ethics (chapter 8). In the end, I hope to have described criticism and writing poised at a moment between deconstruction and some "other heading," a moment at which we set out for some "unanticipatable" future by doing a certain violence to the deconstruction that is its origin.

I have many people to thank for the development of this project. Kit Hume has been a tireless reader of the manuscript from its earliest version as a dissertation through the final revisions for publication. Jeff Nealon likewise read through many versions of this manuscript, and was essential in helping me to transform what started as a formalist study of postmodern worlds into a more timely engagement with deconstruction and materiality. Other readers have contributed to the project by reading the manuscript and offering suggestions, including Kate Cummings, Raymond Federman, Ann Kibbey, Brian McHale, Jim Phelan, Peter Rabinowitz, Sanford Schwartz, Joe Tabbi, and the late Salim Kemal. My thanks as well to the anonymous reviewers for State University of New York Press. Two of the chapters were developed first as journal articles. Chapter 2 was published in a somewhat earlier form in *Postmodern Culture* 11.1 (September 2000) as "Derrida in the World: Space and Post-deconstructive Textual Analysis"; part of chapter 6 appeared in *Genders* 27 (1998) as "The Local Site and Materiality: Kathy Acker's *Empire of the Senseless*." I would like, finally, to express my gratitude to Carol and Sam, both of whom in different ways supported me during the long process of writing and revising this manuscript. My thanks to them for the other headings and futures that they have given me.

chapter one

THE NARRATIVE TURN

Deconstruction and Narrative

In the last decade literary and cultural critics have increasingly turned toward the language of narrative and storytelling to describe the act of assigning meaning to some object or textual feature. Hayden White's once-controversial claim that historiography is a form of narration that is as much concerned with formal closure and generic expectations (expectations of "cohesion") as it is with its "correspondence" to historical fact (*Tropics* 66) has now been extended to many other fields. It has become commonplace to see the analysis of literature as relying on literary histories that are always constructions with their own tendency to create entities such as "American Literature" for their own strategic purposes (McHale, *Constructing* 1). In contrast to White's early assumption that the hard sciences are the antithesis of narration (*Tropics* 30), Donna J. Haraway has mounted a feminist critique of the biological sciences by revealing the operation of "fictive strategies" and "allowable stories" within primatology (85). Perhaps more thoroughly than any of these, postcolonial criticism has associated "nations" and "narration"—claiming that the "social" is entwined with the narratives that members of a society tell about themselves—in its attempt to reveal imperialism and its alternatives in diverse cultural products (Bhabha, *Nation*). In these instances, narrative is equated with the production of historical, literary, cultural, and even scientific knowledge.

Narrative seems to appeal to critics today as an alternative to deconstructive language of textual deferral, slippage, and indeterminacy. Indeed, to refer to narrative as a "turn" from deconstruction is itself an ironic echo of the revolution that deconstruction brought to historical and literary studies two decades ago. An endless spate of books and articles trumpeted the "linguistic turn" that deconstruction was supposed to have introduced into the humanities—a turn that included narrative, ironically, as one form of the deconstructive interest in language.[1] We cannot understand what critics mean when they appeal to narrative in contemporary criticism without recognizing narrative's ambiguous relationship to deconstruction. Although some have suggested that narrative may be part of our basic phenomenological perception of the world (Kerby), in contemporary criticism narrative usually describes knowledge organized through language. Deconstruction has provided the most elaborate theory of how language influences understanding, but critics have seen the infinite textual unraveling of *différance* as a dead end incapable of justifying the need to write and to deconstruct. Like deconstructionists, critics who describe knowledge as a "narrative" are suspicious of claims to objectivity. As Christopher Norris notes, the popularity of describing knowledge as a narrative construction "mostly goes along with a marked reaction against the kinds of wholesale explanatory theory which would seek to transcend their own special context or localized conditions of cultural production" (*Contest* 21). Narrative, however, is a much less threatening model for language's influence on knowledge than the deconstructionist idea that "there is nothing outside of the text." A narrative, after all, usually has a narrator who can take responsibility for the narratives he or she constructs. While describing oneself as a "narrator" admits that one's conclusions are interested, by confessing this bias a writer can indirectly *increase* the ethical force of his or her claims. This paradoxical claim to legitimacy at work within contemporary criticism is noted well by John McGowan in his critique of Edward W. Said. In turning to the deconstructionist language of "otherness" Said returns to a traditional humanism, according to McGowan. We have not recognized, McGowan claims,

> how parasitic the whole concept of an other is on liberal traditions of individualism. To put it another way, to imagine the other as distant and separate is profoundly undialectical. The poststructuralist skepticism about claims made for and about the existence of otherness stems from an acute awareness that the other participates in a relationship that defines him as other. The very notion that otherness affords some kind of purity or freedom rests on an assumption of self-sufficiency, of an identity forged in the absence of social ties. (175)

This valorization of otherness helps to produce an image of the critic as capable of recognizing and admitting one's own bias; the result, according to McGowan, is a contradictory image of the contemporary intellectual as free precisely by virtue of admitting one's place within poststructuralist representational and metaphysical systems. McGowan writes, "Said, like much of the left, wants to maintain a firmer distinction between oppressors and oppressed than poststructuralist theory, with its extremely sensitive notions of appropriation and complicity, would allow. Said posits a version of the postmodern monolith insofar as he finds that worldliness and interest delegitimate all existing social forms and that all cultures have enormous powers of 'identity-enforcement,' but he also claims a heroic disentanglement from such determinants for the critic" (173). In contrast to Andrew Ross's conclusion that postmodernist criticism rejects the "universal intellectual" (Introduction xiii), Said's attitude seems to reflect that of the traditional, humanist literary critic, historian, or social scientist. Precisely this contradiction is at work within the rhetoric of narration in contemporary criticism. Calling one's writing a "narrative" and confessing to being a "narrator" with particular interests and subject to certain formal constraints seems to recognize a real-world multiplicity (and the "otherness" oppressed by prior writing) that readers are asked likewise to accept. In claiming that all knowledge is a narrative construction, literary, social, and cultural critics seem to regain from deconstruction a sense of the value of research and interpretation.[2] Whether these critics are right in their assessment of the limitations of deconstruction—and we will see in chapter 2 that deconstruction's relationship to the world and to the criticism that comes after it is considerably more complex than these comments suggest—this critique has provided the impetus to rethink critical practice.

The apparent contradictions that McGowan observes in Said's writing underlie current arguments about narrative after deconstruction. The debate over the value of this narrative model for knowledge is particularly clear in contemporary feminism, which has been both attracted and repelled by deconstruction. Feminism has been accused of essentialism more than most forms of social criticism, and has tried to come to terms with deconstruction's claim that even a well-intentioned critique of patriarchy is a textual construction. To many feminists, describing knowledge as narrative is no improvement on deconstruction, since both foster skepticism toward the theoretical concepts necessary for the critique of social inequalities. Seyla Benhabib asserts the need for concepts such as "victim" and "oppression" in feminist criticism:

> While it is no longer possible or desirable to produce "grand narratives of history," the "death of history" thesis [i.e., poststructuralism] occludes the epistemological interest in history and in historical narrative which accompany the aspirations of all struggling historical actors. Once this "interest" in recovering the lives and struggles of those "losers" and "victims" of history is lost, can we produce engaged feminist theory? ("Feminism" 23)

Like many feminists, Benhabib is clearly ambivalent about equating narrative and knowledge. Although describing conventional knowledge as a narrative can question traditional values that exclude some individuals and groups, the logical and ethical force of any consequent call for social change is weakened when we admit that those calls likewise depend on narratives. Why should we act on knowledge that is "just a story"? This question haunts contemporary criticism concerned with social change; as Jane Flax remarks, "If there is no objective basis for distinguishing between true and false beliefs, then it seems that power alone will determine the outcome of competing truth claims. This is a frightening prospect for those who lack (or are oppressed by) the power of others" (42). Although the narrative model describes how critics write in a social context, theorists have not been able to explain why knowledge produced through narratives should be more compelling than knowledge produced through a play of *différance*. This is the mystery of post-deconstructive interest in narrative—how narrative can be reinterpreted as a mode of textual construction that straddles the line between language and real-world responsibilities, between textual forms and the writer's political and social location.

The task of this book is to explain why narrative has reappeared as a way of speaking about textual construction after deconstruction and how narrative can be deployed to address the interaction between text and world. In referring to post-deconstructive narrative, I mean just this—narrative that is aware of, and anxious about, deconstruction. Post-deconstructive criticism is defined by its departure from deconstruction—even though, as I will argue in chapter 2, that departure is incomplete and in fact based in part on a self-interested misreading of deconstruction. This is not to claim that all narrative today has a single style or that recent narrative is always motivated by deconstruction; instead I explore how narrative is being re-created by a variety of contemporary critics as a way of thinking about the textual issues raised by deconstruction. In approaching narrative in this way, I am obviously departing significantly from the various ways in which we usually think of narrative—as a particular type of manipulation of narrators and narratees, as the human negotiation of temporality, and so on.[3] The task of this chapter is to sketch out the scope of the term *narrative* in this post-deconstructive context.

Narrative Totality and Narrative Openness

Narrative has elicited an ambivalent response as a model for knowing because critics often use the term *narrative* to refer to two interrelated but distinct qualities of discourse. On the one hand, narrative implies totality and seamlessness; on the other hand, narrative suggests a more open-ended and tentative form of discourse in which the role of the writer is evident. The struggle between these two qualities in the current "narrative turn" is particularly clear in the work of Jean-François Lyotard. Lyotard's well-known characterization of postmodernity as "the incredulity toward metanarratives" (*Postmodern* xxiv) distinguishes two ways of giving authority to discursive knowledge: the traditional authority granted by metanarratives and the more limited authority of language games. Metanarratives are sweeping "stories" in which knowledge claims are given significance and made to seem natural. The "narrative of freedom," for example, was the means by which scientific knowledge rightfully freed itself from "priests and tyrants" by claiming that "all peoples have a right to science" (31). Language games, conversely, depend on discursive rules that are capable of change and that grant authority to knowledge claims only in limited ways. Can some narratives be open-ended like language games, or does narrative by its nature incline toward the sweeping totality of metanarratives? Although narrative draws attention to the poles of communication in the same way that language games do,[4] Lyotard answers this question in different, even contradictory ways. In *The Postmodern Condition* Lyotard assaults "metanarratives" and calls for "local knowledge" based on language games: "any consensus on the rules defining a game and the 'moves' playable within it *must* be local, in other words, agreed on by its present players and subject to eventual cancellation. The orientation then favors a multiplicity of finite meta-arguments, by which I mean argumentation that concerns metaprescriptives and is limited in time and space" (66). In this work, language games remain open and subject to change ("local"), and can achieve this openness only by renouncing metanarrative claims to universal legitimacy. Although Lyotard discusses "little narratives" that are not metanarratives in this early work (60), narrative by its nature seems to resist challenge. In *The Postmodern Condition*, then, Lyotard thinks of narrative primarily as creating wholes and less as revealing the role of a "narrator." Lyotard's *Instructions païennes*, a work roughly contemporary with *The Postmodern Condition*, in contrast sees narrative as more open and not inherently totalizing. Cecile Lindsay summarizes how Lyotard defines narrative as the "stuff" of culture and as the core of language games in this work: "The referents of a narrative are never events or brute facts in themselves, but rather other narratives. A multitude of varying narratives can take their points of departure from any proffered narrative. The question of the greater or lesser 'truth' of the various narratives thus has no general pertinence, just as the universality or omnitemporality of any narrative is undercut by its inscription within a given pragmatic context" (53). In *Instructions païennes* Lyotard celebrates what Richard Rorty refers to as "first-order narratives" (86), stories that circulate within the culture and that are capable of taking on a role in language games. In this work Lyotard seems to be concerned more with narrative's ability to draw attention to its "narrator" and less with how it creates wholes. In more recent writings, however, Lyotard once again emphasizes how narrative creates a sense of totality. In *The Differend*, Lyotard writes, "narrative is perhaps the genre of discourse within which the heterogeneity of phrase regimens, and even the heterogeneity of genres of discourse, have the easiest time passing unnoticed" (151). Lyotard vacillates, then, in his treatment of narrative—at times emphasizing its ability to create wholes, at times more interested in how it draws our attention to its creation by a writer in a specific social context and thus renders the text's claims more tentative.

Lyotard's vacillating treatment of narrative explains why individual critics respond to his work in very different ways. Lyotard's interpreters often focus on one side of his treatment of narrative and fail to recognize his concern for the other; that is, they criticize him either for celebrating narrative as an *act* of construction without being aware of its need for wholes, or for seeing in narrative a concern for wholes without addressing narrative's social production and reception. In their widely reprinted critique of Lyotard, Nancy Fraser and Linda J. Nicholson follow the first course. They assume that Lyotard is interested in the social production of narrative and chide him for failing to see the necessity of narrative totalities:

> A first step [in creating a "postmodern feminism"] is to recognize, *contra* Lyotard, that postmodern critique need forswear neither large historical narratives nor analyses of societal macrostructures. This point is important for feminists, since sexism has a long history and is deeply and pervasively embedded in contemporary societies. Thus, postmodern feminists need not abandon the large theoretical tools needed to address large political problems. (34)

Fraser and Nicholson treat Lyotard as an advocate of narrative's ability to reflect on its own production so that they can make their case for narrative totalities. Other critics approach Lyotard's work from the opposite perspective; they take him as a theorist of narrative totality in order to argue for the importance of how narrative is created and produced. Allen Dunn's reading of Lyotard's notion of the "differend" exemplifies this latter approach:

> [T]he differend's very immunity from the language of adjudication [as an
> example of the language game] threatens to reduce it to mere tautology, to
> a programmatic discontent with systems simply because they are systems.
> According to the logic of the different, there is no way of analyzing the evils
> of hegemony, of explaining why notions of a cognitive totality must neces-
> sarily be harmful, nor can we learn anything about the differend from its
> historical contexts, since the differend is produced by a pure contingency
> that is devoid of cause or historical determination. (197)

For Dunn, Lyotard is concerned with "cognitive totality" and fails to
understand the "historical contexts" in which such language is deployed. Both articles approach narrative through only one of its two
aspects; in this they share Lyotard's inability to bring together narrative's tendency to create wholes and its awareness of its "constructedness." The conflict between these two qualities of discourse is an inherent part of the post-deconstrutive turn to narrative. As I have suggested,
precisely what attracts critics to narrative is its ability to be ambiguously deconstructive. Deconstruction is seen by critics variously as too
much concerned with textual slippage or too much enamored with
inescapable textual laws—a duality neatly embodied in Jane Flax's fear
that the slippage between truth and falsity will end up reifying the current system of power. Narrative seems to accept both textual indeterminacy and totality while bringing this conflict to the surface and—
most importantly—suggesting that these two might be resolved
productively. Striking a balance between textual totality and a self-
reflection that renders the whole text more tentative is the task of post-
deconstructive narrative.

Lyotard himself actually suggests the way in which this balance
might be struck in precisely the text that Dunn so dislikes. *The Differend* studies the most basic level of discourse capable of being judged
true or false: the phrase. For Lyotard, a community defines what will
count as a true statement: "Reality is not what is 'given' to this or that
'subject,' it is a state of the referent (that about which one speaks)
which results from the effectuation of establishment procedures
defined by a unanimously agreed-upon protocol, and from the possibility offered to anyone to recommence this effectuation as often as he or
she wants" (4). Lyotard claims that some phenomena cannot be discussed adequately within a given community's discursive rules. What
does not fit within these rules Lyotard calls the "differend":

> The differend is the unstable state and instant of language wherein some-
> thing which must be able to be put into phrases cannot yet be. This state
> includes silence, which is a negative phrase, but it also calls upon phrases

which are in principle possible. This state is signaled by what one ordinarily calls a feeling: "One cannot find the words," etc. A lot of searching must be done to find new rules for forming and linking phrases that are able to express the differend disclosed by the feeling, unless one wants this differend to be smothered right away in a litigation and for the alarm sounded by the feeling to have been useless. (13)

For Lyotard, the differend is not a statement that challenges the validity of normally accepted discursive rules; within his understanding of discourse, that is impossible, since statements cannot be formulated except through such rules. Rather, the differend represents the inability of the community's "phrase universes" to apply in a given instance. We can never argue directly for social change based on such discursive aporia since, by definition, they cannot be described using traditional moral imperatives. Such instances are instead opportunities for the wholesale change of a discursive system.

A community can recognize limitations within its discursive system because discourse performs two functions that can be at odds with each other. Arguing against linguistic theories that reduce reference to sense (Saussure) or sense to reference (Russell), Lyotard distinguishes between two basic types of phrases necessary for communication: "A cognitive phrase is validated thanks to another phrase, an ostensive one or one which displays. This is formulated as *Here's a case of it*. In every phrase, *of it* refers to the cognitive phrase" (41). Lyotard offers the following example of the differences between the cognitive phrase and the ostensive phrase: "The phrase *Here is a red flower* is transformed into two phrases, a cognitive phrase or definition: 'Red corresponds to wavelengths in the spectrum from 650 to 750 millimicrons of the radiation emitted by an object'; and an ostensive phrase: 'The color of this flower here is a case of it'" (41). For Lyotard, a phrase can be judged true and valid only when cognitive phrases are joined to an "object as an extra-linguistic permanence, as a 'given'" (33) by means of an ostensive phrase: either the direct deictics of spatiotemporal reference (here, now) or the "quasi-deictics" of a proper name. The object designated by a name or a deictic reference cannot be exhausted by a single cognitive phrase: "a named referent is real when it is also the possible case (the object of an ostensive phrase) of an unknown sense (presented by a not yet current phrase)" (47). Such an object makes discussion possible, since it allows many different cognitive phrases to be offered dialogically in a given context. Although these objects might appear to us to be concrete in and of themselves, they are named and designated through discourse and convention: "How can it be known that the referent is the same? *The same* signifies at least that it is locatable at the same place among common and accessible cross-references. This is what the names of chronology, of topography, of anthroponymy, etc. permit us to do. Once placed in these systems, the referent loses the marks of a current 'given'" (38). Ostensive references to concrete objects are just as discursive as cognitive references, and just as much dependent on community convention and rules.[5] The gap between these two types of reference is what creates our sense that the object designated by the name is concrete, that it exceeds the concept: "If the name can act as a linchpin between an ostensive phrase with its deictics and any given phrase with its sense or senses, it is because it is independent of the current showing and signified" (43). The concreteness of the objects that a community might discuss is, then, an effect of the gap between two different types of language use. These two forms of language use, in turn, seem quite similar to the two qualities that critics have associated with post-deconstructive narrative—its totality and self-conscious tentativeness. Cognitive discourse refers to the abstract system of language and concepts which, at least since Ferdinand de Saussure, we have thought about as a complete system that divides up all of experience. Conversely, ostensive reference seems to be the reference to concrete objects that would open language out to the real world and thus encourage new expressions. Obviously, this parallel is not perfect, since ostensive reference is not by itself open-ended. Nonetheless, we can see Lyotard in *The Differend* working through some of the deconstructive problems that will drive critics to an interest in narrative.

Narrative itself has a particularly complex role within the discursive dynamics that Lyotard sketches in *The Differend*. In *The Postmodern Condition*, narrative primarily establishes ostensive reference: "Even before he is born, if only by virtue of the name he is given, the human child is already positioned as the referent in the story recounted by those around him, in relation to which he will inevitably chart his course" (15). Lyotard repeats this association in *The Differend* by quoting Saul A. Kripke's *Naming and Necessity:* "a baby is born; his parents call him by a certain name. They talk about him to their friends. Other people meet him. Through various sorts of talk the name is spread from link to link as if by a chain" (91). Narrative thus establishes ostensive reference, and its objects become the concrete elements that are the basis of dialogue, even though dialogue itself is antithetical to the kind of totalization that Lyotard often associates with narrative. Statements that can be legitimated (i.e., have an ostensive as well as cognitive element) draw on narratives in order to define names, but also contrast themselves to such narratives as dialogically open within a certain discursive community. In *The Differend* Lyotard resolves his earlier vacillation between seeing narrative as totalizing and seeing it as admitting its own construction by making this tension essential to narrative's place within discourse in general. Without narrative's totality we could not firmly define an object's name for an individual discursive community; without narrative's awareness of its own construction we could not use these names as part of a larger system of dialogue and debate. What unites narrative's totality and tentativeness—its availability to other articulations—is the concrete "linchpin" of the named object under discussion. Narrative by itself does not make this object concrete since this object is open to multiple cognitive phrases only when it leaves the seamless narrative of naming and enters into the arena of dialogue and legitimation. A narrative creates a concrete entity, instead, only at the moment when that entity is no longer discussed "narratively"—when narrative's totality is put aside for the sake of a more open form of discourse. Lyotard seems to be struggling here to define a fundamentally different way of thinking about narrative's place in the dialectic of totality and openness. He offers a vision of narrative as one part of a type of discourse that admits its totality while also making its objects available for other articulations—indeed, even encouraging us to recognize how one total system might be rejected for an entirely new way of placing that object in discourse.

By now, it is clear that when I speak of post-deconstructive narrative, I am not implying a distinct genre of writing. Rather, narrative is part of the functioning of discourse in general. For Lyotard, narrative is simply the history that stands behind the given name, a history that *might be* appealed to in order to define and clarify a reference to a concrete entity. Narrative here is part of all language use. Thus in this project when I speak about narrative after deconstruction, I am really describing a certain hitherto unrecognized quality of textuality in general that has appeared to critics to be an answer to some of the problems raised by deconstruction. In particular, as we will see, narrative seems to be a quality of discourse that might be *exploited* to produce texts that better foreground their open-endedness, their availability to other articulations. Lyotard is far from giving us a fully formed theory of post-deconstructive narrative in *The Differend*, since he is writing less about narrative itself and more about how narrative might have a place in the general dynamics of debate. He, nonetheless, signals what narrative promises to do, and suggests that its ability to reference objects and to create a particular sense of concreteness is the essence of its power. That narrative can create such a sense of concreteness is evident throughout post-deconstructive criticism. Simon During's discussion of nationalism and literature in *Nation and Narration* is a good example of how post-deconstructive criticism can use such concreteness to talk about the discontinuity and open-endedness in discourse. During begins his study with the observation that "the nation-state is, for better or worse, the political institution which has the most efficacy and legitimacy in the world as it is" (139); he goes on to argue that the concept of "nation" is necessary even for groups marginalized by its current definition. A given culture, During argues, may have many nationalisms, each claiming to describe the culture totally. To develop a model of culturally disunified totalities, During turns to the "civil Imaginary":

> The term names prose writings which provide representations of social existence from the beginning of the eighteenth century through the period of the classic realist novel and beyond. At its beginnings the civil Imaginary does not cover just what we would today call fiction: Addison and Steele's journalism stand at its point of emergence. What these writings have in common with Defoe, Richardson, and Fielding's novels is the production of narratives, moral cruxes, a linguistic decorum, and character types which cover the social field of the post-1688 world.
>
> The civil Imaginary is an attempt to order what Steele calls "the uncontrollable jumble of Persons and Things" in that society. Thus its purpose is in part ethical in the Foucauldian sense. It produces representations of manners, taste, behaviour, utterances for imitation by individual lives. (142)

During defines the civil in terms of the types of entities that it recognizes. In Sir Walter Scott and Jane Austen, During finds an imaginative and less didactical type of novel that reworks the entities of the civil Imaginary. Scott and Austen, writes During, "[force] their extensions of reality back into the real. However much their techniques and interests differ; for both, to be imaginative is also to be realistic" (148). These writers are able to be more imaginative because the novel's own form allows for a heterogeneity of entities: "The text's unity is the unity of culture—a set of overlapping, unprogrammable connections and analogies within the strictly delimited frame of the work itself" (147). The novel's acceptance of heterogeneous entities, During reasons, allows postcolonial novelists to deploy the idea of "nation" without accepting hegemony. Postcolonial writers, During claims, use "realism's folding of the Imaginary into the real" (151) in order to work toward a "global" but discontinuous civil Imaginary. This paradoxical idea of a total but discontinuous civil space depends on the concrete entities that compose the civil Imaginary. Such concrete entities entail "global" narrative structures ("representations of manners, taste, behaviour" and the ethics on which they rest) to organize them, yet have the capacity to enter into new relations. Such concrete entities allow, paradoxically, the interrelation of many totalities.

Narrative's apparent ability to create such moments of concreteness will be most important to critics as they struggle to resolve deconstruction's totalizing textual system and its attractive power to reveal slippages within hegemony. Nonetheless, even critics not particularly engaged in deconstructive issues have become interested recently in narrative's creation and manipulation of concrete objects. Narratology itself is a case in point. The study of narrative methods developed as a distinct field of study beginning with Vladimir Propp's analysis of the formal patterns within the plots of Russian folktales, but entered the mainstream of American academic study primarily as a tool for stylistic analysis. Gerard Genette's study of temporal ordering in Marcel Proust popularized a new direction for the study of narrative based on how the events of the novel are ordered and presented within the text. Although these concerns are by no means discredited in current narratology, more philosophical issues of fictional reference have developed as an increasingly important area of study.[6] Theorists commonly group inquiry into fictional reference, the organization of fictional space, and the interrelations between real-world and fictional entities under the broad term *fictional semantics*. Thomas G. Pavel has argued that studying the concrete objects of the fictional text can explain how texts bring together many totalities, a "plurality of worlds." For Pavel, narratives work through the clashes between these worlds: "Competition between neighboring [ontological] landscapes always leads to a process of ontological focalization, to a sorting out and ordering of the worlds in place" (139). Contemporary fictional semantics, Pavel argues, arises out of the inadequacy of traditional referential theories, which presuppose a one-to-one relation between name and object. For Pavel, fictional semantics must use richer and more complex models of ontological realms:

> This amounts to a plea for richer models that include realms different from the actual world. The constitution of such models would allow the theory of fiction to look for explanations beyond the level of fictional individuals. . . . [F]ictional beings do not necessarily come into existence through individual gates or blocks in their referential history; rather, their fate is linked with the movements of populous groups that share the same ontological destiny. Fictionality cannot be understood as an individual feature: it encompasses entire realms of beings. (42)

For Pavel "objectness" cannot be defined by an entity's being on the receiving end of a subject's perception or referential act; rather, being an object depends on that object's function within a whole economy of the real and the fictional. Although his image of textual openness is considerably less radical and his understanding of the concreteness of narrative less complex than Lyotard's, nonetheless Pavel's theory of fictional worlds suggests how broadly we have begun to think of narrative as a matter of creating and manipulating textual concreteness.

Recent Theories of Materiality

When I suggest that post-deconstructive narrative works by manipulating textual concreteness, I am raising a broad and tangled philosophical question about what makes an object "concrete." When we refer to "concrete entities" in Lyotard's writing, we really imply two distinct things: that these elements are objects, and that they are concrete. Are objects by their nature "concrete"? Or is "concreteness" produced by an object's context? And just as *narrative* has been a term that has become ubiquitous within post-deconstructive criticism while being used in seemingly contradictory ways, so too has the issue of concreteness—renamed "materiality"—pervaded the post-deconstructive landscape. Indeed, materiality as a concept and issue is deployed currently by critics under the banner of very different theoretical schools. Elizabeth Grosz's book of materialist feminism, *Volatile Bodies*, takes as its starting point Maurice Merleau-Ponty's phenomenological theory of human embodiment. Judith Butler's widely influential *Bodies that Matter* is a postphenomenological study of materialization as a discursive process heavily indebted to deconstruction. Slavoj Žižek's Lacanian discussion of the peculiar materiality of commodity objects in *The Sublime Object of Ideology* is presented as an explicit step beyond poststructural textualism. However, Žižek's psychoanalytic understanding of materialism is directly opposed by Gilles Deleuze and Félix Guattari, whose materialist theory of "desiring machines" is offered as an explicit escape from the psychoanalytic emphasis on lack. Although these conflicting theories of materiality are themselves not *textual* theories and consequently have no direct relationship to narrative, they articulate a network of concerns that illuminate our inquiry into post-deconstructive narrative because they arise out of the same struggle with deconstruction.

Normally we think of "matter" as *the* common quality of natural objects. In his study of the origins of the concept of matter in ancient Greek philosophy, Samuel Sambursky argues that developing a concept of matter was the first step in formulating a scientific inquiry into nature. The theory of matter, Sambursky writes, is the "attempt to rationalize phenomena and explain them within the framework of general hypotheses. The object aimed at [is] giving general validity to the experience obtained from regarding the world as a single orderly unit— a cosmos the laws of which can be discovered and expressed in scientific terms" (4). Recent theories, however, analyze the idea of "the material" in order to challenge the belief that objects are knowable. Materiality has been an especially important concept in recent feminism. Western metaphysics traditionally has drawn a strict line between the body and the mind. Many feminists have noted that the philosophical attempt to locate identity in a disembodied consciousness starts from a male model of the body. In pregnancy, in contrast, we can distinguish body and spirit much less clearly. Theorists have gone on to suggest that examples drawn from the female body could lead to a richer understanding of the "embodiment" of consciousness in flesh (Diprose). The body that we occupy is material and concrete, but not necessarily a distinct and stable object. Understanding how the body might be "material" without being an object is important for contemporary feminism because associating women with the body is a traditional means of marginalizing them. As Grosz writes,

> Relying on essentialism, naturalism and biologism, misogynist thought confines women to the biological requirements of reproduction on the assumption that because of particular biological, physiological, and endocrinological transformations, women are somehow *more* biological, *more* corporeal, and *more* natural than men. The coding of femininity with corporeality in effect leaves men free to inhabit what they (falsely) believe is a purely conceptual order while at the same time enabling them to satisfy their (sometimes disavowed) need for corporeal contact through their access to women's bodies and services. (*Volatile* 14)

To challenge the way in which women have been defined as "more corporeal" than men, feminism must show a relation between the body and the "purely conceptual order" that patriarchal thought seeks to occupy.

This corporeal feminism seeks to connect the body and the "conceptual order" by challenging the traditional distinction between subject and object, a distinction that implicitly undervalues the physical world and severs its connection with the subject. As Grosz writes, "The mind/body relation is frequently correlated with the distinctions between reason and passion, sense and sensibility, outside and inside, self and other, depth and surface, reality and appearance, mechanism and vitalism, transcendence and immanence . . . and so on. These lateral associations provide whatever 'positive' characteristic the body may be accorded in systems where it is the subordinated counterpart of mind" (3). As soon as we define knowledge as the relation between subjective knower and objective reality, knowledge means overcoming a gap between two categorically different spheres. Seyla Benhabib argues that the Cartesian distinction between subject and object underlies modern philosophy's epistemological crisis: "Modern philosophy began with the loss of the world. The decision of the autonomous bourgeois subject to take nothing and no authority for granted, whose content and strictures had not been subjected to rigorous examination, and that had not withstood the test of 'clarity and distinctness,' began with the withdrawal form the world" ("Epistemologies" 109). Benhabib claims that epistemology based on the distinction between subject and object will find the world "lost" and knowledge to be constructed according to the observer's bias. If such suspicion toward knowledge is most fully articulated in deconstruction, corporeal feminism's interest in materiality is post-deconstructive precisely in exploring the possibility of regaining the world, of life without the Cartesian split between subject and object. Rosalyn Diprose's work on female "embodiment" is a good example of how thinking about the material body as something other than a distinct object undermines the Cartesian distinction. By revisiting traditional questions about the nature of our "being in the world," Disprose challenges us to take account of how we inhabit our bodies themselves:

> Underlying all these questions is some assumption about the meaning of "in." An ethics based on universal rational principles assumes that our "being" is a discrete entity separate from the "world" such that we are "in" the world after the advent of both. An ethics based on the problematic of place, on the other hand, claims that our "being" and the "world" are constituted by the relation "in." (19)

Diprose argues that feminists have accepted too readily from a male philosophical tradition the idea that the world is independent of, and radically different than the subject. To conceive of the subject and world as constituted by their relation to each other, as Diprose recommends, means rethinking what we mean by "objectivity."

Corporeal feminism provides a theory not of materiality in narrative but of the materiality of the extra-textual body. Nonetheless, this theory reveals how a nuanced understanding of post-deconstructive narrative's manipulation of textual concreteness will need to be developed. In particular, corporeal feminism raises the issue of how this materiality will appear to us and be recognized. As should already be clear, materiality cannot simply be a stable and objectively knowable quality of the things of the world or discourse, since such concreteness would return us to the traditional language of distinct subject and object.

Instead, corporeal feminism has often turned to Merleau-Ponty's phenomenological theory as a model of subject/object relations based on
interaction rather than on opposition. Grosz draws on Merleau-Ponty's
notion of "touch" to describe our corporeal being in the world. Unlike
sight's tendency to spatialize the world, and unlike the temporal continuity of hearing, touch implies a greater give-and-take between subject
and world: "Touch is regarded as a contact sense. . . . [I]t provides con-
tiguous access to an abiding object; the surface of the toucher and the
touched must partially coincide" (*Volatile* 98). Grosz and other feminist
critics have seen in this idea of "touch" a corporeality that does not fit
easily within traditional ways of understanding the body as an object.
Merleau-Ponty certainly encourages us to believe that "touch" is inherently connected to the body by using the term *flesh* to describe a substance that bridges subject and object:

> There is an experience of the visible thing as pre-existing my vision, but this
> experience is not a fusion, a coincidence: because my eyes which see, my
> hands which touch, can also be seen and touched, because, therefore, in
> this sense they see and touch the visible, the tangible, from within, because
> our flesh lines and even envelops all the visible and tangible things with
> which nevertheless it is surrounded, the world and I are within one another,
> and there is no anteriority of the *percipere* to the *percipi*, there is simul-
> taneity or even retardation. (123)

Merleau-Ponty's rather mysterious idea of "flesh" seems to explain how
subject and object participate in a total world, what phenomenologists
describe as "Being" in general. M. C. Dillon understands Merleau-
Ponty's concept as such an overarching Being: "Merleau-Ponty claims
that there is a continuity between my body and the things surrounding
me in the world I inhabit. Indeed, I can touch worldly things precisely
because I am myself a worldly thing. If I were an incorporeal being, I
could not palpate the things around me or interrogate the world with
my hands" (159). Although Dillon focuses on how subject and object
share in a larger Being, Merleau-Ponty also makes it clear that this
Being allows for heterogeneity in the elements that it holds together.
The world's unified heterogeneity is most clear when Merleau-Ponty
describes the "atmosphere" of Being:

> Far from opening upon the blinding light of pure Being or of the Object, our
> life has, in the astronomical sense of the word, an atmosphere: it is con-
> stantly enshrouded by those mists we call the sensible world or history, the
> *one* of the corporeal life and the *one* of the human life, the present and the
> past, as a pell-mell ensemble of bodies and minds, promiscuity of visages,
> words, actions, with, between them all, that cohesion which cannot be

denied them since they are all differences, extreme divergences of the same something. (84)

For Merleau-Ponty the flesh (total Being) does two things: it overarches all individual elements (objects as well as the subjects that perceive them) while also allowing those elements to remain distinct and to form a "pell-mell ensemble." Merleau-Ponty wants to avoid turning "flesh" into a single all-pervasive substance, a "pure Being" that we can recognize directly; he wants to complicate but not dismiss the distinction between subject and object. Nonetheless, some critics have felt that describing a general substance that subjects and objects share in does indeed erase the distinction between subject and object. Emmanuel Levinas notes the difficulty of applying Merleau-Ponty's theory of flesh to interpersonal relations:

> [C]an the social unity toward which it [Merleau-Ponty's analysis of "flesh"] claims to proceed be thought solely on the basis of an intercorporeity understood as the solidarity of an organism in its *esthetic* unity? Is the meaning of intersubjectivity at the level of sociality attained while being conceived by analogy with the image of the joining of a person's hands, "the right knowing what the left is doing?" Is the handshake a "taking cognizance of" and as it were a coinciding of two thought-worlds in the mutual knowledge of one by the other? Is it not the *difference*—the proximity of one's neighbor? ("Sensibility" 63)

Levinas argues that without a sense of difference between individuals we cannot speak of ethical and communal relations. Any theory of subject/object relations must walk a path, then, between two dangers: accepting the traditional belief that subjects and objects are distinct a priori, and subsuming subject and object into a general "Being" that does not allow us to talk about the very real gaps that exist between objects and subjects, objects and objects, and subjects and subjects.

Merleau-Ponty's theory, contextualized by Levinas's critique, suggests how we will have to approach materiality in narrative texts. Merleau-Ponty defines three different elements of the world: subject, object, and the "flesh" that mediates between them. Dillon's comment that "I can touch worldly things precisely because I am myself a worldly thing" suggests that "flesh" represents the materiality of these other two elements, the fact that objects and subjects are concrete entities that jostle against each other in the world. If we say, however, that everything is material by virtue of the fact that it exists within the world, we have both created a worthless category (since everything is material) and undermined the real distinction between instances when we are aware of an object's materiality and those when we are not.

Materiality cannot be understood as a *static* substance or quality that overarches subject and object. This static understanding of flesh is what Levinas critiques in Merleau-Ponty: "It is in sensibility, according to Merleau-Ponty, that the carnal (or the mental) manifests its ambiguity or ambivalence of the extension or interiority, in which the *felt*, which is out there, is ipso facto a *feeling*. The sensible content is itself inseparable from that incarnation, of which it is, according to Merleau-Ponty, the 'reflection' or the 'counterpart'" ("Intersubjectivity" 57). Levinas focuses on the ambiguity that is the heart of Merleau-Ponty's theory of flesh, that touching also means being touched. According to Levinas, treating the interaction between self and other as a static ambiguity erases the line between inside and outside and makes other people into reflections of one's own feelings. We need, instead, a *dynamic* model of how materiality functions in the relation between subject and object. Samuel Weber has recently argued that individuals work to create "objectivity" rather than merely encountering it. He ignores the normal definition of the word *objective* as what is true or unbiased, and instead treats objectivity as the condition of being an object. Arguing that the object (or "objectivity") is partially produced by the subject suggests a dynamic model of subject and object. Weber writes,

> First, the firm guidance that the object, as the other of the subject, is called upon to provide presupposes a stability that is achieved only at the cost of excluding, fending off, or fencing out others—that is, other possibilities, other ways, other encounters. Second, such exclusions serve the interest of that privileged other of objectivity that turns out to be the subject seeking to stabilize itself. And finally, this stability is not exempt from the tension and tendencies that it seeks to harness. (39)

Weber argues that the subject uses the object for "firm guidance," and that the object itself is created by "excluding, fending off, or fencing out others." These "others" are the unrealized ways of defining and isolating any material object. A material object, Weber suggests, is granted "objectivity" when the many possible ways of circumscribing it are shaped into a single form of "stability." This distinction between the messy network of potentials that surround a material object, and the neat but constructed stability of "objectivity" echoes the distinction in Merleau-Ponty's theory between subject, object, and the materiality (flesh) that overarches them. Both Merleau-Ponty and Weber distinguish between what we can call "objectivity" and "materiality." Using Weber's reworking of the term, we can say that the world is objective when it is made up of individual, self-contained, and stable objects. Materiality, conversely, describes the world as a network of potential objects. Objectivity seeks to separate the subject from the object so that both will appear stable. When we are aware of the materiality of an object, conversely, we recognize our involvement in the outside world, the fact that we may choose different ways of defining objects that in turn affect how we think of ourselves as subjects.

We can observe, then, a complex but cohesive dynamic suggested by Merleau-Ponty's phenomenology and developed by contemporary critics in different, often conflicting ways. A subject cannot simply choose to recognize materiality and avoid objectivity; rather, materiality and objectivity are halves of the same process. The dynamic model of subject/object relations makes us aware of the materiality of the "other," but does not suggest that we can avoid turning others into objects. Levinas writes, "That person [the other] cannot be represented and given to knowledge in his or her uniqueness, because there is no science but of generality. But the nonrepresentable—is it not precisely the inside, which, *appresented*, is approachable? . . . It is, in proximity, all the novelty of the social; proximity to the other, who, eluding possession, falls to my responsibility" ("Sensibility" 66). In demanding that we recognize our "proximity to the other" Levinas does not claim that we can avoid turning other people into objects "given to knowledge." Rather, the proximity that Levinas describes frames and questions objectivity. It exposes our relation to the other and suggests that we have, indeed, created that object according to our own interests. For Merleau-Ponty, materiality (flesh) describes a general Being that encompasses subject and object. Levinas and Weber transform this theory to suggest that materiality is the shadow of objectivity, a penumbra of other possibilities that surrounds any object. Where Merleau-Ponty's static understanding of materiality hints that we might be able to think about Being in general without reference to specific objects, Levinas and Weber insist that materiality and objectivity are locked in a dynamic interaction. Materiality appears only in our act of creating a fixed and stable object, and we cannot create objects without raising the issue of materiality.

This is not, of course, a theory of materiality *in* narrative. As we try to understand post-deconstructive narrative and its appeal to textual concreteness we will need to consider how the dynamics of object, subject, and materiality are shaped and changed by a textual context. Nonetheless, there is a great deal of sympathy between these theories of narrative and materiality that I have discussed. Both see themselves inhabiting a post-deconstructive world; both are unhappy with the dichotomies and dead ends that deconstruction seems to pose; both see an inquiry into our ideas of objects and concreteness to provide a new dynamic for knowledge. What is most exciting for post-deconstructive narrative about the concept of materiality is what Weber describes— the way in which materiality can both reference a whole system of "being" and yet at the same time remind us of the other possibilities that surround the object. Post-deconstructive narrative, we saw, inherited precisely this problem from deconstruction—how texts can be totalizing systems and yet be subject to self-reflection and hence tentative in a way that makes them capable of being used by others to articulate its objects in very different ways. Post-deconstructive narrative, then, can best be understood through its complex engagement with materiality. This is the great challenge of post-deconstructive narrative, a challenge that it pursues by returning to the fundamental problems and contradictions of deconstruction itself.

chapter two

DECONSTRUCTION AND THE WORLDLY TEXT

◆

Localizing Deconstruction

In chapter 1 I have mostly accepted as a starting point the opinion stated by many critics that deconstruction is a dead end, and that for criticism to engage satisfactorily in the world, we must go "beyond" deconstruction to a narrative criticism. To understand what I have called the "post-deconstructive" interest in narrative, however, we must recognize that such claims are based in part on a simplification of deconstruction. Indeed, in this chapter I would like to argue that the best starting point for post-deconstructive criticism is a rich understanding of the way in which deconstruction thinks about the world and the political location of the critic.

When critics appeal to narrative as an alternative to deconstruction, they usually see narrative as a mode of discourse in which the writer is present as a kind of "narrator" and the whole work's "constructedness" is evident. One of the most important and pervasive ways in which this quality of narrative is described is by using the language of critical or writerly "location." Recent critics have insisted that interpretation is constructed from a political and social "location," a concern that seems lacking in deconstruction. Typical is Susan Bordo's comment about deconstruction:

> In theory, deconstructionist postmodernism stands against the idea of disembodied knowledge and declares that idea to be a mystification and an impossibility. . . . The question remains, however, how the human knower is to negotiate this infinitely perspectival, destabilized world. Deconstructionism answers with constant vigilant suspicion of all determinate readings of culture and a partner aesthetic of ceaseless textual play as an alternative

ideal. Here is where deconstruction may slip into its own fantasy of escape from human locatedness—by supposing that the critic can become wholly protean by adopting endlessly shifting, seemingly inexhaustible vantage points, none of which are "owned" by either the critic or the author of a text under examination. ("Feminism" 142)

As a result, Bordo suggests, deconstruction claims to be the "view from nowhere" and falls into a self-delusion about its own "locatedness" within the world. She argues that criticism that speaks of the "location" of the critic accepts from deconstruction the idea that knowledge cannot be objective; it departs from deconstruction in how it explains why objectivity is impossible. Where deconstruction believes that knowledge is not objective because texts themselves are unstable, "local" criticism claims that objectivity is lost because critics are always located *somewhere*. For the "local" critic, knowledge can never be objective because one's location always intrudes into any produced text. Like narrative and materiality, then, location has been a concept around which critics have attempted to build a theoretically sophisticated response to the problems of deconstruction. Indeed, we can say that the spatial language of "location" provides one of the essential means by which post-deconstructive criticism can mark its difference from deconstruction.

"Local" criticism is a particularly good place to examine the relation between deconstruction and post-deconstructive criticism because it has sought to mark its break from deconstruction so clearly. The recognition that interpreters are always "located" somewhere politically and socially has led critics to insist on attending to the local details of the object or event being studied. Such local details, according to Jean-François Lyotard, are an alternative to the "grand narratives" that deconstruction has unraveled. Critics in this sense avoid making any large philosophical claim for an object, and instead consider its details as a way of revealing their personal relation to this object. However, they find almost immediately that the local has no pragmatic, critical value without such broader narratives. In considering how, for example, one might analyze local instances of gender politics, we are immediately confronted by the metaphysical assumptions implicit within terms such as *man* and *woman*, and are forced to construct a larger theoretical apparatus to organize them. Nancy Fraser and Linda J. Nicholson describe the problem this way: "Suppose . . . that one defined that object [of social criticism] as the subordination of women to and by men. Then, we submit, it would be apparent that many of the [metanarrative] genres rejected by postmodernists are necessary for social criticism. For a phenomenon as pervasive and multifaceted as male dominance simply cannot be adequately grasped with the meager critical resources to which they would limit us" (26). Critics are left scrambling for some way to make sense of this tension within the local's rejection of, but need for, larger theoretical narratives, often going to the extremes of claiming that, although master narratives are to be avoided, critics in certain circumstances might be granted a theoretical waiver: "Formulating wrongs, on the other hand, can make use of theory. Victims might turn to existing theories or even themselves theorize when striving to phrase the wrongs signaled by their feelings and so on" (Schatzki 49). Critics make a mistake, I would like to suggest, when they become caught up in debates about how much they can theorize and still remain "local." Rather than treating theory as something at odds with one's political location and thus to be indulged in only with care, I argue that deconstruction allows us to think about being located within the sociopolitical world as inherently involving theory. Critics who debate the use and nature of the local have generally assumed that deconstruction and the world are naturally opposed. Certainly, the use to which deconstruction was put in its heyday—as a tool for a type of close reading, a hyper-New Criticism—supports this opposition. As we move away from this textualism, however, we should reconsider this reading of deconstruction as well.

I would like to argue that the concept of the world—or, rather, the "worldly" as I will define it in this chapter—is reconcilable and indeed crucial to deconstruction. Understanding this worldly quality of deconstruction not only helps to explain and perhaps resolve some of the problems implicit within the concept of the "local," but also forces us to explain what we mean when we say that critics are "narrators" and to define the relation between deconstruction and post-deconstructive narrative.

Rethinking Deconstructive Space

Deconstruction and the post-deconstructive criticism that speaks about "location" share a spatial language of texture, movement, layers, and boundaries.[1] In one sense, post-deconstructive criticism simply shifts these spatial metaphors from the text to the world, reading social relations in the same way that concepts and words were read by the deconstructionist. Consider, for example, Teresa de Lauretis's introduction to her book *Feminist Studies/Critical Studies*, a work typical of the attempt to formulate post-deconstructive critical practice. De Lauretis treats the world as a space in which social relations conflict and transform when she notes in recent feminism "a shift from the earlier view of woman defined purely by sexual difference (i.e., in relation

to man) to the more difficult and complex notion that the female subject is a site of differences; differences that are not only sexual or only
racial, economic, or (sub)cultural, but all of these together and often
enough at odds with one another" (14). De Lauretis implies that individuals within social relations function according to a deconstructive
model to the extent that we can describe them as inhabiting a space of
conflict between overlapping cultural systems and networks. Such a
formulation shifts Jacques Derrida's language of hinge, trace, and
boundary from the text to the culture, paralleling cultural space to textual space and individuals to terms caught within a play of *différance*.
At the same time, however, post-deconstructive criticism also assumes
that social relations function not merely *like* deconstructive textual
play, but also on the basis of it. Thus, de Lauretis quotes Monique Wit-
tig's remark that hegemony "produces the difference between the sexes
as a political and philosophical dogma" (13). This remark bases social
reality on a more literal Derridian play, assuming that within any culture there exists a transtextual space in which gender concepts arise
and on the basis of which social relations are constructed. This latter
way of modeling social reality clearly carries a different emphasis than
the previous passage, where the space of conflict was real and the elements under consideration were not terms but individuals. Post-deconstructive criticism thus imports deconstructive spatiality both as a
model for speaking about social relations and as a textual system by
which those relations are taken to have been constructed in the first
place. The result is a sort of kettle logic, a criticism that uses deconstructive spatiality in overlapping, contradictory ways.

This contradiction plays a strategic role within post-deconstructive
critical praxis. One of the principle charges leveled at deconstruction is
that it allows the individual no room to act against the discursive systems that function within the culture, since the subordination of reality
to textuality implies that no real-world act can affect this textual play.
In the wake of deconstruction, critics are searching for a way to define
the possibility of significant counterhegemonic action—how a text can
be simultaneously caught in system of *différance* and yet also open-
ended, producing objects available to other articulations. The dual way
in which critics have appropriated deconstructive space actually helps
them to open up this possibility. Consider, for example, Chris Weedon's
discussion of the political freedom created by (an appropriation of)
deconstructive space:

> Even when the principles of "*différance*" are inscribed in an historically
> specific account of discourses, signifiers remain plural and the possibility
> of absolute or true meaning is deferred. The precariousness of any attempt

to fix meaning which involves a fixing of subjectivity must rely on the denial of the principles of difference and deferral. The assertion of "truth" involved is constantly vulnerable to resistance and the redefinition of meaning. . . . As individuals we are not the mere objects of language but the sites of discursive struggle, a struggle that takes place in the consciousness of the individual. (105–6)

Weedon here strategically straddles two appropriations of deconstructive space in order to define a type of "discursive struggle" in which the individual can be a conscious and active participant. She accepts the more literal deconstructive notion of space as a textual "field" in which terms undergo *différance*. At the same time, however, Weedon also accepts the analogy between this textuality and social space, defining the space in which individuals interact as merely *like* textual space. This latter, analogical use of deconstructive space allows Weedon to emphasize the role of *individuals* as the site of struggle. To accept either of these spatial models solely would limit Weedon's idea of discursive freedom. To see deconstructive space as purely textual denies the primacy of the individual; to consider it merely an analogy denies the "precariousness" of meaning and limits the individual's ability to fight against hegemony. This dual, contradictory appropriation of deconstructive space thus makes possible a vision of political freedom, but generally remains locked within deconstructive ironies that make this practice contradictory. In the language of location, I will show, is the striving toward a post-deconstructive style of writing, a kind of narrative that will reenvision textual construction in a much more productive and satisfying way.

These contradictions in "local" criticism arise out of the mistaken assumption that deconstructive spatiality has no inherent connection to the concept of world, and thus must be appropriated in various ways. Critics appropriate deconstructive space in these two ways because they misunderstand Derridian space as a metaphor for confrontation and substitution. Both Weedon and de Lauretis assume that when deconstructionists speak of space, they merely describe a plane in which elements (terms or individual subjects) meet, conflict, and transform. This understanding of deconstructive space is not unique to post-deconstructive criticism, but instead can be traced back to the widespread reading of deconstruction as a rhetorical discipline. Barbara Johnson, for example, applies deconstruction to literature in an attempt at "identifying and dismantling differences by means of other differences that cannot be fully identified or dismantled" (x). When she speaks about space within the text she deconstructs, she refers simply to the ways in which terms are incompletely and problematically distinguished from each other: "The differences *between* entities (prose and poetry, man and woman, literature and theory, guilt and innocence) are shown to be based on a repression of differences *within* entities, ways in which an entity differs from itself" (x–xi). Johnson's spatial language is merely a metaphor, a way of defining the lack of self-presence in individual terms and their dependence on a metonymic "differing." This understanding of Derridian space has led critics to reduce textual play to a simple metonymic substitution of linguistic terms, and to see Derrida as cut off from more "worldly" concerns. It is in this sense that Edward W. Said describes Derridian space:

> All this establishes a sort of perpetual interchange in Derrida's work between the page and the theater stage. Yet the locale of the interchange— itself a page and a theatre—is Derrida's prose, which in his recent work attempts to work less by chronological sequence, logical order, and linear movement than by abrupt, extremely difficult-to-follow lateral and complementary movement. The intention of that movement is to make Derrida's page become the apparently self-sufficient site of a critical reading, in which traditional texts, authors, problems, and themes are presented in order to be dedefined and dethematicized more or less permanently. (*World* 202–3)

Said argues that, according to Derrida, the text is a self-contained stage within which terms undergo a ceaseless transformation. Behind this characterization of Derrida's textual stage is the same assumption that Johnson makes: any space attributed to the text must be merely a metaphor, and as a result Derridian space is just another way of speaking about metonymic substitution.

This simplification of deconstructive space is not without its benefits for post-deconstructive criticism. Post-deconstructive criticism defines its own relevance to the world, we can suggest, by strategically keeping deconstruction out of the world.[2] That is, by simplifying deconstructive space into a simple field analogically meaningful, recent critics have made room for themselves to appropriate deconstruction for a more worldly criticism. Yet, in doing so these critics have produced a post-deconstructive space whose contradictions preclude any coherent theory of textual functioning. Reclaiming a fuller understanding of Derridian space, then, is the first step to understanding its involvement in the world and explaining how critical "location" can become the basis of post-deconstructive narrative. That Derrida does not understand textual space as a simple field is quite explicit within his writing. Derrida finds Sigmund Freud's "Mystic Writing Pad" interesting exactly because of its violation of geometrical consistency:

Differences in the work of breaching concern not only forces but also locations. And Freud already wants to think [of] force and place simultaneously.
He is the first not to believe in the descriptive value of his hypothetical representation of breaching. . . . It is, rather, the index of a topographical
description which external space, that is, familiar and constituted space,
the exterior space of the natural sciences, cannot contain. (*Writing* 204)

Derrida's discussion of space departs from classical models of geometric space and thus rejects any notion of a textual "field." Critics have
had difficulty coming to terms with Derrida's nonlinear space because,
as we have seen in Barbara Johnson, attention to the "sliding" and
"exteriority" of terms within a text seems naturally to presuppose some
(metaphorical) field upon which they function. Because he is free from
the need to apply the idea of *différance* to interpretational methodol-
ogy, Rodolphe Gasché's treatment of Derrida as a philosopher is perhaps the most satisfying discussion of Derridian space. Unlike Johnson,
Gasché resists the temptation to reduce exteriority to a way of speaking about rhetorical substitution:

Recall that the relation to an Other constitutive of a self, whose minimal
unit is the arche-trace, presupposes an interval which at once affects and
makes possible the relation of self to Other and divides the self within itself.
In the same way, differance as the production of a polemical space of differences both presupposes and produces the intervals between concepts,
notions, terms, and so on. In that sense, arche-trace and differance, each in
a different manner, are spacing. From the perspective of arche-trace, spacing "is the opening of the first exteriority in general, the enigmatic relationship of the living to its other and of an inside to an outside." (199; citing Derrida, *Grammatology* 70)

According to Gasché, Derridian space is always being produced; it is an
undertaking rather than a metaphorical field. The difficulty of translat-
ing Derrida's claim that space is produced into a theory of how texts
stage the slippage of terms has driven critics, on the one hand, to
Johnson's textualism and, on the other, to Weedon's contradictory
appropriation of deconstructive space.

Producing Space in the Worldly Text

To understand deconstructive space, which will provide the basis
for post-deconstructive narrative, we must avoid treating this space as
a metaphor, and instead see it as something produced by critical praxis

itself. I would like to describe Derrida's elusive notion of space by turning to what is probably Derrida's most direct discussion of space, his
essay "Ousia and Grammē." This essay discusses time and the philosophical tradition that has treated it in spatial terms. Derrida claims
that philosophers have consistently denied temporality for the sake of
the presence implied by spatial forms. He does not, of course, reject
spatiality in favor of some direct understanding of temporality. Temporality can never be self-present, and thus can never be known except by
how it modifies the spatial models that philosophers attempt to impose
upon it. The essay describes, then, a very complex space that results
from the attempt to account for time, a space that comes up against the
limits of presence.

Derrida begins with G. W. F. Hegel's dialectical model of space. Such
dialectics have, for Derrida, a general similarity to the movement of *différance*, thus allowing Derrida to start from an active approach to
space. Two different ways of understanding space arise in three stages
by dividing the initial immediacy and completeness of the ideal term,
space. Derrida writes, paraphrasing Hegel,

> Differentiation, determination, qualification can only overtake pure space
> as the negation of this original purity and of this initial state of abstract
> indifferentiation which is properly the spatiality of space. Pure spatiality is
> determined by negating properly the indetermination that constitutes it,
> that is, by itself negating itself. By *itself* negating itself: this negation has to
> be a determined negation, a negation *of* space *by* space. The first spatial
> negation of space is the POINT. (*Margins* 41)

In this passage, Derrida considers how an initial term (*pure space*) contains within itself an implied distinction that transforms it into a different understanding of space (the point) in many ways opposed to that
initial term. The first and third stages represent two different ways of
understanding space—"pure" space and the point. The middle stage of
this textual transformation involves postulating a certain ground on
which these two terms interact, the stage upon which this transformation occurs—what Derrida refers to elsewhere as "opening up of its
own space, effraction, breaking of a path against resistances, rupture
and irruption become a route" (*Writing* 214). For Hegel, concrete space
is the product of the work of negation, the third stage of the dialectic.
Here, however, Derrida departs from Hegel and defines what appears to
be the more concrete and fundamental space as a textual ground that
allows the movement between the first and third positions. This transitional space is implied by the active terms that this passage employs, in
which the terms "space" themselves: "As the first determination and

first negation of space, the point spatializes or *spaces* itself. It negates itself by itself in its relation to itself, that is, to another point. The negation of negation, the spatial negation of the point is the line. The point negates and retains itself, extends and sustains itself, lifts itself (by *Aufhebung*) into the LINE, which thus constitutes the *truth* of the point" (*Margins* 42). Dialectical transformation produces a space by virtue of the force implicit within that transformation, a force that demands a ground upon which to function. Derrida, then, borrows from Hegel the idea that space is produced by the ongoing transformation of concepts; he departs from Hegel by seeing this production as, paradoxically, what allows the movement in the first place.

Derrida's model of this paradoxically produced and preconditional space is the "gramme." Literally the gramme refers to a line or trace; more generally it is the spatial rendering of temporal movement. The gramme spatializes time by treating it as the accumulation of moments. Each moment within the gramme is understood as "in act"—that is, as moving toward some end and thus referring to a telos that unifies these moments into a whole. Understood in this way, the gramme treats each point as self-present and simply repeats the metaphysical tradition of spatialization and presence. However, Derrida is able to reaccentuate the gramme in a way that allows it to function in a less self-present, more temporal fashion. To do this, Derrida emphasizes how individual points within the gramme depend on the limit toward which they move: "But if one considers now that the point, as limit, does not exist *in act*, is not (present), exists only potentially and by accident, takes its existence only from the line in act, then it is not impossible to preserve the analogy of the gramme: on the condition that one does not take it as a series of potential limits, but as a line in act, as a line thought on the basis of its extremities *(ta eskhata)* and not of its parts" (59–60). Derrida argues that the space that the gramme provides should be understood as comprising a whole movement that passes through each point "accidentally." Thus, the presence of each point is always deferred to this whole, which itself is not self-present but potential and multiple. The gramme, then, is a nonlinear space, a space produced temporarily by reference to the "extremes" and out of the movement of signification.

How is this temporally produced space related to textual slippage, to the play of *différance*? We already saw some connection between the production of space and textual play in the gramme. The text creates its space—defines the gramme—by recognizing potential limits toward which it moves. In the same way, we might say, the terms within a text indirectly "defer" to other terms, moving toward them in a way that creates a space of semantic slippage. But in formulating textual play this way, we come up against the problem I noted in Barbara Johnson and others: the reduction of Derridian space to a flat field in which a term and its others exist. Critics assume that textual space must be a stable field because they homogenize the ontology of textual elements—that is, they assume that the one element and its others "exist" in a similar way. This ontological homogenization can perhaps be traced back to a general critical tendency to understand the play of difference and alterity on the model of an individual's confrontation with his or her social, sexual, or racial "other." The first description of *différance* in Terry Eagleton's widely used *Literary Theory: An Introduction* follows this pattern: "Woman is the opposite, the 'other' of man: she is non-man, defective man, assigned a chiefly negative value in relation to the male first principle. But equally man is what he is only by virtue of ceaselessly shutting out his other or opposite, defining himself in antithesis to it, and his whole identity is therefore caught up and put at risk in the very gesture by which he seeks to assert his unique, autonomous existence" (132). Despite the validity of Eagleton's summary, this example is dangerous as a general model for *différance* because it treats the ontological status of the two elements (self and other) as equivalent— they are, ultimately, both people with equal rights and identities. Such equivalence demands that the ontological ground of their confrontation be fixed, since that defines the very possibility of these terms acting as "others." Actual people, after all, always meet "somewhere." In formulating the gramme as a model for the produced space of deconstruction, however, Derrida works against exactly this presupposition of ontological equivalence between the elements of *différance*. He is careful to avoid claiming that the various points within the gramme are self-present; rather, he emphasizes that the gramme marks out a play of potential or accidental points. For Derrida, the "other" toward which a text moves is never simply something like the original term, and the text never constructs a space upon which these two "others" can meet equally. Only by recognizing an ontological difference functioning within the elements of textual play can deconstructive space avoid being fixed and instead function as something in process.

The ontological complexity that is the basis of *différance*, I would like to suggest, can be described more generally as a fluctuation between the concrete and conceptual. Indeed, one of the principal things that Derrida gains by beginning "Ousia and Grammē" with Hegel is the ability to cast his discussion in terms of concreteness. The importance of the issue of concreteness is clear in Derrida's summary of Hegel: "Space . . . has become concrete in having retained the negative within itself. It has become space in losing itself, in determining itself, in negating its original purity, the absolute indifferentiation and exteriority that constituted itself in its spatiality. Spatialization, the accomplishment of the essence of spatiality, is a despatialization and vice versa" (*Margins* 42). Whereas the concrete is something produced for Hegel as the end of a teleological process, the concrete functions much more as an ambiguous moment within this movement for Derrida. The play of space in "Ousia and Grammē" that we just discussed stages a tension between the concrete and the conceptual. The space that arises in the play of terms is concrete because it is the larger space where these two abstract definitions of space meet and clash. This space is conceptual, however, because it is the concreteness of this term *(space)* that opens up the possibility of polysemy and the slippage between two different understandings of the term; such a transitional space appears to be a conceptual supplement to a concrete term. This concrete/conceptual tension is implicit within the "pure space" from which Derrida (and Hegel) start: "Nature, as 'absolute space' . . . knows no mediation, no difference, no determination, no discontinuity. It corresponds to what the *Jena Logic* called ether: the element of ideal transparency, of absolute indifferentiation, of undetermined continuity, of absolute juxtaposition, that is, the element without interior relations" (41). What opens "pure space" up to deconstruction and analysis is its attempt to blend the *concrete* (the immediate) and the *abstract* (its ideality) necessary for full self-presence; as we have seen, these two terms introduce an ontological split that ultimately creates a textual space. As this example makes clear, neither of the two elements is the more basic, stable, or given. Rather, textual elements constantly fluctuate between these two different ontological conditions.

This fluttering between concrete and conceptual makes possible the *différance* of the text. Gregory Ulmer has generalized this concrete/conceptual fluctuation and described Derrida's methods as essentially "allegorical," stressing that textual elements constantly operate as both concrete and abstract.[3] Ulmer suggests that the allegorical nature of *différance* is clearest when Derrida discusses the mechanical "apparatus" of writing (*Applied* 81–83). Derrida describes the ontological problems introduced by the apparatus of writing most directly in his Mystic Writing Pad essay:

> Writing, here, is *technē?* as the relation between life and death, between present and representation, between the two apparatuses. It opens up the question of the technics: of the apparatus in general and of the analogy between the psychical apparatus and the nonpsychical apparatus. In this sense writing is the stage of history and the play of the world. It cannot be exhausted by psychology alone. (*Writing* 228)

Freud's model of the Mystic Writing Pad is interesting for Derrida in part because it introduces the issue of the apparatus which, as this passage suggests, can never remain simply a metaphor—it is always both an actual machine and a way of speaking. We can see this hesitation between the concrete and the conceptual of a textual element as the basis of writing and its deconstructive effects. Without this concrete/conceptual ambiguity, a term could not be described as undergoing the kind of slippage that Derrida describes in "Ousia and Grammē" and elsewhere. In *Speech and Phenomena*, for example, Derrida's treatment of the opposition between expression and indication depends on the issue of the concrete. In that analysis, Derrida opposes the concrete, situational indication to the ideal, "nonworldly" expression. What drives Derrida's deconstruction of these terms is how the concrete nonetheless reappears out of the movement toward the ideal. Thus, expression shifts from being an ideal "nonworldliness [that] is not another worldliness" (76) to become reentangled within the concrete world: "The opposition between form and matter—which inaugurates metaphysics—finds in the concrete ideality of the living present its ultimate and radical justification" (6). In all of these instances Derrida treats the opposition between the concrete and the conceptual as an inevitable problem around which the text will be constructed.

Textual space itself embodies the ontological ambiguity essential to *différance*, since it is a metaphor applied by a critic but also one form of space in general. Derrida's *Edmund Husserl's "Origin of Geometry": An Introduction* concerns itself with the problem of the origin of space in the science of geometry: "There is then a science *of* space, insofar as its starting point is not *in* space" (85). Geometry conceives space in contradictory terms: space is concrete within current geometry and metaphorical in the early geometer's proto-idealizations of space. Similarly, Derrida ends *Positions* with the problem of space and the degree to which it can be taken as equivalent to alterity—that is, the degree to which it is a metaphor for an incomplete distinction between terms. Derrida notes that "In effect, these two concepts *do not signify exactly* the same thing; that being said, I believe that they are absolutely indissociable" (81). Derrida elaborates further:

> *Spacing/alterity:* On their indissociability, then, there is no disagreement between us. I have always underlined at least two characteristics in the analysis of spacing, as I recalled in the course of the interview: (1) That spacing is the impossibility for an identity to be closed on itself, on the inside of its proper interiority, or on its coincidence with itself. The irreducibility of spacing is the irreducibility of the other. (2) That "spacing" designates not only interval, but a "productive," "genetic," "practical" movement, an "operation," if you will, in its Mallarméan sense also. (94)

Derrida seems to have in mind an opposition between, on the one hand, space as a metaphor for alterity (the impossibility of identity) and, on the other, space as something concrete and productive in its own terms.

Because space is ontologically ambiguous, it mediates between text and world. Space's position between text and world is explained most clearly when Derrida describes the "topos" or occasion of writing. In his early essay, "Force and Signification," Derrida distinguishes between the topographical and the topological, arguing that we cannot directly correlate space and textuality: "Now, stricto sensu, the notion of structure refers only to space, geometric or morphological space, the order of forms and sites. . . . Only metaphorically was this *topographical* literality displaced in the direction of its Aristotelean and *topical* signification (the theory of commonplaces in language and the manipulation of motifs or arguments)" (*Writing* 15–16). Rather than accepting topographical space as a natural part of the text or rejecting it as a misunderstanding of textuality, Derrida considers how textual space is produced out of a self-reflection built into all textual language: "How is this history of metaphor possible? Does the fact that language can determine things only by spatializing them suffice to explain that, in return, language must spatialize itself as soon as it designates and reflects upon itself?" (16). A text becomes spatial whenever the linguistic slippage at work in *différance* forces the text to reflect on itself. Why textual self-reflection produces textual space is most clearly explained by Derrida's notion of *lieu* as both a spatial site and a rhetorical topos. What Alan Bass translates in this passage as "the theory of commonplaces in language," Derrida describes in the original as "théorie des lieux dans le langage" (*L'écriture* 28). The use of the word *lieux* allows Derrida to suggest a necessary complicity between textual articulation and the creation of textual topography. Derrida makes this association clear elsewhere: "The *topoi* of the dialogue are never indifferent. The themes, the topics, the (common-)places *[les lieux]*, in a rhetorical sense, are strictly inscribed, comprehended each time within a significant site *[des sites chaque fois signifiants]*. They are dramatically staged, and in this theatrical geography, unity of place corresponds to an infallible calculation or necessity" (*Dissemination* 69; *La Dissémination* 77). In this passage Derrida exploits the parallel between the rhetorical topos and the physical site, implying that the topos allows the working-out of the geography dictated by the topography. The topos here is the means by which the topography manifests itself and textual conflicts play out. In "Force and Signification," Derrida suggests that the topographical depends on a previously existing topos: "Structure is first the structure of an organic or artificial work, the internal unity of an assemblage, a *construction;* a work is governed by a unifying principle, the *architec-*

ture that is built and made visible in a location" (15). The *lieu* can hold together text and the "occasion" within the world where it is analyzed because the *lieu* is ontologically unstable and flutters between the concrete topographical site and the rhetorical topos.

This notion of the *lieu* is very similar to what critics have described as the "local site," and is the point at which we can bring together deconstruction's law of *différance* and theories concerned with critical "location." Elspeth Probyn suggests the ontological indeterminacy of the local site: "the concept of 'locale' will be used to designate a place that is the setting for a particular event. I take this 'place' as both a discursive and nondiscursive arrangement which holds a gendered event, the home being the most obvious example" ("Travels" 178). Probyn recognizes that the "locale" must exist in a problematic way as both part of discourse, and as something opposed to it—or, in the terms I have used, as *conceptual* and *concrete*. The difference between place and event (Probyn's example is the distinction between home and the family) marks the fluctuation between concrete space and the interpellating (conceptual) representations that appear within that space. As Derrida suggests it will, this concrete/conceptual ambiguity arises when space comes up against its limit and recognizes the temporal—summarized nicely by Probyn's casting of the concrete/conceptual ambiguity in terms of place and event. Probyn inherits this concrete/ conceptual tension and its formulation as the play between place and event from Lyotard. When Lyotard suggests that "any consensus on the rules defining a [language] game and the 'moves' playable within it *must* be local, in other words, agreed on by its present players and subject to eventual cancellation" (*Postmodern* 66) he claims that discourse hesitates between using and changing the "rules" of this interaction. Any reference, then, fluctuates between taking this "locale" concretely as a given base for communication, and renegotiating the boundaries of discourse conceptually. Lyotard explains that the locale produces knowledge by (the possibility of) negating its starting point: "working on a proof means searching for and 'inventing' counterexamples, in other words, the unintelligible; supporting an argument means looking for a 'paradox' and legitimating it with new rules in the games of reasoning" (54). The very possibility of rejecting the site, of switching from the concrete to the conceptual understanding of this local space, is the means by which the contradictions that drive Lyotard's discursive "game" are worked through. Probyn follows the same reasoning in her use of Lyotard:

> In this formulation the bricoleur actively pieces together different signs and produces new (and sometimes unsanctioned) meanings; the bricoleur is always in the process of fashioning her various locales. The concept of

"locale" then serves to emphasize the lived contradictions of place and event. In acknowledging that we are daily involved in the reproduction of patriarchy we can nonetheless temper a vision of strict interpellation with the recognition that discourses are negotiated. Individuals live in complex places and differentiate the pull of events. (182)

According to Probyn, the site or locale holds contradictions and allows their analysis precisely because of the difference between "place" and "event"—that is, because of the ontological ambiguity of the site under analysis. Probyn does not simply suggest that the locale can be valued over the event or representation—that is, that we can strip away the representation for the sake of this concrete place. Rather, she recognizes that the very space in which women operate is constructed as part of a necessary duality with representation. Thus, to use Probyn's example, one can have a proper "home" (as a space) only to the extent that one has a family of some sort—that is, only to the extent that space is bound to, and even produced from, representation. The "reproduction of patriarchy" thus is not seamless but reveals its contradictions through the ontological ambiguity of the space in which it appears.

The ontologically ambiguous local site positions the critic between text and world. Perhaps Derrida's most concise comment on the notion of "world" comes at a point in his book *Of Grammatology* where he considers the material basis of the trace and what it means for signification: "It is therefore *the game of the world* that must be first thought; before attempting to understand all the forms of play in the world" (50). This passage occurs in the context of considering Ferdinand de Saussure's claim that the connections among elements of a signifying system are arbitrary, a claim critics have often used to characterize *différance* as a shapeless "freeplay." Derrida, in contrast, claims that treating linguistic elements as arbitrary assumes that they are concrete things in the world whose existence is independent of the meaning given them. Instead, Derrida suggests, we must see writing as caught up within a whole system of making these terms *worldly* and thus arbitrarily inserted within a phonetic system: "From the very opening of the game, then, we are within the becoming-unmotivated of the symbol. With regard to this becoming, the opposition of diachronic and synchronic is also derived. It would not be able to command a grammatology pertinently. The immotivation of the trace ought now to be understood as an operation and not as a state, as an active movement, a demotivation, and not as a given structure" (50–51). For Derrida, the system of language as pure difference depends on the move into the world, on stripping away motivation and treating signifieds as concrete individuals. It is because we can treat signifiers as concrete that their association with signifieds is arbitrary. De Saussure's fundamental distinction between signifier and signified is, then, the product of "the game of the world," the functioning of a process of "worlding." It is exactly this play of the *idea* of the world, the always incomplete movement toward the world, which makes the text fluctuate between the concrete and the conceptual:

> Since consciousness for Freud is a surface exposed to the external world, it is here that instead of reading through the metaphor in the usual sense, we must, on the contrary, understand the possibility of a writing advanced as conscious and as acting in the world (the visible exterior of the graphism, of the literal, of the literal becoming literary, etc.) in terms of the labor of the writing which circulated like psychical energy between the unconscious and the conscious. The "objectivist" or "worldly" consideration of writing teaches us nothing if reference is not made to a space of psychical writing. . . . [W]e perhaps should think that what we are describing here as the labor of writing erases the transcendental distinction between the origin of the world and Being-in-the-world. Erases it while producing it. (*Writing* 212)

For Derrida, then, the world as a problem defines the apparatus of the text and thus introduces a slippage between the concrete and the conceptual. Texts are always "worldly," always involved in the extra-textual in complex and incomplete ways.

The Multiple Spaces of Post-Deconstructive Narrative

I would like to suggest that recognizing textual worldliness provides a way of thinking about the relation between a critic's extra-textual "location" and the contradictions that he or she finds within the text. The relation between these two elements can be understood as the very problem that post-deconstructive criticism tries to theorize, and the tension that narrative seems to capture. In chapter 1 we saw that deconstruction seemed both to define a totalizing textual system and yet also to make texts indeterminate and radically incomplete; narrative promised a textuality which, while systemic, constantly opened outward to new articulations in more productive ways. Although my discussion in this chapter has suggested that critics have failed to appreciate the complexity of deconstruction's engagement in the world, the task of articulating a model for the relationship between text, critic, and world is only vaguely sketched by deconstruction. Narrative, we will see, can balance an awareness of a deconstructive system of slippage with the critic's position in relation to that system, a position that allows these contradictions to become the basis for any number of ways of developing an interpretation.

Derrida makes the relation between textual indeterminacy and readerly location clear in "Ousia and Grammē" when he discusses how the gramme can "hold" the force of textual play because of the action of an observer: "The impossible—the coexistence of two nows—appears only in a synthesis—taking this word neutrally, implying no position, no activity, no agent—let us say in a certain complicity or coimplication *maintaining* together several current nows which are said to be the one past and the other future" (*Margins* 55). In this passage Derrida associates the now *(maintenant)* and the act of "maintaining" contradictions within a text. In describing how the observer participates in "maintenance," Derrida stresses the observer's role in balancing the physical textual forces in terms of which Derrida describes space and time earlier in the essay: "*Ousia* as *energeia*, in opposition to *dynamis* (movement, power) is presence. Time, which bears within it the already-no-longer and the not-yet, is composite. In it, energy composes with power" (51). The observer's external position transforms the temporality of the text into a force that it "maintains" within an overall balance. Indeed, Derrida's description of the text as an apparatus—so basic to the text's concrete/conceptual ambiguity—is itself dependent on some external position from which this system is used as a tool. Derrida writes, "The machine does not run by itself. It is less a machine than a tool. And it is not held with only one hand. This is the mark of its temporality. Its *maintenance* is not simple" (*Writing* 226). Derrida argues that the functioning of the whole text depends on a "hand" that holds it and operates it. Drawing on the conclusions that we have reached already, we can say that the dynamics of the textual "machine" involve three elements: the fundamental slippage between the concrete and conceptual understanding of basic concepts, the spatial "site" or *lieu* in which this slippage is staged, and the external position from which an observer "maintains" this slippage and allows it to appear as a force within the text. The external position of the observer here creates an overall arc of the text's slippages, a gramme of its limit, and thus allows us to recognize that play in a way that the pure temporality of *différance* by itself would not.

The tripartite structure of *différance*, topos, and observer in Derrida's theory defines a relatively fixed system that arises from the worldliness of the text. Each of these elements is interrelated and refer to the others. The topos in which we discover the slippage of the text points back to its core play of linguistic *différance*. Likewise—and this is what critics have missed in claiming that Derrida does not address the issue of the "location" of deconstructive praxis—this topos and its dependence on textual conflicts also reference an extra-textual, analytic position from which these conflicts become visible. Because this analytic position is essential to the functioning of the text's topos Derrida has claimed that deconstructive criticism is not simply arbitrary, a product of what the observer hopes to find. Consider Derrida's often-cited description of deconstruction in his book *Of Grammatology:*

> The movements of deconstruction do not destroy structures from the outside. They are not possible and effective, nor can they take accurate aim, except by inhabiting those structures. Inhabiting them *in a certain way,* because one always inhabits, and all the more when one does not suspect it. Operating necessarily from the inside, borrowing all the strategic and economic resources of subversion from the old structure, borrowing them structurally, that is to say without being able to isolate their elements and atoms, the enterprise of deconstruction always in a certain ways falls prey to its own work. (24)

Derrida's description of the trace emphasizes not merely *différance* and its spatial articulation in the text as a structure, but also the position that this space creates for a critic to "inhabit." The trace is not defined arbitrarily by the reader, but instead revealed jointly by the location of the observer and the site upon which the trace appears. Derrida particularly stresses the critic's dependence on this interconnected system in the following description of deconstruction:

> The *incision* of deconstruction, which is not a voluntary decision or an absolute beginning, does not take place just anywhere, or in an absolute elsewhere. An incision, precisely, it can be made only according to lines of force and forces of rupture that are localizable in the discourse to be deconstructed. The *topical* and *technical* determination of the most necessary sites and operators—beginnings, holds, levers, etc.—in a given situation depends upon an historical analysis. This analysis is *made* in the general movement of the field, and is never exhausted by the conscious calculation of a "subject." (*Positions* 82)

Here, the position of an observer (the incision he or she makes), the space of the text (its lines and forces), and slippage that the terms undergo (the "general movement of the field") are all mutually dependent. If Derrida lacks Weedon's optimistic post-deconstructive model of the self-conscious critic, he also refuses to believe that textual play is independent of a reader. Rather, language, space, and reader are interconnected by the text's worldliness.

Derrida's theory of the tripartite structure of deconstructive praxis relies on the space of the site as its core, but we can see the whole of the tripartite structure as a collection of several spaces. This is a structure that Probyn herself suggests in using the term *locale* for a specific site, and *location* for a more theoretical space: "By 'location' I refer to the methods by which one comes to locate sites of research. Through location knowledges are ordered into sequences which are congruent with previously established categories of knowledge" ("Travels" 178). If Probyn's distinction between locale and location seems appropriate to Derrida, we should recognize in deconstruction the seed of a radical approach to an individual's negotiation of textuality and sociopolitical involvement. Derrida offers us an image of criticism based on a space that is constantly being constructed, which always gestures beyond itself, and that finally depends upon its continual transformation into other kinds of space. The radical implications for criticism of this spatial multiplicity are never treated directly by Derrida, and indeed we can say that the exploration of these spaces is precisely what is being promised by the post-deconstructive turn to the language of the critic as narrator who is "located" somewhere. One place where the positive connotations of spatial multiplicity have been explored is Michel de Certeau's writing on the negotiation of space in "everyday life." In particular, de Certeau's emphasis on social space speaks to the liberatory potential that exists within these multiple spaces precisely by returning to the post-deconstructive question of how a text can be subject to a fixed textual law and yet also be available to new articulations. De Certeau thus allows us to link Derrida's discussion of the textual dynamics of worldliness back to the goals of post-deconstructive narrative.

De Certeau's work on everyday life takes as its point of departure the premise that everyday actions are a tactical bricolage of "making do" that always works against traditional notions of power. Because he is interested in locally limited tactics rather than in broad systems of power, de Certeau's approach to everyday life is thus broadly in sympathy with local criticism's interest in the positive political effect of occupying a critical "position" in a certain way. But de Certeau also echoes Derrida in treating such locations as constantly opening out into other forms of space. De Certeau's liberatory criticism depends on complicating the social space upon which traditional and some poststructural images of social power and authority depend. When Michel Foucault argues that modern society develops "a certain policy of the body, a certain way of rendering the group of men docile and useful" by locating individuals in isolated spaces where they can be observed and disciplined (*Discipline* 305), he associates strict spatial organization with the operation of power. De Certeau agrees that power operates by virtue of certain "proper places" that it defines, but he also explores social spaces that fall outside of proper disciplinary arrangement.

Distinguishing the hegemonic "strategy" from the "tactics" of the weak, de Certeau writes, "strategies are actions which, thanks to the establishment of a place of power (the property of a proper), elaborate theoretical places (systems and totalizing discourses) capable of articulating an ensemble of physical places in which forces are distributed. They combine these three types of places and seek to master each by means of the others" (38). De Certeau contrasts fixed places to the practice of operating within space, a practice that by its nature undermines stability and the power that it supports. His focus is urban geography, where individuals use city spaces "tactically": "the street geometrically defined by urban planning is transformed into a space by walkers" (117). Such spatial practices are inherently temporal. De Certeau is worth quoting at some length:

> At the outset, I shall make a distinction between space *(espace)* and place *(lieu)* that delimits a field. A place *(lieu)* is the order (of whatever kind) in accord with which elements are distributed in relationships of coexistence. It thus excludes the possibility of two things being in the same location *(place)*. The law of the "proper" rules in the place: the elements taken into consideration are *beside* one another, each situated in its own "proper" and distinct location, a location it defines. A place is thus an instantaneous configuration of positions. It implies an indication of stability.
>
> A *space* exists when one takes into consideration vectors of direction, velocities, and time variables. Thus space is composed of intersections of mobile elements. It is in a sense articulated by the ensemble of movements deployed within it. Space occurs as the effect produced by the operations that orient it, situate it, temporalize it, and make it function in a polyvalent unity of conflictual programs or contractual proximities. . . . In contradistinction to the place, it has thus none of the univocity or stability of a "proper."
>
> In short, *space is a practiced place.* (117)

De Certeau distinguishes between a defined place *(lieu)* and a more general and abstract space produced by "proper" places' confrontation of time. He imagines that one's everyday actions cut across places, introducing a temporality and bringing many spaces into contact. This idea of spatial practice at first seems to echo the later writings of Foucault, whose emphasis on individual practices has seemed to many critics to be a productive alternative to the image of panoptical power in works like *Discipline and Punish*.[4] But rather than treating practice as an alternative to disciplinary spaces, I would like to suggest, de Certeau follows Derrida and explores how practice creates a second level of space.[5] Specifically, de Certeau concludes in this passage rather surprisingly that undermining place reveals a more abstract space that "occurs as the effect produced by the operations that orient it." This is, of course, just the opposite of what we would expect, since we usually think that it is the "concrete" that has the potential to undermine discourse and representation. Like Derrida, de Certeau refuses to believe in some fundamental concrete "thing" that troubles concepts or abstract spaces. De Certeau is suggesting that the shifts between places are freeing precisely because they allow us to recognize a broader notion of space that overarches individual places. Against calls for localization, de Certeau suggests that attention to "sites" (places) is valuable only because of the crossing of boundaries that they necessitate, crossings that allow us to glimpse a more abstract notion of space. De Certeau makes clear that this abstract space cannot be inhabited in any permanent way; rather, the importance of this abstract space is that it makes possible a certain kind of action, a practice. When we recognize a space that overarches individual places, we grasp our ability to act in ways not predetermined by those places and by the power relations that they support.

One form of spatial practice is narrative. De Certeau writes, "every day, [stories] traverse and organize places; they select and link them together; they make sentences and itineraries out of them. They are spatial trajectories" (115). For de Certeau, narrative is at work within the movement between "proper places" of any sort—including the discursive topoi that legitimate scientific knowledge. He emphasizes the practice of narrative by turning to the model of the folktale: "the folktale provides scientific discourse with a model, and not merely with textual objects to be dealt with. It no longer has the status of a document that does not know what it says, cited (summoned and quoted) before and by the analysis that knows it. On the contrary, it is a know-how-to-say exactly adjusted to its object" (78). Narrative in this sense is always the practice of discourse, a practice that sets into play the movement between proper places. When we understand the abstract space that de Certeau suggests, we recognize our own role within the construction of objects of knowledge. And once we recognize this role and the larger space upon which it depends, de Certeau suggests, we can begin to formulate new trajectories for analysis. Thus, quite against local criticism's demonization of theory, de Certeau argues that only through a kind of epiphany-like glimpse into abstract space can critics move beyond the political locations from which they initially approach their object of study. If de Certeau is right, then critics' willingness to participate in the dialectic of location and textual "site" is precisely what allows interpretation to spin off into new directions. Indeed, we will recall Derrida's insistence in "Ousia and Grammē" that the point always gestures toward the whole movement of the line. The nexus between critical location and textual site thus resembles the confused space of the city, where many paths overlap and new trajectories constantly appear. Here we finally have some concrete statement of how critics can respond to the problems of openness in the whole textual dynamic of deconstruction. De Certeau suggests that precisely the movement between the spaces of this dynamic is what opens a text up to having its objects articulated in new ways.

Although using narrative to refer to the practice of negotiating social space is a very idiosyncratic definition of this complex term, de Certeau's theory actually illuminates the appeal to narrative in a post-deconstructive context and suggests the relevance of Derrida's theory of textual worldliness in general. De Certeau treats narrative as a form of discourse in which the practice of constructing and organizing that discourse is evident. The same is true of definitions of narrative in a post-deconstructive context. One way to define narrative is as that form of discourse that both claims the authority to describe an object or event and yet also makes clear that it *is* the product of a certain person speaking or writing. The "narrator," after all, is a figure for the act of ordering and shaping a text; narration, by implication, is that mode of discourse where the ordering of the text is represented within the text, where the text folds back and represents its own exterior (the act of constructing the text) within itself. Of course, many other definitions of narrative come to mind—as rhetorical means of assigning legitimacy, as a model of historical ordering, as the human struggle with temporality, and so on. In a post-deconstructive context, however, it is easy to see how narrative's other qualities are allowed to fall into the background so that it can come to function as par excellence the act of constructing the worldly text. Derrida defines this construction through the play of *différance*. Even though critics in the past have seen a categorical difference between deconstruction's idea of a textual system and the issue of how critics are "located" within the political and social world, my discussion has shown that both are concerned with textual "worldliness." Critics who use the language of location make the worldliness of the text more explicit and help us to recognize a tension within deconstruction otherwise easily overlooked. Deconstruction suggests that the critical language of "location" exploits tensions between concrete and conceptual textual elements that "local" critics themselves may not have recognized. These tensions can become the basis for a post-deconstructive criticism that attempts to place such "worldliness" at the center of its theory, and that labels the attempt to exploit that worldliness and to construct more open-ended texts *narrative.*

Derrida after Deconstruction

De Certeau provides a way of reading deconstruction as containing the seeds of a response to the problems that critics have seen in it. It is certainly important to note that, although many of its problems and dynamics are defined by deconstruction, post-deconstructive criticism marks a distinct attempt to foreground that dynamic and to exploit it to produce texts open to other articulations by emphasizing the writer or critic as one of many "narrators." It is appropriate to conclude this chapter by noting that Derrida's own writing has evolved recently toward precisely these post-deconstructive concerns. In particular I am interested in how his recent work on Karl Marx reflects a change in emphasis in his theory, or at least a change in his tactics in presenting that theory. One of the most remarkable things about *Specters of Marx* in the context of this study is its narrative quality. Indeed, in turning to a figure like Marx, Derrida not only finds an opportunity to discuss the politics that so many critics have suggested are lacking in his theory, but also addresses a subject deeply entwined with history and almost demanding a narrative of influence and causality: "among all the temptations I will have to resist today, there would be the temptation of memory: to recount what was for me, and for those of my *generation* who shared it during a whole lifetime, the experience of Marxism, the quasi-paternal figure of Marx, the way it fought in us with other filiations, the reading of texts and the interpretation of a world in which the Marxist inheritance was—and still remains, and so it will remain—absolutely and thoroughly determinate" (13–14). Derrida is certainly not constructing a traditional narrative; indeed, we should not expect him to, since a large part of the attraction of narrative as a concept in post-deconstructive criticism has little to do with history and temporality. Instead, as we have seen, critics redefine narrative as discourse that places the "worldliness" of the text at the forefront. Derrida's way of speaking about Marx in this passage suggests something of this, since he obviously wants to treat Marx not as an historical person but as a figure that shuttles back and forth between real-world influence and textual construction. Derrida escapes the "temptation of memory" precisely by investigating these ontological ambiguities of the "specter" of Marx: "We believe that this messianic remains an *ineffaceable* mark—a mark one neither can nor should efface—of Marx's legacy, and doubtless of *inheriting*, of the experience of inheritance in general. Otherwise, one would reduce the event-ness of the event, the singularity and the alterity of the other" (28). Derrida casts the "specter" of Marx as ontologically indeterminate, both concrete and conceptual, and actual and ideal. It is this "specterality" that fascinates Derrida, both as a condition of Marx's "presence" within intellectual debates today, and as an issue thematized by Marx. Indeed, when Derrida defines deconstruction as an extension of Marxism— "Deconstruction has never had any sense or interest, in my view at least, except as a radicalization, which is to say also *in the tradition* of a certain Marxism, in a certain *spirit of Marxism*" (92)—he seems to have in mind just this shared concern for the "spectral" and how it complicates the self-presence of everyday objects. Derrida associates the specter with the concrete/conceptual ambiguity of *différance* directly. Discussing the difference between the specter and spirit, Derrida writes, "it is a differance. The specter is not only the carnal apparition of the spirit, its phenomenal body, its fallen and guilty body, it is also the impatient and nostalgic waiting for redemption, namely, once again, for a spirit" (136). The tension that Derrida offers here between the ideal presence of the spirit and the physicality of the specter is just the tension that we have seen throughout between the conceptual and the concrete.[6]

Derrida's recent work departs from his earlier writing on *différance* by representing this ontological ambiguity differently. The specter is not merely ontologically ambiguous; it is a textual figure that embodies everything material that cannot be treated as a simple object. This characterization is clear when Derrida contrasts spectrality and the ideality of spiritual presence: "For there is no ghost, there is never any becoming-specter of the spirit without at least an appearance of flesh, in a space of invisible visibility, like the dis-appearance of an apparition. For there to be ghost, there must be a return to the body, but to a body that is more abstract than ever. The spectrogenic process corresponds therefore to a paradoxical *incorporation*" (126). In this "spectrogenic process" Derrida defines how the movement to embody the spiritual ends up producing a "spectrality" opposed to that spirit. Relatively new in this book is Derrida's claim that this spectrality is a textual element against which one must act. Derrida returns to the language of force and "maintenance" (3) to suggest that one's relation to such specters is always a matter of "work": "the work of mourning is not one kind of work among others. It is work itself, work in general, the trait by means of which one ought perhaps to reconsider the very concept of production—in what links it to trauma, to mourning, to the idealizing iterability of exappropriation, thus to the spectral spiritualization that is at work in any *technē*?" (97). Understanding an object (in this case, the object of mourning) always involves actively participating in "spectral spiritualization," which creates self-present and stable (spiritual) entities but that also produces a kind of "materiality" that haunts the text. In chapter 1 we saw that materiality named ontological ambiguities in the physical body, but noted that it applied vaguely to textual construction. Derrida here seems to be appealing to just such a materiality as part of a method of representing *textually* Marx's legacy.

This theory of textual materiality that seems to be developing in Derrida's recent work can be seen as a response to some of the questions raised about deconstruction, and suggests that Derrida's recent work participates in what I have called the "post-deconstructive" project. Slavoj Žižek offers a familiar critique of deconstruction as insufficiently concerned with politics and ideology, but does so very insightfully through a discussion of its difficulty of dealing within material objects. He sees Jacques Lacan's theory of the symptom as challenging poststructuralism: "[T]he fundamental gesture of post-structuralism is to deconstruct every substantial identity, to denounce behind its solid consistency an interplay of symbolic overdetermination—briefly, to dissolve the substantial identity into a network of non-substantial, differential relations" (72). By ignoring our sense that some things are concrete, poststructuralism blinds itself to the operation of ideology, whose objects exploit a contradictory materiality. According to Žižek, individuals treat ideological objects (e.g., money) as if they were real, even through theoretically individuals understand that these objects merely stand for abstract relations and values: "So, on an everyday level, the individuals know very well that there are relations between people behind the relations between things. The problem is that in their social activity itself, in what they are *doing*, they are *acting* as if money, in its material reality, is the immediate embodiment of wealth as such" (31). Žižek sees in these "sublime" objects of ideology a dangerous acceptance of irony. For Žižek, ideology encourages and exploits an ironic understanding of the contradiction between knowing and doing. Any counterhegemonic theory that uses irony as a strategy simply plays into the hands of hegemony: "in contemporary societies, democratic or totalitarian, that cynical distance, laughter, irony, are, so to speak, part of the game. The ruling ideology is not meant to be taken seriously or literally" (28). Instead, Žižek suggests that we might look for gaps in the functioning of ideological objects—attend, in other words, to the materiality that these objects try to deny.

It is not difficult to see Derrida responding in what we might call the "post-deconstructive" style of *Specters of Marx* to the problems raised by Žižek. In turning to the material complexity of the specter, Derrida seems to respond to the problem of textual objects in poststructural criticism. Indeed, we can go further and suggest that Derrida's recent writing is actually quite similar in its explanation of when and how materiality becomes apparent in objects. Žižek treats the material not as a precondition of the objective—some brute "stuff" that has been shaped into an object by an observer—but as an *effect* of creating and maintaining stable and fixed ideological objects. In treating materiality as an effect and not a precondition, Žižek is true to his psychoanalytic assumptions. For him, it is the very contradictions in the ideological object that are the source of its attraction. Žižek calls these contradictions the "symptom" of one's functioning within ideology (23) and, following Lacan, describes such a symptom as the source of enjoyment itself: "The symptom is not only a cyphered message, it is at the same time a way for the subject to organize his enjoyment—that is why, even after the completed interpretation, the subject is not prepared to renounce his symptom; that is why he 'loves his symptom more than himself'" (74). Žižek sees the gap between doing and knowing itself as a kind of symptom, and thus as part of the enjoyment of the commodity. The real leap in his theory is using this definition of the symptom to describe our feeling that deep down we have some undeniable material basis for our place in the world:

> What do we do with a symptom, with this pathological formation which persists not only beyond its interpretation but even beyond fantasy? Lacan tried to answer this challenge with the concept of *sinthome*, a neologism containing a set of associations (synthetic-artificial man, synthesis between symptom and fantasy, Saint Thomas, the saint . . .). Symptom as *sinthome* is a certain signifying formation penetrated with enjoyment: it is the signifier as a bearer of *jouis-sense*, enjoyment-in-sense.
>
> What we must bear in mind here is the radical ontological status of symptom: symptom, conceived as *sinthome*, is literally our only substance, the only positive support of our being, the only point that gives consistency to the subject. (74–75)

For Žižek, the materiality of the *sinthome* is an indirect effect of our enjoyment of ideological objects. Symptoms *seem* to be caused by a root desire that underlies the relation between an individual and the ideological objects of the world. Symptoms for Žižek are not, however, created by some inherent desire, but are instead the product of the contradictory attitudes that ideological objects demand of individuals. The desire (our "substance") which seems more fundamental than our involvement in the social world of objects and others is actually a construct. Rather than treating materiality as a precondition of objects and the world, Žižek argues that our sense of materiality is actually created by contradictions within the "objective" world.

In the idea of spritualization Derrida echoes Žižek's notion that materiality is produced out of one's relation to ideological objects; in both cases, this production of a counterobjective (or for Derrida, counterspiritual) materiality is a trace left behind when one makes sense of the world. Where Žižek is concerned with the "immaterial" objectivity of ideological objects (e.g., money that can never become worn), Derrida is concerned with how objects granted self-presence are spiritually disengaged from the world. Where Žižek sees this ideological objectivity creating a counterobjective materiality of the bodily symptom, Derrida sees all spiritualization as the movement toward an embodiment that reentangles it in the spectral. For Derrida (drawing on the ghost in *Hamlet* to explain the contradictions of the specter), the spirit hidden within ghostly armor quickly gives way to a spectrality that blurs the line between spirit and what serves to protect it from the real world: "This protection is rigorously *problematic* (*problema* is also a shield) for it prevents perception from deciding on the identity that it wraps so solidly in its carapace. The armor may be but the body of a real artifact, a kind of technical prosthesis, a body foreign to the spectral body that it dresses, dissimulates, and protects, masking even its identity" (8). Like Žižek, then, Derrida suggests that the very movement toward a self-contained objectivity produces a counterobjective materiality.

Derrida becomes interested in the textual figure of materiality at the same moment when he is struggling to define his own political position in relation to Marxism. This is not a coincidence. The complex textual materiality that we see in Derrida as well as in writers discussed earlier like Lyotard and Elizabeth Grosz appears on the post-deconstructive scene as a way for critics to think about *both* the textual construction of knowledge and the continuing power that that knowledge has to shape political action and drive us to articulate these objects of knowledge in new ways. If, as I have suggested in this chapter, post-deconstructive narrative obeys a complex system of textual dynamics for negotiating the relation between world and text, the materiality of its objects becomes the clearest and most forceful embodiment of those dynamics. The movement from deconstructive irony to post-deconstructive exploitation of those ironies demands that we find a way to capture them and use them as part of a larger text. Materiality accomplishes precisely this, and thus represents the textual figure through which all these issues of worldliness and multiple textual spaces are arranged.

chapter three

THE SEARCH FOR
FORM IN AMERICAN
POSTMODERN FICTION

◆

Problems in the Poetics of Postmodern Fiction

It has been a critical commonplace in the last twenty years to refer to contemporary experimental, avant-garde fiction as "self-deconstructive." Typical is Linda Hutcheon's characterization of postmodernism in general as using self-contradiction for critique:

> Willfully contradictory . . . postmodern culture uses and abuses the conventions of discourse. It knows it cannot escape implication in the economic (late capitalist) and ideological (liberal humanist) dominants of its time. There is no outside. All it can do is question from within. It can only problematize what Barthes has called the "given" or "what goes without saying" in our culture. History, the individual self, the relation of language to its referents and of texts to other texts—these are some of the notions which, at various moments, have appeared as "natural" or unproblematically common-sensical. And these are what get interrogated. (xiii)

When we think of the unraveling stories about storytelling written after modernism by writers like John Barth, Jorges Borges, or Italio Calvino, we do indeed seem to have a corollary to deconstruction. Both postmodernist fiction and deconstruction challenge the kinds of traditional metaphysical beliefs that Hutcheon lists. Both approach this critique through self-reflection, producing difficult works that often baffle casual readers.

And yet, especially in America, when these writers describe their own goals, they rarely emphasize deconstruction as desirable in and of itself. Indeed, these writers often speak in seemingly traditional terms about discovering the natural aesthetic bases for new fiction. Ronald Sukenick, for example, calls for a return to fundamental aesthetic principles in fiction: "we must go back to the sources of fiction, stripped of inessentialities and historical trappings, so that we can recognize the fundamental virtues of the novel though they may appear in odd recombinations and unaccustomed forms. New fiction requires new criteria, but such criteria will be rooted in the essentials of the medium" (*Form* 243). Sukenick's hope of developing a new aesthetics of fiction in postmodern America is a motivation for much of this seemingly "self-deconstructive" writing, a motivation that has largely been unrecognized by critics. Postmodern experimental fiction in America has sought to develop a notion of form appropriate to fiction. Amiri Baraka's introduction to his collection of fiction, *The Moderns*, explains this search:

> "It is a commonplace though always a surprising fact that, in the literary countries generally, the subtleties of poetic technique have been mastered earlier than the simplicities of prose . . . ," which was Douglas Bush talking about the differences between Chaucer's prose and his poetry. I take this to be a generalization displayed often enough to have some meaning. It has certainly been the case with recent American literature, at least in its public entrance. (Jones x)

For Jones, writers simply do not understand the formal principles of fiction. Almost two decades later, Gilbert Sorrentino makes the same observation about fictional form: "American poets have solved literary problems that prose writers, except for those who are also poets, have not even begun to grapple with" (O'Brien 5). Although an interest in formal concerns is characteristic of postmodernism in all the arts, contemporary American writers hope to return to the fundamental principles of form because fiction according to these writers has treated form so inadequately in the past. Gertrude Stein's writing attracts William H. Gass, for example, because it raises basic formal questions: "None of the literary innovators who were her contemporaries attempted anything like the revolution she proposed, and because her methods were so uncompromising, her work cannot really be met except on the finest and most fundamental grounds" (*Fiction* 87). In searching for a new aesthetic and formal basis for fiction, postmodern writers often turn to other arts. Donald Barthelme has spoken of the importance of painting for his approach to fiction (LeClair and McCaffery 39). Ishmael Reed and Raymond Federman have spoken about the influence of jazz as a model of textual construction.[1] We can say, then, that despite the disruptive self-reflexivity evident in a great deal of postmodern fiction, the writers of this fiction believe that they are pursuing a positive aesthetic goal, and that this goal entails an attempt to define a notion of form appropriate to prose fiction.

Postmodern fiction in American, then, occupies a fascinating relation to deconstruction, a relation that we can call "post-deconstructive" in the sense that I have defined in chapter 1. This fiction accepts deconstructive principles, embracing the idea that discourse is always incomplete, that subjectivity is at least partially illusory, and so on.[2] But at the same time, this fiction obviously wants to go beyond these deconstructive assumptions to produce a new kind of writing that does more than merely restate textual paradoxes. We have seen precisely the same thing in post-deconstructive criticism's turn to narrative, which we have noted embodies the hope of accepting but transforming deconstructive binds to produce a type of text whose objects are available for other articulations. Clearly the search for form in *fiction* does not lead inevitably to an inquiry into *narrative* as a model for that aesthetic form. But I will show that these postmodern writers do indeed develop a post-deconstructive fiction in much the same way that we saw critics develop post-deconstructive narrative—by emphasizing the relation between the text and the outside world and by using the problematic materiality of textual elements as an emblem of that "worldliness." In particular these writers think about fiction as a mode of writing in which the author negotiates a position between the text and the real world, echoing the concern for the narrator that we have seen in post-deconstructive criticism. If, as I have suggested throughout, the interest in post-deconstrutive narrative arises from the attempt to find a way to construct texts that are responsible for how they take a role within a political context, turning to a genre of writing that is highly self-conscious about how it is being constructed and how it will affect readers is bound to clarify textual construction after deconstruction. In the process we will help to rethink the interpretation of a number of contemporary American writers as merely "self-deconstrutive."

Defining Form in Postmodern Fiction

When postmodern American writers describe fictional form they usually emphasize the temporal, ongoing character of fictional composition. Indeed, writers of postmodern fiction in America are quite explicit in claiming that fictional form must not be a static structure within the text, but rather must arise out of a tension between the real world and the fictional text. This fiction, we can say, searches for a *dy-*

namic understanding of form that does not sever the process of composition from the final textual "product." Sukenick describes a new
type of form that arises out of the process of composition: "if there is
one thing that I hope characterizes my thinking about form, it is in considering form a dynamic, rather than inert, element of composition. In
contemporary work important to me, form is not a given but an object
of invention, part of the content and, like it, determined only in composition" (*Form* ix). Guy Davenport likewise has remarked that "every
force evolves a form"—both in the history of ideas, and in artistic creation (151–55). Paul Auster comments similarly on how the structure of
his works evolve out of composition: "At this point I'm not even thinking about anything beyond doing the books themselves. They impose
themselves on me, so it's not my choice. The only thing that really matters, it seems to me, is saying the thing that has to be said. If it really
has to be said, it will create its own form" (264). For all of these writers, fictional form reflects how the text came into being. These writers
do not aggrandize the creative act, but rather recognize that writing
negotiates between the demands of the socially "located" writer *and*
textuality. Walter Abish's essay, "The Writer-to-Be: An Impression of
Living," describes how fiction negotiates between the demands inherent to the text and the extra-textual impulses of the writer. His essay
discusses the moment of coming to write, the time before publication
when one's definition of writing is all potential: "How does one explain
that sudden intrusion in one's life of that singular resolve to become a
writer, someone who passes his or her days in a kind of self-imposed
isolation concocting a fictitious world peopled by fictitious characters?" (101). Abish's claim in this essay is that for the writer-to-be, "the
book-to-be is both a text as well as a prescription for the journey of self-
discovery" (102). His definition of writing suggests that a story is both
a textual construction and a stage upon which the author acts—both
textual and extra-textual. For these postmodern writers, the poetic
structure of the text has a real-world origin, but this structure also
reflects the textual context in which this "journey" is to be pursued.

We hear in these descriptions of the interaction between text and
world in postmodern fiction an echo of Derrida's concept of textual
worldliness. Derrida too is struggling with the issue of textual form to
the extent that he tries to explain how space and time *shape* the text.
We saw that textual worldliness is mediated by a play between different kinds of spaces—what I called the "local site" and one's critical
"location." In much the same way, Sukenick describes fictional form as
the *continuity* of text and world when he describes the "poetics of
experience":

Fiction as improvisation, all that old beatnik stuff, we've heard it before, you say, and it only opens the door to mediocrity. The door is always open to mediocrity, and no theory can close it. It is true, however, that the idea of fiction as defined by the act of composition raises formal problems that the beatniks did not even approach recognizing, much less resolve. Kerouac was simply an explosion out of the going commercial-academic complex in fiction in the direction of what was happening in the rest of the arts—the rest of the world, for that matter. However, the work of Kerouac, taken together with that of Burroughs and of the poet-theorists with whom they are associated, should not be minimized. It represented a return to what might be called a "poetics of experience," in which art tends to be considered not about experience but part of it, and which could be argued as the most vital tradition in American writing. (*Form* 7)

Sukenick admits that writers are often unaware of the practical problems that their poetic pronouncements raise. In claiming that fiction must not be about experience but part of it, he pares down these writerly claims to one basic definition of fictional form: the real world and fictional text must be continuous. As Sukenick notes, "If art is continuous with experience, there is no frame. Art is free, at least, actually to merge with life" (43). If fiction does not imitate the world, then a writer need not *impose* a structure upon it; structures will evolve in a text in the same way they evolve in our experience of the world. Postmodern fiction, then, is given form by its points of continuity with the world, just as we saw how the deconstructive text was shaped by the way in which critics moved back and forth between real and textual "locales."

Critics have occasionally recognized this postmodern interest in fictional worlds, but have treated this interest largely as a thematic issue. Most often it is assumed that postmodern writers describe the nature of a "world" (McHale, *Postmodernist* 10), or that they are challenging any totalizing world system (Hutcheon 141–57). The comments of writers like Sukenick and Abish have suggested that American postmodern fiction is interested, instead, in how a text's relation to the world affects its notion of form. The lack of awareness of these formal issues is one of the reasons why self-reflective postmodern fiction has received relatively less attention in recent years. Indeed, we can distinguish between two traditions within recent experimental American fiction: the historical and self-reflexive. In the former category we can place writers like Thomas Pynchon, Don Delillo, and E. L. Doctorow; in the latter, we can place writers like Raymond Federman, Clarence Major, and Sukenick. Although early criticism tended to celebrate the radical formal experiments of the latter group—in part because this group was more insistent on offering the explanations of their own formal goals that I have quoted in this section—the former group has garnered the lion's share of recent study. Hutcheon's theory of postmodernism makes clear why critics have shifted their attention. Working against early criticism that placed writers like Federman at the center of the postmodern canon, Hutcheon writes, "Much contemporary metafiction is indeed almost solely concerned with its own artifice, its own aesthetic workings. But self-reflexivity has a long history in art, and, in fact, the label of 'self-begetting novel' has been used to describe both modernist fiction and the New Novel. The postmodernist art I have been and will be describing in this book is historical and political in a way that much metafiction is not" (52). She encourages critics to choose between historical and self-reflexive types of contemporary fiction. Given the apparent choice between politically engaged texts that are "about" specific historical events and issues, and those texts that are self-reflexive and often obscure, critics have usually embraced the former and neglected the latter.[3] This neglect is in part a post-deconstructive condition: critics feel that self-reflexivity is a dead end, and consequently turn to historical fiction for an alternative. But let us recall what we saw in Jacques Derrida's writing, that the basis of a rigorous post-deconstructive criticism was implicit within the earlier deconstructive writing, and that more recent writing works to create a distinction for the sake of its own self-definition. The same, I think, is true of postmodern fiction: the distinction between reflexive and historical postmodernism, while common, is to some extent a construction that serves the purpose of defining the relevance of postmodern fiction after deconstruction.[4] Although the deconstructive self-reflexivity that Hutcheon criticizes may be frustrating, the writers who attempt to solve the problems raised by deconstruction for fiction from within this tradition are likely to be those that produce the most satisfying response to those problems.[5] Thus, I will focus on American postmodernism in its self-reflexive strain, and especially on those works that appeared after the first flush of this reflexive writing. Such fiction provides an example of post-deconstructive writing not only in this chapter but throughout the remainder of this book. To focus on *post*-deconstructive writing, I will not discuss the early (1960s) works from the self-reflexive strain of postmodern writing in America—works like John Barth's *Lost in the Funhouse*, Robert Coover's *Pricksongs and Descants*, and Sukenick's *Up*—but instead will concentrate on the more recent writing of the 1970s and 1980s. Although I have suggested that postmodern fiction in America is from the outset interested in formal issues, we would expect that more recent writing has been able to work through deconstructive issues more fully. Just as the issue of worldliness essential to post-deconstructive criticism is implicit in Derrida's early work but not fully

expressed as a method of analysis and writing until his book on Karl
Marx, so too can we say that the most recent postmodern fiction manages to articulate a post-deconstructive fictional form with which earlier texts only struggled.

Trying to move beyond the negative implications of textual worldliness—the instability of the text, the inability of the writer to define
some objects as "concrete," the difficulty of taking a single "position" in
relation to the text, and so on—to construct a positive aesthetic of this
fiction leads experimental postmodern writers to emphasize the mo-
ment-by-moment development of the text. Postmodern texts evolve:
authorial choices affect, but also are translated by, a developing text
that has sequence, but that lacks traditional hierarchies or static patterns. This idea of narrative as an open-ended sequence that may evolve
a form as it goes grows in part out of the Beat theory of "Spontaneous
Prose" and in part out of musical, especially jazz, models to which many
experimental writers in fiction have turned. As Federman writes, "if
one admits from the start (at least to oneself) that no meaning preexists language, but that language creates meaning as it goes along, that
is to say as it is used (spoken or written), as it progresses, then writing
(fiction especially) will be a mere process of letting language do its
tricks" ("Surfiction" 8). Federman's improvisational aesthetics challenges our traditional belief that a text must have a fixed structure that
an author conceives and inserts into a text. Often critics describe the
rejection of such hierarchies in postmodern fiction as a matter of "parataxis" (Hayles)—that is, the juxtaposition of items within the text—but
such a characterization misses what is essential in postmodern temporality. Unlike a paratactic text, which usually explicitly rejects cohesion
and order, this postmodern narrative leaves open the possibility that
order might evolve out of the text's temporality. Peter Nichols has
argued that experimental writers like Federman and Sukenick are following a distinctly temporal strand of postmodern American fiction:
"Another form of postmodernism has turned its attention very deliber-
ately to questions of temporality and narrative, and specifically to what
Lyotard has called the 'event,' the singular moment which can be spoken about only after it is over, and which is composed of 'simultaneous
and heterogeneous temporalities'" (14; citing Readings 24). The textual
temporality that Nichols and Federman describe is less a matter of the
represented events of the narrative—although these may be part of the
work's open-ended, developing quality—and more a matter of its own
development during the time of reading and writing. That postmodern
writers understand textual temporality very broadly is clear in Kathy
Acker's interview observation: "Any prose writer, even if he doesn't use

narrative the way narrative is traditionally used, is concerned with narrative. I mean the reader has to go from A to Z and it's going to take a long time and that's narrative. There's no way to get around it; that's the form" (Friedman, "Conversation" 14). Even a writer as "structural" as Gass emphasizes the time of reading when he remarks that "the book is more like a building which you're trying to get someone to go through the way you want him to" (LeClair and McCaffery 25). Auster's comment on Charles Reznikoff suggests that he too is interested in the temporal development of the text: "Art, then, for the sake of something—which means that art is almost an incidental by-product of the effort to make it. The poem, in all instances, must be an effort to perceive, must be a moving *outward*" (37). Although Auster, Acker, and Gass think about space differently, all three associate postmodern fiction with temporality and see that temporality as existing against some kind of background thrown into relief by this movement. This background appears to provide a sort of form for their fiction—although it is clearly a "form" in a very untraditional sense.

I would like to argue that time and space are the constants that shape the continuity of world and text, and that they are therefore the "forms" through which post-deconstructive fiction, like post-deconstructive criticism, is organized. In chapter 2 we saw that the play between many spaces, especially as they are mediated by an often-suppressed temporality with which texts cannot fully come to terms, provided the underlying structure for the organization of textual worldliness. Postmodern fiction often has a more positive, even essentialist notion of textual temporality, but it shares with Derrida's writing an insistence that space and time organize the text's relationship to the extra-textual world. For many of the postmodern fiction writers that we have discussed, what remains constant between world and text is the time of reading and writing. Postmodern fictional narrative brings together two different kinds of time: the time of the "act of composition" and the time of the "experience" of reading. There is a continuity between world and text because both are essentially temporal: the time of writing is manifested in the temporality of the text, which in turn is manifested in the time of reading. Other writers like Gass see space as providing continuity between world and text; Gass describes the act of writing as constructing a "house" through which a reader then moves. When Joseph Frank writes about "spatial form" in narrative, he recognizes that space is both an internal part of the work, and an external structure for the reader's interaction with the text.[6] Contemporary writing in American has approached form through space and time in part because of its own literary history. Indeed, some of the best and earliest writing on postmodern fiction defined the formal use of space in postmodern writing as an inheritance from nineteenth-century American fiction. Charles Caramello summarizes Richard Poirier on this inheritance:

> In *A World Elsewhere: The Place of Style in American Literature*, Poirier explores the "effort to create a world in which consciousness might be free to explore its powers and affinities," the effort, that is, to create a world of language in which consciousness can realize itself independent of the constraints of historical time and politico-sexual space. Anticipating modernism, Poirier's argument runs, classical American literature proceeds "as if only language can create the liberated place." The radical separation of self and world promises the possibility of *re*creating the world in language and, further, of *creating* a new self that can inhabit that world. (57; citing Poirier ix, 5)

Caramello and Poirier are correct in noting that postmodern fiction constructs textual spaces to reflect on the relation between text and world. Narrative form is usually defined through technicalities of narration (the relation between text and its narrators), the organization of a given plot (symmetry or asymmetry between the beginning and ending points of the narrative), or details of the presented characters and places themselves (structural balance between types of characters or locations visited). Time and space are considerably more abstract elements of a fictional text, but for that reason are better able to move back and forth between text and reality. In offering his model of postmodern fiction as "obopshebam," Major is attracted to space and time as formal elements because they are abstract and can take many different shapes:

> Reality as an idea contains all the difficulties anybody could ever want to tackle. Even the most ambitious readers of, say, Beckett's *Malloy* or a later work like *Ping* would have trouble discovering the exact ways space and time are employed and represented in these texts. But reality itself—which, let us say, *contains* time and space—as a model for inter-textual obopshebam fiction is particularly problematic because it refuses to stop changing; or being a million different things at any given point; or disappearing before one's eyes. ("Meditation" 170)

Real-world space and time are not simply represented within the text, since space and time themselves are not static things—they refuse to stop changing. Rather, space and time provide Major with a way of talking about how world and text are similarly unstable. Because time and space can take so many different shapes, they are able to move between world and text: "[Time] is a physical thing. It both occupies and possesses a terrain; it can be seen, felt, held and released. A lemon—real or in a Paul Cézanne—possesses time as a seasonal metaphor. The space of that real lemon, unlike a literary text . . . is a time-matrix charged with metaphysical processes. It is, however, a key aspect of literary history that the measure of all the time states of written texts must be seen within those metaphysical boundaries" (169).

Clearly post-deconstructive fiction and criticism understand the nature of textual worldliness differently, and consequently define the role of space and time in negotiating that worldliness in very different ways. For Derrida texts constantly offer up a kind of spatial completeness that supported traditional notions of presence for him; temporality consequently remains an element of the text that can be recovered only with a great deal of difficulty. Indeed, Derrida suggests that temporality will only be recognizable in the gaps between spatial constructions. Postmodern fiction, conversely, seems to take the opposite approach. Although, as I have just noted, different writers emphasize either space or time, time seems to be fundamentally less mysterious and more an integral part of composition and reading. Space has often seemed to be less a presence insisted on in everyday discourse and more a background upon which this temporality functions. Indeed, we could say that spatiality is the very condition of form in postmodern fiction, since we only get a glimpse of something organizing composition when we sense a space behind this temporality. Although this contrast appears to make a fundamental distinction between deconstructive criticism and postmodern fiction, let us note first that it suggests a deeper relationship between time, space, and the worldly text. In both cases we see textual worldliness being revealed though a tension between space and time in which at certain moments one gives way to the other. Thus, postmodern fiction clarifies the spatiotemporal dynamic that Derrida describes by suggesting that textual time need not be the ineffable or mysterious element in this dichotomy. Rather, space and time appear as qualities at work in ambiguous ways *both* in texts and in the real world. Literary interest in the act of reading will place emphasis on space as the mysterious quality that is constructed out of this temporality; philosophical interest in the metaphysics assumed by texts will treat spatiality and presence as the basis of representation, and make temporality the ineffable textual quality to be explored. In both types of textuality, however, we see a movement toward a positive understanding of textual construction that does not simply refuse the problems raised by deconstruction, but instead attempts to use them to produce a new kind of textual construction which, I have argued, is usually associated with narrative in this post-deconstructive context. We saw that post-deconstructive criticism hoped to produce a kind of text that recognized the omnipresence of textual dynamics and yet managed to make its own objects available to new articulations. Postmodern fiction seems to share in this dual goal when it describes the author's location within the dynamics of textual production while insisting that the ongoing nature of fictional composition leaves the text suspended and forward-looking. The tone of Abish's "writer-to-be" essay captures this duality nicely: here is an image of unescapable textuality in which the author's position as a writer is always-already articulated, and yet this position points toward futurity and suggests that this is a text yet to be developed. We can say, then, that postmodern fiction engages the same post-deconstructive problems that draws critics to the textual model of "narrative."

Negotiating Materiality in Postmodern Fiction

Throughout this study I have suggested that the kind of narrative being developed after deconstruction emphasizes the material ambiguities of its textual objects. These narratives do this because such ambiguities provide a way of thinking about what we can now call the "worldliness" of the text—its complex relation to the real world. The materiality of its objects is not merely a philosophical corollary to the issues of worldliness; it is also a textual feature that can be used to foreground and negotiate these issues. We saw how important this was in Derrida's recent work, where materiality became a figure through which all of these issues could be raised. The materially complex figure of Marx in this work allowed Derrida to embody the problems of worldliness while throwing the whole dynamic of critical location into the foreground. Is there an equivalent interest in textual materiality in the post-deconstructive writing of postmodern fiction? Since, as we have seen, post-deconstructive narrative names a certain way of exploiting textual problems, we can say that discovering materiality as an issue used in this fiction may well mean that we can rightly call the aesthetic goals of postmodern fiction a form of post-deconstructive "narrative."

Gass's critical essays often reference the spatiotemporal tensions that I have used to characterize postmodern fictional form in order to discuss issues of textual materiality. Although he is rarely considered a major figure in postmodern writing, his background in analytic philosophy naturally attracts him to issues of textual objects and thus encourages him to explore textual materiality as a tool for post-deconstructive narrative in his critical writing and interviews much more explicitly than other writers. Gass's primary concern is how everyday words, the "raw materials" of a text, come to be transformed when they are inserted into the fictional text: "It seems a country-headed thing to say: that literature is language, that stories and the places and the people in them are merely made of words as chairs are made of smoothed sticks and sometimes of cloth or metal tubes" (*Fiction* 27). He asserts the word's ability in and of itself to project a world with spatial and temporal dimensions: "the sentence . . . is entirely surrounded by logical space like parking lots around a bowling alley" (*World* 318). Art functions by foiling language's normal reference to fixed, conventional locations and times: "The poet struggles to keep his words from saying something, although, like the carrot, they want to go to seed" (297). The restraint that Gass associates with poetic writing is essential for his understanding of formal coherence in a work. According to Gass, the tensions between restraint and forward-movement transform a text's basic materials into a represented object. When he applies these observations about the philosophy of language to aesthetics he is thus returning to the issues of space and time, and suggests how the issues of materiality dovetail with postmodern fiction's formal concerns. Behind the tension between the natural disposition of language and the restraint exerted by the writer is a conflict between space and time. Gass uses the example of a statue to describe the tensions of the fictional work:

> On the other side of a novel lies the void. Think, for instance, of a striding statue; imagine the purposeful inclination of the torso, the alert and penetrating gaze of the head and its eyes, the outstretched arm and pointing finger; everything would appear to direct us toward some goal in front of it. Yet our eye travels only to the finger's end, and not beyond. Though pointing, the finger bids us stay instead, and we journey slowly back along the tension of the arm. In our hearts we know what actually surrounds the statue. The same surrounds every other work of art: empty space and silence. (*Fiction* 49)

For Gass, a literary work is defined formally by the tension between the forward development of the text (the goal in front of the statue) and the background presupposed in that movement (the limit of the statue-space)—in other words, by textual space and time. The formal coherence that Gass describes is not static; instead, it arises from the temporal movement through the work that at some point turns back and reveals the "tension" in the movement. In the tension between a whole textual space and our temporal movement through it we know how this

object is constructed. Gass claims that through spatiotemporal conflicts we realize "what actually surrounds the statue," the "silence" of
those elements of it that have been excluded in order to give the statue
shape. Without enclosing this space and suspending the statue's reference to its goal, we could not construct a distinct art object, an entity
that we can stand before and view. Here Gass raises questions about
the work's *materiality* in the sense that I used the term in the first
chapter—he questions how an object comes to be seen as a distinct,
fixed thing and suggests all those things that have been left out of that
object. But just as we have seen in critics interested in the concept of
materiality, Gass also suggests that these exclusions themselves are
part of what makes us feel that the object *is* concrete. Without the foil-
ed movement of the statue, Gass suggests, it would seem inert and without interest. Precisely the material conflicts within the statue make it
seem so compelling a *thing*.

Gass imagines the spatiotemporal conflicts that draw our attention
to the materiality of the statue in fairly traditional, formal terms. He has
something of the New Critic in him, and consequently produces an
account of form that makes the statue appear almost a self-contained
thing. These spatial conflicts need not, however, emphasize formal closure. Indeed, it may be more appropriate to postmodern fiction to
emphasize the way in which these spatial tensions open the work up,
rather than close it down. This certainly is the emphasis in Edward W.
Soja's account of contradictions within postmodern spaces. Soja inaugurates his account of postmodern space in his well-known study, *Postmodern Geographies* by observing that the spaces that make up the
contemporary city—embodied in one of his other works on Los
Angeles—do not obey traditional geographic logic. He writes,

> the historical development of urbanization over the past century has been
> marked by a selective dispersal and decentralization, emptying the centre
> of many of the activities and populations which once aggregated densely
> around it. For some, this has signaled a negation of nodality, a submergence
> of the power of central places, perhaps even a Derridan deconstruction of
> all differences between the "central" and the "marginal." Yet the centers
> hold. Even as some things fall apart, dissipate, new nodalities form and old
> ones are reinforced. (234)

For Soja, postmodern cities do not simply discard the notion of spatial
organization, but instead create a constant circulation of spaces that
create "new nodalities" even as old centers and margins shift. He has
more recently offered this image of spatial transformation as part of a
more general theory of space. In *Thirdspace*, Soja describes the move-

ment of "trialectics," a logical progression modeled on dialectics in which a third term emerges not as a synthesis of the earlier two, but as a radical alternative. He writes, "Thirding introduces a critical 'other-than' choice that speaks and critiques through its otherness. That is to say, it does not derive simply from additive combination of its binary antecedents but rather from a disordering, deconstruction, and tentative reconstitution of their presumed totalization producing an open alternative that is both similar and strikingly different" (61). Soja applies this idea of an "otherness" arising out of initial terms to traditional notions of space, and argues that we can see radical new ways of thinking about space arising out of traditional definitions: "Such thirding is designed not just to critique Firstspace and Secondspace modes of thought, but also to reinvigorate their approaches to spatial knowledge with new possibilities heretofore unthought of inside the traditional spatial disciplines" (81).

Soja's account of postmodern space as arising from an ongoing transformation of spatial definitions to produce new ways of thinking about space is a useful corrective to the narrowly formal model that Gass offers. Soja, too, offers a way to think about the formal construction of the work, since he is interested in the ways in which thought is given shape by spatial models. Unlike Gass, however, Soja implies that the movement of composition and reading opens up the work to new types of spaces rather than turning it back into a closed, tension-filled whole. Soja's account of postmodern space seems to me especially appropriate for writers like Federman and Sukenick, who emphasize improvisational composition and see the temporal movement through the text as the key to postmodern fictional form. Indeed, Marcel Cornis-Pope has recently suggested that the these writers are trying to develop a poetics that specifically rejects such self-contained texts. As Cornis-Pope argues, this fiction can "be described as a polemical, process-oriented form of narration that continually reformulates its modes of articulations, 'push[ing] out to the edge of culture and of form' in order to 'allow more reality into the work'" ("Innovation" 225; citing Sukenick, *Form* 135). Soja's understanding of the constant transformation of spaces seems to keep the formal principle that Gass articulates while at the same time making clear that postmodern space can open the work outward to new spaces, rather than becoming a self-contained whole.

Despite its limitations, Gass's account of space is important because it locates this spatial transformation as the place at which the work's materiality comes into question. We can see the same entwining of space, time, and the materiality of textual objects in a great deal of postmodern fiction, and this network of connected issues suggests that this fiction does indeed share in the general textual goals of post-decon-structive narrative. Let us consider Sukenick's novel *Blown Away*. As a relatively recent self-reflexive novel, Sukenick's story is clearly post-deconstructive in the sense that it appeared after the first flush of self-reflexivity in fiction and seems to be struggling to use this self-reflexivity in new ways. Indeed, what is most striking is the way in which Sukenick has backgrounded his own act of writing and instead has located the novel's self-reflexivity in its concern for how individuals are positioned within and between narratives in everyday life—specifically, in this case, through the stories created by the Hollywood film industry. Late in the novel a character notes that he wants to create "experimen-tal fiction that everybody can understand. Why should the masses be deprived of elite art?" (138). Although Sukenick is aware of the contra-diction of this last sentence, this goal is consistent with one that he has articulated since the publication of this novel: a critique of mass media that nonetheless refuses to believe that individuals can simply ignore the narratives that novels, news, and film provide.[7] *Blown Away* tells the story of Boris Ccrab, a psychic; Clover Bottom, a starlet; and Rob Drackenstein, a movie director. The story opens with Ccrab hypnotiz-ing the vapid Bottom and "selling" her to Drackenstein, who produces an unexpected hit with Bottom as the star. The bulk of the novel con-cerns the attempt to create a second vehicle for Bottom's budding star-dom, a film that itself becomes entangled in the "real-life" stories of Bottom's romance and success. The problems that Drackenstein en-counters when he alternately tries to exploit and exclude these stories in making Bottom's second film are reflected in how the story is told. Ccrab is a very good psychic, and generally knows what will happen in the novel. Ccrab also predicts events to others within the novel, which we later see "repeated" in their original occurrence. Ccrab can, too, project himself into other places and times (and consequently can be at several places at once), as well as into other people in order to influ-ence their decisions—most notably Drackenstein's decisions about Bottom's second film. Interwoven with these foretellings is the con-struction of the movie itself, which increasingly mirrors Bottom's life, and the writing of a book about the making of the film, which itself is part of the final film Drackenstein tries to produce. Although the narra-tive begins in a relatively realistic way by following Ccrab's perspective, as this perspective becomes caught up in events that he anticipates and in the hypothetical plots of the film, the overall effect is that of a web of dizzyingly interwoven narratives. As Sukenick turns to think about narrative itself as a form, I would like to argue, he suggests how the aes-thetic goals of postmodern fiction dovetail with the post-deconstructive narrative mode that I have described in chapter 1.

The novel's dizzying convolutions reflect the overlapping and unstable narrative roles that individuals occupy. A college student at the beginning of the novel, Clover is "discovered" and taken over by a larger-than-life role from which the film draws its power. Although she is typical of the homogeneity of contemporary media society ("There are a thousand Cathy Junes in this city, including Clover Bottom," remarks Drackenstein [47]), she paradoxically becomes unique through the role that she adopts. Ccrab discusses Clover's role directly: "In principle there's only one sex goddess, periodically called up from the underworld in the person of yet another doomed avatar. The Director as necromancer, sustaining dead spirits with blood rites. He drains her till she becomes a completely empty medium for his own evil schemes. It's a traditional vampire theme" (98). The fact that Clover occupies a role that exists independently of her is quite evident in the novel. Clover herself is merely a look-alike for the original actress in Drackenstein's first film; by the end of the novel, Drackenstein is again planning to use a look-alike stand-in for Clover on his second film (172). Sukenick is less interested in commenting on the film industry than he is in explaining how individuals occupy narrative roles in general. The narrator describes Ccrab's schizophrenia, which develops because he occupies many different narrative roles. "Crab's eyes don't converge anymore," remarks the narrator:

> There's another Crab who is more disengaged, who can see more of what's going on because he's less involved, he's hardly there, a vague embodiment, passing from visibility to invisibility from body to body taking possession like a loa, a spirit. He's less interested in given destinies than Crab, including his own, he has more authority. That's because he's closer to me. I'm Ccrab. I'm the omniscient narrator. The Father, the Son, and the Holy Ghost was basically the solution to a narrative problem. (96)

Ccrab's voice and perspective begin to disintegrate because he occupies several roles in the same narrative. It is not just Ccrab who accepts multiple narrative roles; rather, the multiplicity of these roles is part of contemporary society in general. Victor Plotz (Drackenstein's scriptwriter) explains the pervasiveness of narrative roles in contemporary society: "[R]eading about yourself is always a bummer. It's like hearing yourself on tape or seeing yourself on TV. It never seems like your self to yourself. That's because your self from the outside isn't yourself. It's a third person, a him. All media induces schizophrenia, or what we used to call schizophrenia. Now multiple personality is becoming the norm. Everyone is becoming everyone. And no one" (101). Film's creation of transpersonal roles is part of the saturation of contemporary life by narratives—film, news, novels, and so on. Clover's own doomed role as a "sex goddess" is merely an extreme instance of a general cultural phenomenon.

Thus far I have characterized *Blown Away* much like any other critic would describe a self-reflexive novel—by emphasizing textual inconsistencies and metafictional paradoxes. Sukenick's novel departs from this reflexivity by struggling to define how characters might escape these narrative entrapments. This, I would suggest, makes the novel *post-deconstructive* in the sense that I have used the term in chapter 1: it is a novel that confronts the claims and problems of deconstruction, and that tries to resolve or transform them into a positive, open-ended image of textuality that we have associated with post-deconstructive narrative. Most remarkable here is that Sukenick develops this post-deconstructive novel precisely by turning to the material complexity of the "objects"—in this sense the novel's characters—that narratives define and orchestrate. Sukenick's goal of discovering and escaping from some of these narrative convolutions is clear in the novel's ending where Drackenstein visits Henry Miller, who advises him to accept the task of "unwriting": "[L]ife is not a book, don't you see. If everything that's going to happen is already written it makes a rotten story, a story it's up to us to unwrite. And from another point of view everything is unpredictable, and even when I wipe my nose, that's something that never happened before and nobody could have thought up ahead of time" (177). This advice ends the novel, and we can assume that it reflects Sukenick's own goals.[8] How Sukenick hopes to "unwrite" his characters' plots and to grant them some freedom within their narrative roles is hinted at early in the novel. The story itself opens with Ccrab realizing that he is becoming caught up in a tragic romance with Bottom and is loosing control of his life. In response to another's comment that Ccrab's predictions about himself are always wrong, Ccrab says, "They're not wrong. They have a statistical probability. If they don't happen to me they'll happen to someone else. . . . Astrology is a flat system. Like life, it doesn't refer to anything beyond itself" (43). Ccrab suggests that narratives and the roles they create cannot be changed or challenged, but that there is always a gap between the individual and the role; as Ccrab notes, "The macroconditions conform. . . . The microconditions are always chaotic" (71). This gap between individual and role introduces some indeterminacy into these otherwise inescapable narratives. *Blown Away* is a novel of "unwriting" and thus exploits this gap to help free its characters. While accepting the roles that mass media provide for its characters (e.g., repeating typical stories of tragic movie starlets; "Monroe, Mansfield, it's all the same story" [160]), the novel unwrites these outcomes, leaving the reader with an ambiguous ending. Although Clover appears to die (in several ways, in fact) she reappears in the last chapter entitled "Revision," which is concerned with the burial of Plotz. Amid the increasing chaos of the story, Clover's place within this tragic plot gradually becomes less certain; her last line in the novel is that "It's beautiful to be back in the world again" (163). Although it would be a mistake to say that she "overcomes" her fate, as an individual she seems to sidestep a narrative role that remains doomed.

Characters like Bottom can sidestep their narrative role because narrative progression itself is a contradictory idea. The chaos of the novel's overlapping plots is, after all, a kind of hyper-ordering of the story. Sukenick takes the notion of plot and order to an extreme where progression folds back upon itself and creates a kind of textual space. The narrator refers to the story as a "network" (52), but Sukenick only explores this spatialization of narrative late in the novel with Plotz's death. Plotz dies before completing either the film or his novel about the making of the film; the remarks of the person from whom Dracken-stein buys a grave for Plotz draw attention to the spatial implications of Plotz's name:

> He concludes a deal, for cash, in a Hamburger Hamlet in West Hollywood, with a curious little man who advises him against cremation. "There's nothing like a good plot," he tells Drackenstein. "You put a body in, you cover it with six feet of real estate, you know what you got. No surprises. You ever got to check up on something you can always dig it up. With cremation what have you got? Ashes. You sneeze at the wrong time and you could all blow away." (169)

"Plot" is a necessary anchoring device, a permanent space that stops the "blowing away" of Sukenick's title. Clearly Sukenick means to suggest some similarity between narrative plot and this burial plot; both, we can say, hold disparate elements together that otherwise might blow away. Sukenick also seems to intend some irony by having this "plot," which holds together all the novel's elements, appear only at the end of the novel. The irony of the plot's belated appearance is likewise evident in how Plotz meets (one of) his death(s). Plotz dies on his way to a hotel that embodies the plot of the novel he is writing: "And of course he was after the gothic touch in the Winchester House. Mazes, rooms within rooms, stairways leading nowhere. Which is a lot like his crazy plots, come to think of it. Is that what he had in mind?" (137). Plotz's plot (his life as well as his writing) concludes when it finds a way of embodying itself. Sukenick suggests that the end of the plot itself is tied to death, since death "never fits into the plot" (23). Like the hotel that embodies Plotz's writing, characters grow toward a death which, while outside of their life, becomes a monument (a burial plot) that embodies that life. We can apply Sukenick's observations about characters' lives to narrative plot in general. The shape of a novel's progression, we can say, will appear only when that progress stops and is replaced by a spatial embodiment. Paradoxically, narrative time is complete only when it becomes narrative space. In turn, as Soja might suggest, this "completed" spatial plot becomes the occasion for more rewriting and further narration, as characters continue to develop other, tangential plots.

Characters escape the destinies that cultural narratives provide for them by taking advantage of the paradox of narrative time and by exploiting their own material complexity as narrative objects. Escape from a narrative role can seem to be an act of suicide, since the ending of a plot is associated with death. Perhaps the association of embodying a narrative and ending one's life is most explicit in the novel's ironic comment about Plotz's own "genius": "He [Plotz] can come up with brilliant story ideas but unfortunately is already dead at this point, of his final stroke of genius" (160). Plotz's genius *is* being dead; he has found a way to step outside of the narrative. This way of escaping narrative plots is hardly practical outside of a metafictional novel, however, and Sukenick suggests an alternate method: some characters control narrative by manipulating others. Already I have quoted Ccrab's comment about the "Director as necromancer, sustaining dead spirits with blood rites" (98); elsewhere Ccrab describes his own manipulation of Clover as "corpomancy" (38). The novel's vampire-necromancer theme suggests that one's power and self-control depends on being able to treat others as objects, brute bodies to be manipulated; Drackenstein's producer is, indeed, referred to as an "energy vampire" (71). Constructing a narrative and manipulating others within it gives one a sense of control; one stands outside of this narrative much like someone who has found a way to embody a narrative into a spatial structure. Nonetheless, this system of vampirism is not as simple as it seems, since the bodies manipulated resist being treated as simple objects. Plotz's burial plot holds his physical remains, and we can say that plots in general protect and revere the body so that it cannot "blow away." But a plot is also a site of decomposition; it breaks down a body from a unified thing into an amorphous "matter." The larger "plot" of Sukenick's novel likewise celebrates and disintegrates the body of Clover. Drackenstein's films break Clover down into body parts: "Reviewers have almost totally ignored the film as a whole and have focused attention on parts of Bottom's body" (49). Clover becomes so popular and appears to take on a role as a "sex goddess" because her body parts have the power to affect viewers. If fracturing the (female) body seems to be a typical form of media objectification, it also can destabilize narrative roles and the vampirical manipulation of others. Sukenick describes an object with an ambiguous existence when Clover visits a glass chapel: "Its glass admits sheets of radiance that dissolve the barrier between interior and exterior space, and looking at a wall, you see not a painting of the world as in other churches, but the world itself of which the Chapel, through its transparency, declares itself part" (123–24). This passage describes an object both seen and seen-through, both part of the world and a means of understanding it. Clover describes herself as a kind of "glass house" (124), and she can affect audiences because she is never a simple object delimited within a frame. Instead, as sex goddess she crosses the line between object and viewer and involves others in narratives with her. Ccrab seems to recognize that his body is not a simple object late in the novel, when he remarks on his love for Clover:

> He feels like something inside him is going to split open. Like a cocoon. Falling in love is not to make you happy, it occurs to Crab. That's not the point. Happiness is overrated, there are more important things than happiness, even in Southern California. Falling in love is a mode of self-destruction, he thinks. For the first time he understands the old connection between joy and insanity. Love and death. (149–50)

Ccrab gradually recognizes that he and Clover are not simple objects. Their bodies instead are "material": unstable, only relatively fixed, and able to enter into new narratives with the others around them. If his fractured identity suggests little control over these narratives, he is neither trapped within permanent roles nor guilty of the "corpomancy" of manipulating Clover.

Ccrab discovers that narrative objects have a materiality that complicates any simple plot or narrative role. Specifically, Ccrab comes to recognize how a narrative space (the novel's "plot") makes characters material in a way that undermines the economy of necromancy. It is no surprise that Sukenick ends the novel with Drackenstein's visit to Henry Miller, for no character more needs to "unwrite" plots and the kind of hierarchical relations of control they can foster. Sukenick suggests that the narratives that we occupy everyday can often be more open-ended than those provided by film. Ccrab's schizophrenia shows that the wrenching of narrative roles and the deconstructing of narrative objects is part of everyday life. Ccrab's understanding of the "old connection between joy and insanity. Love and death" suggests that our intimate involvement with others means accepting narrative objects that may "split open" and self-destruct. When taken seriously, our relations with others always exceed the roles we occupy in narratives of our own and others' construction; in this excess, roles can fracture into new stories and identities. Being aware of materiality means recognizing the "proximity" of subject to object that Emmanuel Levinas described. Materiality is capable of mediating but not undermining the distinction between subject and object, between individuals in a larger social context. Film, conversely, does not allow us to take our relation with actors seriously. The fans of Clover's films experience the power of Clover's bodily materiality, but they cannot undergo the personal "splitting" that Ccrab's more intimate involvement allows. Film's visual quality, which frames the body and allows viewers to concentrate on its parts, provides a particularly powerful illusion of the intimate connection and materiality that Ccrab experiences with Bottom.

Sukenick offers us a vision of identities and relationships always mediated by narrative roles. Although we always "objectify" others into narrative objects to be fit into a story, this act raises issues of materiality which, when properly treated, open to new relations and new narratives. I have argued the same thing about the appeal to narrative in a post-deconstructive context in general: narrative can use the issues of materiality surrounding its objects to suggest the horizon of their other possible articulations. This is the promise of post-deconstructive narrative, whether in criticism or in fiction. We have seen that deconstruction implies a degree of textual openness and indeterminacy useful for social critique but also problematizes any philosophical or moral grounds upon which that critique could be constructed. The post-deconstructive narrative that we have seen here clearly accepts that textuality is a condition from which we cannot escape. Nonetheless, it also defines how individuals can imagine new ways of articulating their present circumstances without appealing simply to an unending indeterminacy. Sukenick's novel, then, is not a radical break from the problems of textuality in deconstruction, but it does represent the attempt to use textual worldliness and the complex materiality of textual objects to reimagine deconstructive "openness" in more productive ways.

chapter four

A GENERAL OR LIMITED NARRATIVE THEORY?

Universal Narrative Forms?

Like deconstruction, the appeal to narrative that has appeared in its wake often seems to make broad claims about the nature of textuality in general. The problems that deconstruction poses for interpretation and critique are of course necessarily abstract. The deconstructionist mantra that the system of *différance* is "always already" in place suggests concisely how dependent deconstruction is on the universality of textual laws. Jacques Derrida defines *différance*, for example, as "the movement according to which language, or any code, any system of referral in general, is constituted 'historically' as a weave of differences" (*Margins* 12). It should be no surprise, then, that the textual dynamics that arise in response to deconstruction should be likewise sweeping. When Hayden White writes about narrative as inherently referencing a social center that gives meaning to historical events (*Content* 11), or when Jean-François Lyotard claims that narrative "is the quintessential form of customary knowledge" (*Postmodern* 18), they seem to be speaking about narrative in general, without reference to particular periods or poetics where it may be used differently. In chapter 2 I have suggested that post-deconstructive narrative turns to textual space and time as a way to give shape to its reflections about the "worldliness" of all texts. Should we say that all texts will draw on or at least deal with these spatiotemporal forms? That is, do post-deconstructive critics and writers reveal some *essential* condition of narrative that applies to every period and context?

The question here is especially complex since we are speaking about a number of different kinds of universality. Most fundamental is Derrida's claim that all texts *necessarily* encounter problems with textual worldiness. Of course, the degree to which texts can refuse to attend to these issues, and thus the degree to which some texts are easier or more fruitful to deconstruct, has always been an issue within deconstructive criticism.[1] On top of this universal claim about *différance* and textual worldliness rests a more specific narrative dynamic that exploits textual space and time in order to direct attention toward worldliness. We may, then, be describing an historically specific poetics in post-deconstructive narrative, in contrast to the general, metaphysical problems that Derrida seems to be describing. And yet, this narrative seems to accept the same abstraction that we see in deconstruction when it claims that all knowledge is a narrative or is at least legitimated through narrative. Does post-deconstructive narrative reflect the fundamental conditions of narrative discourse in general? In this chapter I would like to consider this, narrative's relationship to narrative theory in general, and to describe how we might balance the universalizing claims of this narrative with its limitations as an historically specific mode of constructing texts.

Revisiting Spatial Form

A good way to approach the question of how post-deconstructive writing raises questions about narrative in general is to begin with a specific work and to consider the scope and methods of its criticism of past narrative categories. An excellent example of how post-deconstructive narrative returns to such basic questions is Raymond Federman's novella *The Voice in the Closet*, a story that uses the problems of textual space to discuss the difficulty of representing the past. Typical of post-deconstructive narrative, Federman's novel looks to theoretical narrative issues to provide the conditions for opening a seemingly dead-end textual problem to new articulations. The novel itself describes Federman's escape as a child from the Nazi troops that killed the rest of his family during World War II. How, Federman asks, can one describe this senseless and incomprehensible event without giving it some symbolism and significance, without turning it into "just" a story? Charles Caramello explains the parallel that Federman draws between writing and the extermination of his family: "The object of the boy's loss—his family—is no more recoverable to him than the object of the man's loss—the 'primary phenomenon' of the boy's loss—is to him. The loss for 'federman' is double and recuperation doubly impossible" (136). Federman's typography embodies the problems of narrating this childhood event. This novella comprises twenty pages of eighteen lines of text, with each line made up of uncapitalized and unpunctuated prose. Federman keeps the number of letters and spaces constant in each line (68), a strict typographical scheme that forces him to choose words based on their letter count. Such restraints reflect the ambiguous value of enclosure in the novel. The closet in which Federman was hidden as a child was both a prison and a means of escape, since by being locked in the closet Federman was overlooked by the Nazis. The novel's typography, similarly, imprisons Federman in strict requirements but also frees him from traditional narrative unity and coherence that would simplify his past. As a result, Federman seems to be returning to our conventional definitions of textual space and revealing problems and contradictions in its goals. In chapter 3 I argued that postmodern writers are frequently interested in how spaces emerge and evolve through the temporality of the text. Federman's novella brings this temporal poetics to bear on narrative space, in the process revealing problems in traditional narrative categories. Let us examine more closely the problems that Federman's story reveals.

Stylistically, *The Voice in the Closet* resembles a dialogue between Federman the writer who tells the story, and a critical voice, who points out lies and half-truths in this account. The voice, for example, criticizes how Federman surrounded his childhood escape with symbolism in an earlier novel: "what a joke the soldiers quick sssh and all the doors slammed shut the boots in the staircase where it should have started but not him no instead calmly he shoves the statue of liberty at us very symbolic" (4).[2] The voice resists the symbols that the writer "shoves at us." The voice's attempt to escape from symbolism is much like Federman's childhood escape from the Nazis: "I will step into the light emerge run to some other refuge survive work tell the truth I give you my word resist" (14). Hiding within the closet seems to protect the voice from symbolism that accrues when it steps "into the light." The closet sustains mystery and does not allow images to be attached to this event: "never a primary phenomenon to end again reducible to nonsense excrement of a beginning in the dark I folded the paper into a neat package for the birds smelling my hands by reflex or to disintegrate years later but he ignores that too obsessed by fake images" (7). "Fake images" symbolically reconstruct the past and posit a moment of beginning, a point from which the narrative of Federman's life develops. Image and narrative thus work together to create the illusion that senseless events are meaningful: "I wait in the dark now down the staircase with their bundles moaning yellow stars to the furnace the boots my father mother sisters too to their final solution when I needed him the most last image of my beginning to the trains to be remade unmade to shade the light and he calls me boris when I stood on the threshold boris my first false name" (6). The writer repeats the crime of "remaking" his family by creating "false names" and by ignoring the incomprehensible loss itself. The voice is able to criticize the writer's narrative reconstruction by occupying the closet, a space that shields the past from images and symbols that would make sense of it.

Although the voice uses its position inside the closet to resist the writer's symbolism, space itself has both symbolic and antisymbolic qualities. The space of the novel resists symbolism most obviously in how it undermines the normal narrative links between textual elements. Because words are simply placed side-by-side on the page, the links between words and images are often ambiguous. For example, the meaning of the line, "he waits for me to unfold upstairs perhaps the signal of a departure in my own voice at least a beginning after so many detours" (1), depends on whether the phrase "in my own voice" refers to the signal or to the beginning. If the voice is the "signal" for a new departure, it merely awakens the writer; if it is the "beginning" of the departure itself, then the voice represents an entirely new method of storytelling. Although the space of the page destabilizes meaning in the novel, Federman must nonetheless create a space within which symbols will be located and across which they will "correspond." Throughout the novel, Federman plays the two meanings of the word *correspond* off against each other: to communicate and to resemble. In the course of the novel's self-reflexive dialogue, the writer and the critical interior voice correspond—communicate with and mirror each other. The voice observes, "I move now toward my birth out of the closet unable to become the correspondent of his illusions in his room where everything happens by duplication and repetition" (11), and describes itself as "that which negates itself as it creates itself both recipient and dispatcher" (11). Symbolism depends on a certain textual distance that allows us to recognize the "exchange" and "correspondence" between elements. It is precisely because space has a role in symbolism that it enables the voice to resist symbolism. Throughout the novel, the voice exploits ambiguities in the text's spatial references to destabilize symbolic connections that the writer seeks to create. The voice complains at the end of the novel, for example, "here now again at last" (1)— speaking metaphorically about having "at last" described the past, and literally about being "here now" at the end of the book. Likewise, the voice remarks, "not again" (3), which is both a complaint about starting a new page and a claim that this novel will not exploit the childhood tragedy in the way that Federman's other novels have. Both passages make statements celebrating the power of this new account of Federman's past, but both also can be reduced to comments about the writer's location on the page. By playing the space of the page off against metaphorical uses of space, Federman multiplies the meaning of spatial references and destabilizes the text's language. The instability of language in the novel is exactly what helps the voice to escape the symbols that the writer associates with the past. Space is not antisymbolic but rather *ambiguously* symbolic, and thus a means of questioning symbolism. Marcel Cornis-Pope remarks that "*The Voice in the Closet* makes clear [that] the narrative act starts in *sequestration*" ("[Dis]articulation" 84), but we can say more precisely that narrative becomes ambiguous when it is sequestered, when it turns back and considers its own spatiality. As Cornis-Pope suggests, Federman gets the energy for his composition from spatial complications that narrative traditionally ignores. As Edward W. Soja implied in chapter 3, the transformation of these spaces moves the text foward.

Cornis-Pope's reference to "the narrative act" makes it clear that Federman is raising questions about the nature of narrative space in general. Given the extremity of Federman's problems as a reporter of the past, we are certainly encouraged to treat these questions as universal and consequently having profound implications for how we think about space in all narrative. Indeed, when Federman turns to space as a universal condition of textuality, he seems to be following a general trend within criticism of the last generation to emphasize space and time as the basis for narrative form. Critics of the last thirty years have avoided theories, like Nothrop Frye's *Anatomy of Criticism*, which define literary form according to inherited motifs or themes precisely, I think, because space and time provide a greater sense of universality. Frye's well-known theory describes archetypal "mythoi" that provide the underlying formal basis of individual genres and modes; these mythoi make artistic creation "a half-involuntary imitation of organic rhythms or processes" (344). As literary forms, Frye's mythoi exist independently of individual texts. The shift toward space and time as components of fictional form in mainstream American criticism can be traced back to Wayne C. Booth's *Rhetoric of Fiction*. For all that Booth's work claims to reject prescriptive theories of novelistic form, it prescribes the spatial issue of *point of view* as the key term within the analysis of the rhetorical structure of fiction.[3] The abstract category of space seems to forgo any specific theory of artistic construction; it appears theoretically neutral in a way that Frye's archetypal forms do not. For Booth, Frye's mythoi may be useful for categorization, but they lack a grounding in reader response: "Frye's ten types are of limited use as a basis for judgments on technique, since they give us groups of works still unmanageably large and heterogeneous, groups distin-guished from each other less by an induction from their common effects than by a deductive classification of the materials represented" (37). Booth's spatiotemporal narrative form is not external to the work and hence not something to be categorized; it arises naturally out of the interaction of reader and text. Booth's decision to use space (and, to a lesser degree, time)[4] as the basis of fictional form treats it as *worldly* in the sense that Derrida uses the term. Form is part of both the text and the world, an element of the work that can be recognized only because it has an effect outside of the text on the reader. Frye's archetypes, con-versely, appear within a text without reference to the outside from which they came. While the seasonal terms that he uses in analyzing tragedy and comedy, for example, appear both in the text and in the real world, they do not require that we be aware of the movement *from* world to text. Space and time, conversely, draw attention to this move-ment. Readers understand the "point of view" they are given by a fic-tional text by drawing on their real-world experience with "perspec-tive"—both literally in how space and time limit our knowledge of an object, and figuratively in how attitudes shape one's response to a per-son or topic. Although Federman is clearly pushing the relationship between text and world further and seeing in it much deeper problems, both this novel and recent criticism see literary space and time as inter-esting because of their complex connection to the extra-textual world.

This ontological complexity is especially clear in theories of literary space, in part because such space does not seem to be a "natural" part of the literary text. Traditionally, literature has been understood as a "temporal" art; defining a "spatial form" within a literary text, therefore, has always been a difficult undertaking. W. J. T. Mitchell summarizes Gotthold Lessing's distinction between spatial and temporal arts:

> Reading occurs in time; the signs which are read are uttered or inscribed in a temporal sequence; and the events represented or narrated occur in time. There is thus a kind of homology, or what Lessing calls a "convenient rela-tion" between medium, message, and the mental process of decoding. A similar homology operates in accounts of visual art: the medium consists of forms displayed in space; these forms represent bodies and their relation-ships in space; and the perception of both medium and message is instan-taneous, taking no appreciable time. (*Iconology* 98–99)

Painting is a spatial art, says Lessing, and literature is a temporal one. We will struggle if we try to define a spatial component in a written text because the medium is inherently temporal. As Gabriel Zoran remarks, space does not "have a recognized and clear-cut status within the text.

It can be understood in various ways, but none is as clear and unambiguous as the term *time*" (310). Because space seems so foreign to writing, a theorist must simply do more work to define and analyze spatial form in a literary text. But because of this, space seems to be the element that gives shape or provides literary form to the more natural, temporal process of reading. Where reading time seems inevitable, literary space must be shaped and defined by writers and readers.

The ontological complexity of space is precisely the point at which theories of spatial form encounter problems. Indeed, critics have found tremendous problems in the concept over the last ten years. Michael Spencer, in reviewing the state of spatial form theory, remarks that most of the inadequacies within these theories arise from "an awareness that—whatever it is—spatial form is somehow inherent in the work and also 'outside' it (the reader or critic), but an inability properly to define or relate these two aspects" (187).[5] The ontological ambiguity of textual space accounts for why critics have defined spatial form in so many different ways. Ivo Vidan summarizes the debates over spatial form in narrative by describing two basic types of spatial form: "Spatial form in fiction is achieved either through a network of recurring motifs (when there is no continuing developing social or physical action in the forefront—basically this includes the mental action of reminiscence and anticipation), or through a pattern of forward and backward-moving that plays against the chronological order of events" (155). The first definition of spatial form as a "network of recurring motifs" treats spatial arrangement as independent of time, as a-temporal. The second definition of spatial form as "forward and backward-moving" treats textual space as violations of causality, as antitemporal. The a- and antitemporal conceptions of spatial form depend on two different ways of understanding the "location" of spatial form within the literary text. A-temporal spatial form defines a structure that exists above the level of the text, in the mind of the reader and author; this spatial form is atemporal because it exists completely only before composition or after reading. Antitemporal spatial form, conversely, is part of the text itself, a quality of the writing like the choice of narrator or the type of setting.

In searching for a way to save the past from the homogenizing effect of textual symbolism, Federman's novel clearly shows the positive power of deploying several forms of textual space. We saw at the outset that ambiguities in the ontological status of space allow the voice to resist the writer's symbols, but they also motivate the composition of the novel itself. Federman associates the unfolding of his narrative with the search for spatial boundaries: "now I stoop on the newspapers groping to the walls for the dimensions of my body while he stares at his selectricstud humping paper each space within itself becoming the figure of our unreality scratched from words" (5). This passage links writing ("his selectricstud humping paper") to the process of understanding and shaping space ("groping to the walls for the dimension of my body"). Spatial contradictions, rather than the search for narrative resolution or symbolic closure, drive Federman to keep writing. We saw much the same thing in chapter 3, where Soja's theory of postmodernist space described the ongoing transformation of one space into another. Here, multiple spaces are essential to the temporal movement of Federman's writing. *The Voice in the Closet* uses space in two distinct ways; spaces in this novel are both places and objects. The closet, for example, is a space to be occupied but also a symbol that the older Federman uses to describe the problems of writing. As the novel meditates on spaces like the closet, it often ends up folding one space back upon another by treating one as an object and one as a habitation. The following passage, for example, transforms the literal space of the closet into an object in order to develop a fable about writing and disgrace: "they grabbed me and locked me in a box dragged me a hundred times over the earth in metaphorical disgrace" (8). This passage turns the "realistic" space of the closet (as the hiding place for the voice) into a symbol (the box) and inserts it into a surrealistic fable. This fable creates a new space where the symbol appears, a space where Federman is "disgraced." Spaces, then, fold back upon each other to produce new stories. I just quoted Federman's comment, "each space within itself becoming the figure of our unreality" (5). Throughout the novel, we can say, each new space recontextualizes the last and reveals that the whole narrative is driven by purely textual demands—it is "unrealistic." Federman has long admired Samuel Beckett, and has described his writing as an attempt to "go on" despite the apparent pointlessness of using writing to construct the past (LeClair and McCaffery 140). Writing for Federman is inherently valuable as an existential act: "To write . . . is to *produce* meaning, and not *reproduce* a pre-existing meaning. To write is to *progress*, and not *remain* subjected (by habit or reflexes) to the meaning that supposedly precedes the words" ("Surfiction" 8). Federman's struggle to re-create the past, in the end, cannot be a goal but a process—a constant reworking of the past that is both painful and necessary. Federman has accused himself of "remaking" this past, but the spatial convolutions that he follows will not allow the past to become a static object.

Although we might assume that, because they speak about literary space in several different ways, critics have been theoretically sloppy, Federman suggests that these multiple types of space are essential to the functioning of spatial form. It is space's own ability to be both symbolic and antisymbolic that make it so valuable for Federman's critique of representation. In exploiting the ontological ambiguity of narrative space, Federman suggests a certain narrative poetics by which texts can be constructed more effectively. Precisely in this idea that spatial multiplicity might be exploited productively, however, Federman's novel raises the question with which I began this chapter: is the space described by post-deconstructive narrative the space of all narrative, or merely one particular way of thinking about such space? Are earlier, predeconstructive texts merely uninformed about textual dynamics that they are nonetheless subject to, or are these dynamics the result of writing in a post-deconstructive context? Crucial to answering these questions is deciding whether the multiplicity of space is an essential part of spatial form or if it is merely something insisted on by certain writers.

Recent theories of spatial form have recognized that space takes many shapes in the literary work, but most treat this multiplicity as incidental rather than as what makes spatial form a valuable concept. Mitchell's approach is typical of how spatial form theories treat this multiplicity; he simply suggests that there are four distinct types of space in the literary text. He defines these as (1) the space of the page; (2) the represented (literal) space of narrative events; (3) the more abstract "space" in which motifs and symbols are organized; and (4) a metaphysical space that might be equated with what we often speak of as the world of the text, "those patterns [that] are not merely the formal principles which govern the temporal unfolding of his story but the very metaphysics which lies behind a story told about *this* world in *this* particular way" ("Spatial" 553). What motivates this four-part distinction is the problematic ontology of the literary text. Mitchell writes,

> If we turn our attention from the seemingly hopeless tangle of spatial metaphors which riddle the languages of criticism and focus our attention on that problematic object, "the work itself," we note that spatial metaphors intrude at the outset. The ontology of the work, either as a unique object (the autonomous icon of formalism) or as a member of a class (the concentrically arrayed "backgrounds" of contextualism) is elucidated by regarding it as an object in an appropriate field of relationships. A closer look at this curious object inevitably reveals it as a complex field of internal relationships, the most common of which is the phenomenon of stratification, or what is usually called "levels" in literature. (549–50)

The "tangle" of spatial metaphors that we use in discussing literature leads Mitchell to believe that texts comprise multiple strata. Although his theory makes intuitive sense, it fails to explain why these aspects of the literary work should be grouped together under the term *space* in the first place. Although the page is literally a space, and although the actual events of a realistic text usually occur in some place within the story, the spatiality of the other two textual "strata" is far from obvious. Why is the interrelation of motifs inherently spatial? Why is an author's metaphysics spatial? Behind these queries is a more general question, How do we decide to label some textual elements as spatial? Although some critics have argued that real and textual spaces are continuous (Gullón 12), most have recognized that textual space is only loosely connected to what we usually refer to as space in the real world. Zoran describes the gap between real and textual space: "it is important to distinguish between the 'spatial' point of view and the spatial object viewed. Moreover, although the connection between the components is a permanent one, this connection can certainly not be perceived as a correlation. The spatial pattern of the text does not stand in any kind of correlation with the space of the world" (312). Frank Kermode notes the gap between real and fictional space, and concludes that there is no such thing as spatial form: "Forms in space, we should remember, have more temporality than Lessing supposed, since we have to read them in sequence before we know they are there, and the relations between them. Forms in time have an almost negligible spatial aspect (the size of the book). Their interrelations had much better be studied by reference to our usual ways of relating past, present and future . . . than by the substitution of a counterfeit spatial for the temporal mode" (*Sense* 178). Kermode's suggestion that we should not speak about textual space seems extreme, since our everyday ways of thinking about stories and poems involve spatial ideas like "structures" and "patterns." Zoran offers a compromise between Mitchell and Kermode by claiming that *critics* correlate real and textual space, and that they do so in certain ways for specific reasons. Mitchell himself notes how Lessing's distinction between spatial and temporal arts has been transformed by critics to serve other purposes: "It is Lessing's readers who have turned his irregular, associative argument into a system, converting his embattled, value-laden terms into 'neutral critical fictions'" (*Iconology* 111).

Joseph Frank's essay on spatial form shows how grouping several aspects of a literary text using the term *space* can serve other interpretive goals. Frank hopes to define the poetics of a particular literary period (modernism), while arguing that this poetics exploits qualities of literary experience in general. As a result, he must define several spaces: the spatial form that we recognize as a style in the work, and the space through which we as readers apprehend any text. These two types of space are evident when Frank describes the historical specificity of spatial form:

For modern literature, as exemplified by such writers as T. S. Eliot, Ezra Pound, Marcel Proust, and James Joyce, is moving in the direction of spatial form; and this tendency receives an original development in Djuna Barnes's remarkable book *Nightwood*. All these writers ideally intend the reader to apprehend their work spatially, in a moment of time, rather than as a sequence. And since changes in aesthetic form always involve major changes in the sensibility of a particular cultural period, an effort will be made to outline the spiritual attitudes that have led to the predominance of spatial form. (10)

In treating spatial form as typical of a literary movement, Frank must define it as a choice made by a particular group of writers reflecting the "sensibility of a particular cultural period." Spatial form thus must be recognizable within the text if we are to grasp this sensibility and understand its assumptions and concerns. Since it also describes a structure for apprehending the text, however, spatial form cannot merely reside in the text. Rather, spatial form must exert control over the process of reading. This latter quality makes spatial form independent of any individual objects or events in the text and recognizable only in the extra-textual effects it has on the reader. Frank's theory of spatial form, then, holds together at least two different types of space, one inside the text and one outside of it. Recent critics, hoping to describe narrative poetics in general, have criticized Frank's use of spatial form to define a particular literary movement. Spencer notes, for example, that "spatial form, like some manna or disease, is found lurking between the covers of the most unlikely books" (184). He suggests that, although it may be more important to modernist writing, space is an element of any text. Describing space in literature so abstractly, however, can make us forget that textual space must be produced *as space* by someone for some reason. Although, as Spencer notes, we can find spatial elements in any text, critics must choose to do so according to their theoretical and interpretive strategies.

We can go further and suggest that Frank's multiple types of spatial form are contradictory, and that contradiction is in fact a necessary part of any theory of textual space. My discussion has already suggested that Frank is doing two contradictory things when he argues that a specific period's aesthetics rests on universal principles of textual construction. Frank Kermode is troubled by the role of generalizations about all texts in Frank's theory of one period's aesthetics; as Kermode writes, "Frank's commitment to 'spatial form' is much more extensive than he himself allows and much deeper than his claim that it is only a way of describing 'a particular phenomenon of avant-garde writing' suggests" ("Reply" 580). Frank hopes to use spatial form to describe qualities apparent within the texts of European modernism. But if this movement's aesthetic choices control our apprehension of the work, they must affect us from the first moment of reading, before a reader can observe individual qualities within the text. Textual form itself is a contradictory concept: it is both our ingress to the text and a quality within the text that we discover through study and interpretation. The contradictions of Frank's spatial form theory arise not simply because spatial form can never be located in just one way, but because its significance arises only out of its multiplicity. To locate space merely in represented places, or in the space of the page, or in the space of an atemporal structure of motifs—any one of the "strata" that Mitchell defined—denies space the chance to perform a "formal" role in mediating reader/text relations. That the novel is "spatial" because it is written on the space of the page, for example, is completely uninteresting. Likewise defining a spatiality in language's synchronic nature (Genette, *Figures* 44) or recognizing spaces represented within the text (Ronen, "Space") tells us little about the meaning, structure, or effect of a literary work. It is only when we ask how these spaces are connected, how the represented places of the novel resonate with the synchronic structure of motifs or the space of the page, that we begin to speak of a spatial form. Frank is clearly bringing together several spaces when he interprets the famous county fair scene from *Madame Bovary:*

> As Flaubert sets the scene, there is action going on simultaneously at three levels; and the physical position of each level is a fair index to its spiritual significance. On the lowest plane, there is the surging, jostling mob in the street, mingling with the livestock and brought to the exhibitions. Raised slightly above the street by a platform are the speechmaking officials, bombastically reeling off platitudes to the attentive multitudes. And on the highest level of all, from the window overlooking the spectacle, Rodolphe and Emma are watching the proceedings and carrying on their amorous conversation in phrases as stilted as those regaling the crowds. . . . "*Everything should sound simultaneously,*" Flaubert later wrote, in commenting on this scene; "one should hear the bellowing of cattle, the whispering of the lovers, and the rhetoric of the officials all at the same time." (16–17)

In this passage, Frank correlates the literal space of the scene's physical locations (the mob, the platform, the window) to the atemporality, the spatiality, of perceiving these sounds simultaneously. Only by asserting a continuity between the scene's space and the synchronous way we perceive can Frank apply Flaubert's comment about his aesthetic goals to the specific construction of this scene. As this example suggests, to be useful in the analysis of literature, spatial form must encompass many types of textual space—some literal and concrete, others metaphorical and abstract. Spatial form, then, is by its nature an ontologically unstable concept. As Zoran notes, "an important characteristic of total space, which concerns all the levels of structuring, to a certain extent, is *lack of ontological clarity*. . . . [T]otal space is a kind of no man's land bridging different ontological areas. It is perceived not only as the direct continuation of the reconstructed world in the text, but also as a continuation of the real space of the reader, of the external field of reference, the act of narration, and possibly more" (332). As a form, space must be ontologically incoherent; any theory of spatial form is, then, an attempt to exploit this incoherence for an interpretive or theoretical purpose.

Federman's temporal poetics of the evolving postmodernist text allows us to see how spatial contradictions function as a productive part of spatial form theory. We can go so far as to say that Federman's post-deconstructive narrative *completes* or makes conscious what is incompletely stated in spatial form theory. That is, Federman seems to be more aware of the problems of literary space than even the theorists who describe that space. Indeed, I would like to suggest that Federman exploits in a systematic way the spatial multiplicity that spatial form critics appeal to unconsciously. Federman thus can be seen as working in but also commenting on the tradition of spatial form theory. This will seem strange since, when I call *The Voice in the Closet* post-deconstructive I imply that it is resolving or reshaping problems that it has inherited from deconstruction. Spatial form theory certainly would be considered deconstructive by few critics but there are reasons to see some sympathy between the two. Spatial form theory is part of the American literary milieu in which deconstruction was embraced and flourished for a short time as a mode of textual analysis. Indeed, spatial form theory attracted its most intense interest not after Frank's original publication in the 1940s, but during the 1970s and 1980s when deconstruction flourished as a mode of textual analysis. Frank himself noted in 1977, "In recent years . . . there has been a renewed discussion of spatial form and a reconsideration of the merits and deficiencies of the theory as a whole. A new generation, I have become aware, still finds it stimulating and controversial" (69). Certainly the degree to which spatial form raises the issue of textual worldliness suggests how it resonates with deconstructive criticism. Remarking that an interest in space and time is "one sign of reflexivity" in literary studies at the time (1980), Alexander Gelley suggests clearly how spatial form theory resonates with deconstruction: "What is particularly interesting in the present context is the way in which the use of spatial concepts tends to expose a kind of impasse in the metadiscourse. In pointing to the spatiality at work at various levels of the literary text, much contemporary discourse tends to mime rather than analyze the spatial metaphors. Here is an issue that offers exceptional insight into the way criticism will avoid, as if by incapacity, any systematic consideration of its own language" (471). At the heyday of deconstruction in American criticism, Gelley clearly marks the relationship between spatial form theory and deconstructive issues of metalanguage, textual slippage, and worldliness. Spatial form, then, was reevaluated at this time as a way of thinking through deconstruction. As a result, we should not be surprised that Federman's post-deconstructive narrative would imply a reading of those same problems and dynamics in spatial form theory.

Spatial form's relationship to deconstruction makes clear that Federman's indirect commentary on narrative space is, in a certain way, historically limited. While his way of writing certainly seems to have application to our ways of thinking about literary space in general, his writing resonates best with work that shares a certain deconstructive or post-deconstructive interest in the worldliness of the text. The seemingly ahistorical question in Federman's narrative—how does a narrative represent spaces?—arises primarily and most forcefully in an atmosphere informed by deconstruction. Could we apply Federman's poetics of literary space to an earlier narrative—an eighteenth-century novel or a classical epic? We could, but doing so would partially miss the point of post-deconstructive narrative. The purpose of this narrative style is to resolve felt contradictions, to respond to paradoxes recognized within the theoretical landscape, and to give them more productive and positive ways of being articulated. While Federman's novel might imply a way of reading much older narrative, the dynamics would no longer be post-deconstructive in any meaningful way. This is true in a literal sense of the term, but also in the deeper spirit with which the narrative is developed. Post-deconstructive narrative recuperates hope from textual dead ends precisely by mining and extending the contradictions in those dead ends. To see this operation in periods where an awareness of these dead ends is lacking is to describe a fundamentally different mode of theorizing and constructing stories.

The Feel of Multiple Spaces

Before we end this chapter, allow me to add one more wrinkle to this discussion of the limitations of the post-deconstructive narrative style by turning to the issue that runs throughout this study—textual materiality. In suggesting that post-deconstructive narrative is a poetics of textual construction limited to a particular historical moment, we run the risk of suggesting that this mode of writing is experienced merely as one choice among others. Precisely the opposite is the case, I think. Not only do the problems of textual worldliness confront writers and critics as a representational crisis with which they must deal, but the very nature of these poetics is to appear to be tapping into some more fundamental, even physical condition of the text. As a way into thinking about these multiply spaced texts, we should note that our experience of space in the everyday world is not as unified or coherent as we like to think. Susanne K. Langer's claim that even paintings are only artificially "spatial" implies that real-world space is more complex than we usually recognize. Langer writes,

> [T]he space in which we live and act is not what is treated in art at all. The harmoniously organized space in a picture is not experiential space, known by sight and touch, by free motion and restraint, far and near sounds, voices lost or re-echoed. It is an entirely visual affair; for touch and hearing and muscular action it does not exist. For them there is a flat canvas, relatively small, or a cool blank wall, where for the eye there is a deep space full of shapes. This purely visual space is an illusion, for our sensory experiences do not agree on it in their report. (72)

According to Langer, the space of the visual arts is ultimately artificial and severed from real, everyday spatial experience. Langer goes on to claim, much as I have done, that artistic space is produced rather than inherent in a medium: "All accents and selections, as well as radical distortions or utter departures from any 'actual form' of objects, have the purpose of *making space visible and its continuity sensible.* The space itself is a projected image, and everything pictured serves to define and organize it" (77). For Langer, each artwork defines its space (what she calls "virtual space") in a way coherent with its overall purpose. She unintentionally suggests, however, that an artwork comes closer to our experience of real-world space when it holds together many different kinds of space. Langer's criticism of artistic space, after all, is that it is severed from touch, sound, and motion—qualities that complicate and enrich everyday spatial experience. The text with several different kinds of space that Frank describes similarly complicates and refracts our spatial understanding of that work. Langer describes, we could say, the materiality of everyday space—the fact that space does not provide simple or unified access to objects of the world. We will recall that Mitchell claims that the multiplicity of spatial form helps to account for "that problematic object, 'the work itself'" ("Spatial" 549). The multiplicity of space reflects the material complexity of the text that it organizes. In both real and textual space, objects have a place in many different kinds of space (for Langer, visual, aural, and tactile; for Frank, the space of the scene and the atemporality of perception). In a way, then, a work appears material only when it escapes from any single spatiality that would define it neatly as an object, and instead opens out to a multiplicity of spaces.

Federman's introspective and emotionally distraught narrative draws our attention to the experience of these conflicting textual spaces as they construct and deconstruct the past. Derrida has certainly provided a more elaborate and sophisticated explanation of the reasons why texts are worldly and why materiality appears as an element of those texts. Nonetheless, Federman significantly adds to our discussion of this materiality by describing the experience of confronting these texts and discovering their materiality. Federman himself is clearly ambivalent about narrative and, more than the theorists of spatial form that we have discussed, tries to understand the mixed attraction of textual space. As Federman explores the "closet" of the text, he discovers a voice that exposes his emotional ambivalence to the act of "remaking" his past into a well-formed story. Federman's attitude toward his narrative is very much a relation of *abjection* in Julia Kristeva's sense of the term. Kristeva defines abjection as the subject's ambivalent desire to distance itself from an object: "The abject is not an ob-ject facing me, which I name or imagine. Nor is it an ob-jest, an otherness ceaselessly fleeing in a systematic quest of desire. What is abject is not my correlative, which, providing me with someone or something else as support, would allow me to be more or less detached and autonomous. . . . [The abject is] the jettisoned object, is radically excluded and draws me toward the place where meaning collapses" (1–2). In *The Voice in the Closet*, the voice is an unwanted reminder of what has been jettisoned in the construction of the past. The voice does indeed "draw" Federman "toward the place where meaning collapses"—it baits Federman's writer to continue on and explain the past, but it also raises problems that undermine any simple narrative that the writer might hope to construct. Kristeva's term is particularly helpful because it makes sense of the language of bodily materiality associated with the voice. The voice, for example, describes writing as "crapping me on his paper" (4). David Dowling notes the importance of bodily images in *The Voice in the Closet*: "The final lines—'upstairs in his closet foutaise to speak no more my truth to say from fingers federman here now again at last'—suggest that the soul is forever inaccessible. What *is* accessible is the body, Federman's body, its functions and productions—crap and words" (355). Words for Federman are like crap because, although necessary, they "soil" the past. Kristeva suggests that abjection in its "most elementary and most archaic form" is the loathing of food and excrement:

[R]efuse and corpses *show me* what I permanently thrust aside in order to live. These bodily fluids, this defilement, this shit are what life withstands, hardly and with difficulty, on the part of death. There, I am at the border of my condition as a living being. My body extricates itself, as being alive, from that border. Such wastes drop so that I might live, until, from loss to loss, nothing remains in me and my entire body falls beyond the limit—*cadere, cadaver.* (3)

According to Kristeva, excrement is typical of the subject's ongoing creation of external objects, a process that cannot be as complete as it claims to be. The voice, likewise, is a kind of waste by-product of the act of creating an external object of the past, a by-product that also reveals the writer's continuing involvement in this external object. The voice is said to "hide inside his own decomposition" (6) and thus to exist by undermining the objects that Federman tries to construct. According to Federman, then, creating a textual object (the past) always involves excluding the writer's continuing relation with this seemingly self-sufficient entity. Like any act of abjection, this relation continually resurfaces in troubling ways. Federman helps us to see that textual space functions both to present and to complicate a textual object, and that as readers and writers our movement through complex textual space is always charged by our desire for stasis and simplicity.

The materiality evoked as we negotiate the many spaces of Federman's novel makes these abstract spatial contradictions seem concrete and compelling in a way that easily gets lost in summaries of spatial form theory and philosophies of textuality. Federman shows us that the multiply spaced text seems to be an object more physical and hence more spatial than an object more easily defined. Thus, the experience of a post-deconstructive narrative, while no doubt built and organized through abstract textual laws, appears to us as a matter of understanding a concrete, material condition. Thus, when we note that post-deconstructive narrative is merely one mode of textual construction among others, we should not conclude that our experience of such texts is less compelling or that we are aware of these other possibilities. Indeed, the issues of materiality raised by these narratives keep these texts and their paradoxes immediately within our attention. This may well be one of the reasons why post-deconstructive narrative so often makes broad philosophical claims with little reference to their historical specificity—the very mode of this narrative is to develop an experience of the material through such abstraction. More generally we can say that materiality will function in these narratives to make concrete and compelling these more abstract textual laws. We noted, for example, that Derrida's writing became more concerned with textual materiality in his work on Karl Marx. It is not at all a coincidence that this work is also when Derrida tries to discuss the ethics of our complex relation and debt to Marx. Materiality appears in that work, as in Federman's novel, as a figure that renders abstract textual laws more compelling. Textual materiality, in other words, is a way of insisting that we not view post-deconstructive narrative through the lens of simple relativism. Materiality appears as a textual figure precisely as criticism and narrative attempt to rethink deconstructive laws but also to embrace our involvement in those laws and the future forms of textual development opened up by them.

chapter five

RESISTING POST-DECONSTRUCTIVE SPACE

Space and Commodity Culture

If space is an important textual figure within post-deconstructive narrative, we could find no more important sphere in which space is being debated than in cultural theory. Indeed, interest in spatial from in literature has waned somewhat since its heyday of debate in the early 1980s; theories of postmodern culture have revived interest in space as a critical term. Postmodern culture owes its definition as spatial in large part to Jean Baudrillard's theory of the "precession of simulacra" in contemporary society: "Simulation is no longer that of a territory, a referential being or a substance. It is the generation by models of a real without origin or reality: the hyperreal" (*Selected* 166). Baudrillard describes "hyperreality" as images without reference to actual objects. Postmodern hyperreality simply juxtaposes these images spatially, and makes no reference to history, change, or origin. Although critics have attacked other aspects of Baudrillard's writing, his claim that post-modernity is spatial has become an accepted starting point for both critique and defense of this culture.[1] Cultural critics disagree about how much of the spatiality of postmodern culture can be attributed to simple economic changes. David Harvey describes postmodern spatiality as the result of the acceleration of production and consumption:

[A]ccelerating turnover time in production would have been useless unless the turnover time in consumption was also reduced. The half-life of a typical Fordist product was, for example, from five to seven years, but flexible accumulation has more than cut that in half in certain sectors (such as textile and clothing industries), which in others—such as the so-called "thought-ware" industries (e.g. video games and computer software programmes)—the half-life is down to less than eighteen months. . . . The relatively stable aesthetic of Fordist modernism has given way to all the ferment, instability, and fleeting qualities of a postmodernist aesthetic that celebrates difference, ephemerality, spectacle, fashion, and the commodification of cultural forms. (156)

As Harvey suggests, the search for greater efficiency of production has demanded a greater efficiency of consumption and a shift toward "products" that are more quickly consumed (e.g., services). Harvey agrees with Baudrillard that these changes in production and consumption bring with them "time-space compression" as a fundamental change in the nature of postmodern life,[2] but not all critics believe that culture need necessarily reflect these economic changes. Fredric Jameson, for example, has sought out objects that respond to, rather than merely embodying, postmodern space-time compression. He sees E. L. Doctorow's novel *Ragtime*, for example, as problematic because it is unable to represent the historical condition of postmodernity in a way that allows for analysis. Jameson argues that "the kind of reading this novel imposes makes it virtually impossible for us to reach and thematize those official 'subjects' which float above the text" (*Postmodernism* 23). Doctorow, according to Jameson, has had to convey the disappearance of the American radical past "formally (since the waning of the content is very precisely his subject) and, more than that, has had to elaborate his work by way of that very cultural logic of the postmodern which is itself the mark and symptom of his dilemma" (25). Jameson believes that some contemporary writers use postmodern "symptoms" self-consciously for the sake of critique. For Brian McHale, the distinction between complicit and critical strains of postmodernism is problematic: "If postmodernist texts are, like all cultural products in all periods, from a dialectical perspective both complicit with the dominant culture and critical of or resistant to it, then what are the grounds for making the complicit moments stand synecdochically for the *texts as a whole* in one case . . . while choosing to have the critical moments do so in another?" ("Anxiety" 28). Jameson believes that cultural artifacts can respond to economic changes without simply embodying them, but McHale argues that this distinction is untenable. Steven Connor rephrases McHale's criticism and asks of Jameson's theory, "How can a culture which is allegedly defined by the decisive abandonment of originality and authenticity possibility be exemplified in any 'original' or 'authentic' way?" (49).

Among other things, Jameson's writing raises an important question about post-deconstructive narrative. We recognize that not everything written after deconstruction need be post-deconstructive; we would be hard-pressed to find an awareness of deconstructive issues and the resulting narrative dynamics in most popular fiction, for example. What are the limits, then, of turning a blind eye to deconstructive issues? Might we not simply be better off in some political sense to ignore deconstruction and construct traditional narratives? Jameson is an interesting test for such an idea since he clearly has a sophisticated understanding of the problems of deconstructive criticism but also clearly rejects many of the consequences that seem to follow in its wake. In examining Jameson's writing and the idea of space that he constructs, we see post-deconstructive textual dynamics despite his best intentions because of the deconstructive problems with which he starts. In other words, an analysis of Jameson's writing will reveal that post-deconstructive narrative is not merely a genre, but rather a set of textual conditions that produce a style of writing that is not easy to avoid once one becomes involved in thinking through those conditions.

Jameson's Resistance to Postmodern Space

Behind Jameson's resistance to postmodern hyperreality is the larger question of to what extent objects resist or instance the larger culture that has produced them. Indeed, as McHale and Connor suggest, postmodernism problematizes precisely this relation between culture and its objects. For Harvey, postmodernism is characterized not only by space-time compression, but by the transformation of the objects produced economically. These objects are not the concrete "goods" that we traditionally associate with industry, but more abstract "services" that are immediately consumed. Similarly, Baudrillard argues that postmodernism transforms how we think about objects. When postmodern "hyperreality" suppresses history and change it creates a landscape within which objects have particular significance and power. This significance is clear in the American landscape:

> Speed creates pure objects. It is itself a pure object, since it cancels out the ground and territorial reference-points, since it runs ahead of time to annul time itself, since it moves more quickly than its own cause and obliterates triumph of instantaneity over time as depth, the triumph of the surface and pure objectality over the profundity of desire. Speed creates a space of ini-

tiation, which may be lethal; its only rule is to leave no trace behind. Triumph of forgetting over memory, an uncultivated, amnesic intoxication. (*America* 6–7)

Elsewhere Baudrillard remarks, "[w]e are living the period of objects" (*Selected* 29). Baudrillard describes consumption not as the attempt to satisfy preexisting needs, or even as the pursuit of the desires that advertising creates. Rather, Baudrillard argues, the objects of postmodern society form a larger structural system in which the consumer operates:

> We can observe that objects are never offered for consumption in an absolute disarray. In certain cases they can *mimic* disorder to better seduce, but they are always arranged to trace out directive paths. The arrangement directs the purchasing impulse towards *networks* of objects in order to seduce it and elicit, in accordance with its own logic, a maximal investment, reaching the limits of economic potential. Clothing, appliances, and toiletries thus constitute object *paths*, which establish inertial constraints on the consumer who will proceed *logically* from one object to the next. (31)

For Baudrillard, the contemporary "network of objects" creates a cultural space where individuals follow logical "paths" of consumption. Unlike Harvey, for whom the abstract objects of the service economy are the result of simple changes in production and consumption, Baudrillard believes that the problematized relation between object and landscape makes postmodernism mysteriously attractive. Baudrillard starts *America* by speaking of the attraction of the postmodern landscape: "We'd have to replay it all from end to end at home in a darkened room, rediscover the magic of the freeways and the distance and the ice-cold alcohol in the desert and the speed and live it all again on the video at home in real time, not simply for the pleasure of remembering but because of the fascination of senseless repetition is already present in the abstraction of the journey" (*America* 1). Baudrillard describes how objects (ice-cold alcohol) and space (freeways) work together to make the postmodern landscape peculiarly appealing. Paradoxically, this landscape appeals because its objects violate all of our expectations about meaningful space and distinct, concrete entities. This landscape is "senseless," "repetitious," and "abstract." At least according to Baudrillard, the postmodern landscape has power not because it functions according to *different* rules of space and objects, but because it *violates* our expectations of space and objects.

Jameson theorizes the possibility of resistance to the postmodernism that Baudrillard describes precisely by rejecting the appeal of this confused postmodern landscape and returning to a more basic understanding of postmodern objects and, especially, the space in which they appear. We can see the way in which Jameson approaches postmodern space in his often-reprinted interview with Anders Stephanson: "I . . . link these two sets of features (surface and fragmentation) in terms of the spatialization of time. Time has become a perpetual present and thus spatial. Our relationship to the past is now a spatial one" (6). Here Jameson describes postmodernity as spatial because it lacks a temporal continuity. He makes postmodernism's suppression of time clearer early in the interview: "We are approaching a logic of subliminality there and your example [of shortening attention spans] effectively illustrates this new logic of difference to which we are being programmed—these increasingly rapid and empty breaks in our time" (5). We might follow Kermode's critique of Frank discussed in chapter 4 and argue that Jameson should characterize postmodernity not as spatial but as suppressing time, as antitemporal. Jameson, however, hopes to "solve" postmodernism's loss of temporal continuity by turning to something that does appear more literally spatial—mapping. Jameson argues that postmodern culture is fragmented because we have no way to "map" it cognitively. Jameson's description of "cognitive mapping" is worth quoting at some length:

> I have found it useful, for an earlier stage of this historical dissolution of place, to refer to a series of once-popular novels which are no longer very much read, in which (essentially for the New Deal period) John O'Hara charts the progressive enlargements of power around but also away from the small town, as these migrate to the higher dialectical levels of the state and finally the federal government. Could one imagine this migration now projected and intensified at a new global level, some new and more acute sense of the problems of contemporary "mapping" and of the positioning in this system of the older individual, might be achieved. The problem is still one of representation, and also of representability: we know that we are caught within these more complex global networks, because we palpably suffer the prolongations of corporate space everywhere in our daily lives. Yet we have no way of thinking about them, of modeling them, however abstractly, in our mind's eye. (*Postmodernism* 127)

For Jameson, postmodernity is fragmented and denies temporal continuity precisely because its space cannot be visualized. Individuals need models of the networks in which they function so that they can understand their place within a whole culture. The global networks of contemporary society have become so complex that individuals have lost the models or "maps" that they had been able to draw on in the past. Jameson's desire to argue that postmodern society *can* be visualized motivates his decision to characterize postmodern antitemporality as a kind of space. As soon as he manages to describe postmodern experience as spatial, he has implied that it is inherently capable of being mapped. Clearly, if postmodern culture is merely antitemporal, then reordering according to some global structure is by no means necessary.

In turning to the notion of mapping, Jameson can be seen as responding to the whole trend of appealing to narrative after deconstruction. Although mapping accomplishes many of the same things that narrative does—it is a traditional means of providing a sense of wholeness, for example (White, *Content* 1–25)—it seems not to partake of the kind of spatial complexities and ontological problems that other critics find so intriguing in post-deconstructive narrative. Indeed, mapping seems so straightforward and concrete that any deconstructive critique seems perverse. And yet Jameson's space is more complex than it first appears. In fact, he sees a fundamental tension between the abstract space of the map and the concrete space that we navigate using the map. Jameson's discussion of maps begins by returning to their "pre-cartographic" form: "A return to the history of this science (which is also an art) shows us that Kevin Lynch's model does not yet, in fact, really correspond to what will become map-making. Lynch's subjects are rather clearly involved in precartographic operations whose results traditionally are described as itineraries rather than as maps: diagrams organized around the still subject-centered or existential journey of the traveler, along which various significant key features are marked" (*Postmodernism* 51–52). For Jameson, itineraries become maps only when they "introduce a whole new coordinate: the relationship to the totality" (52). For all its abstraction, any total space we envision is constructed to help us with the mundane (itinerary) activity of navigating a particular landscape. The abstract space of the map, then, depends on the concrete space that individuals move through temporally; thus, Jameson concludes, "it becomes clear that there can be no true maps" (52). Cognitive mapping helps individuals to order their experiences in cultural space through time: "If, indeed, the subject has lost its capacity actively to extend its pro-tensions and re-tensions across the temporal manifold and to organize its past and future into coherent experience, it becomes difficult enough to see how the cultural productions of such a subject could result in anything but 'heaps of fragments' and in a practice of the randomly heterogeneous and fragmentary and the aleatory" (25). Cognitive maps reassert the importance of time within postmodern space by allowing individuals to place everyday actions within a cultural whole; once an individual has an image of the whole culture he or she can plan actions to have recognizable continuity and significance. Individuals move through the concrete space of everyday life by reference to the abstract space of the cognitive map.

We saw in chapter 4 that, confronted by the complex existence of the literary text, spatial form theories were forced to treat textual space as having several manifestations within a single text; Jameson's use of two different kinds of space in his theory of postmodern culture develops out of an awareness of a similar material complexity in the objects of postmodern culture. As we have seen, Baudrillard argues that postmodern space draws our attention to the "objectness" of objects—what Baudrillard calls "objectality"—by suppressing depth and time. Jameson uses similar terms in describing how we become aware of the materiality of signifiers when time is suppressed in postmodern texts: "the breakdown of temporality suddenly releases this present of time from all the activities and intentionalities that might focus it and make it a space of praxis; thereby isolated, that present suddenly engulfs the subject with undescribable vividness, a materiality of perception properly overwhelming, which effectively dramatizes the power of the material—or better still, the literal—signifier in isolation" (27). Like Baudrillard, Jameson believes that when space suppresses time, we become aware of the "objectal"—the object stripped of any connection to larger patterns of meaning and thus able to draw our attention to its materiality. In chapter 2 we saw that the issue of materiality arises at those moments when objects are revealed to be products of knowing; drawing on Jacques Derrida and Michel de Certeau, we concluded that these moments will occur when our ways of thinking about space and time clash or reveal their limitations. Jameson cannot condone these flashes of materiality because they are the effect of the isolation and dehistoricization of textual or cultural elements. He implies that being aware of an object's materiality undermines our appreciation of its historical context.

As a result, Jameson must rely on a rather unsophisticated model of objects as discrete entities. In his interview with Stephanson, Jameson remarks, "Normal space is made up of things, or organized by things" (7). As a model for inhabiting social space, the itinerary reflects Jameson's belief in distinct objects; completing a journey means learning to move between independent, concrete landmarks. His belief that the world is made up of distinct objects is clear even when Jameson writes about less concrete entities. His discussion of Frank Gehry's house constructs a grammar of the traditional home by assuming that its basic elements are predetermined: "the first questions are those of minimal units: the words of built space, or at least its substantives, would seem to be rooms, categories which are syntactically or syncategorematically related and articulated by the various spatial verbs and adverbs—corridors, doorways, and staircases, for example—modified in turn by adjectives in the form of paint and furnishings, decoration, and ornament" (*Postmodernism* 105). Like the itinerary mapped according to landmarks, Jameson's grammar of the traditional home starts with independent elements. By insisting that the units organized within space are discrete, Jameson hopes to define a shared and stable cultural field in which individuals operate. The fact that individuals operate within a stable field of discrete entities is particularly clear in Jameson's theory of "allegorical transcoding." As the equivalent of cognitive mapping in literary criticism, allegorical transcoding explains how texts are transformed and made significant by different cultures. In *The Political Unconscious*, Jameson describes "a vast interpretive allegory in which a sequence of historical events or texts and artifacts is rewritten in terms of some deeper, underlying, and more 'fundamental' narrative, of a hidden master narrative which is the allegorical key or figural content of the first sequence of empirical materials" (28). The goals of Jameson's theory of allegory are similar to those of his theory of cognitive mapping. Just as he argued for the importance of a concept of totality in cognitive mapping, so Jameson hopes to counter a "war on totality" in contemporary literary theory (*Postmodernism* 401). According to Jameson, an allegory provides an overall context for interpreting all the elements of a text. Like cognitive mapping did with the elements of social space, Jameson's allegorical model assumes that the basic elements of the text are discrete entities. An example of allegorical transcoding makes the discreteness of these elements clear:

> So the interpretation of a particular Old Testament passage in terms of the life of Christ—a familiar, even hackneyed, illustration is the rewriting of the bondage of the people of Israel in Egypt as the descent of Christ into hell after his death on the cross—comes less as a technique for closing the text off and for repressing aleatory or aberrant readings and senses, than as a mechanism for preparing such a text for further ideological investment, if we take the term *ideology* here in Althusser's sense as a representational structure which allows the individual subject to conceive or imagine his or her lived relationship to transpersonal realities such as the social structure or the collective logic of History. (*Political* 30)

By defining interpretation as allegory, Jameson suggests that textual elements are concrete before they enter into interpretation. Christ's life is made up of discrete and recognizable events that will be given new meaning when his life is taken as an allegory for the bondage of the Israelites. Because these events are discrete, readers can recognize the gap between them and the interpretation they have been given in the past, and thus can see new ways in which they could be "transcoded." Jameson notes the dangers of an interpretive system without this gap: "What happens is that the more powerful the vision of some increasingly total system or logic—the Foucault of the prisons book is the obvious example—the more powerless the reader comes to feel" (*Postmodernism* 5). Texts for Jameson, then, are like children's blocks, which remain a set of independent entities even when they are arranged as the elements of make-believe objects.

Jameson cannot, however, keep his claims about objects so simple. Indeed, he relies on a notion of bodily materiality that is radically different from the discrete objects that are the basis of his theory. If one side of cognitive mapping is the discrete landmarks that make up social space, the other side is the body of the individual who moves through this space: "distance in general (including 'critical distance' in particular) has very precisely been abolished in the new space of postmodernism. We are submerged in its henceforth filled and suffused volumes to the point where our now postmodern bodies are bereft of spatial coordinates and practically (let alone theoretically) incapable of distantiation" (48–49). Social space becomes animated by time when individuals move physically through that space. The human body is neither a discrete object like the landmarks of the space, nor a conceptual representation like the map that organizes and interprets the landmarks. The body functions, rather, as a bridge between discrete objects and their conceptual representation; it is material without being fixed, dependent on maps without being conceptual. The materially complex body appears throughout Jameson's writings as a necessary but backgrounded element of mapping and allegory. When Jameson describes the way in which Gehry's house "cognitively maps" architectural space, bodily "habitation" is the means by which traditional and new forms of domestic space come together: "Le Corbusier's 'free plan' may be said in much the same sense to challenge the existence of the traditional room as a syntactic category and to produce an imperative to dwell in some new way, to invent new forms of living and habitation as an ethical and political . . . consequence of formal mutation" (107). Why does Jameson need such a materially complex entity, when discrete entities have been so important to his theories of cognitive mapping and allegorical transcoding? In chapter 4 we saw that when Frank sought to treat space as a "form" mediating text and reader response he described a tissue of several different kinds of space. Like Frank's theory of spatial form, Jameson's theory of "mapping" correlates two different kinds of space—a physical location in social space and the abstract spatial map that an individual constructs of that space. In Frank's theory, space is meaningful only because several different kinds of space come together. For Jameson, likewise, a map becomes meaningful when one uses it to navigate the real-world corollary of the map's abstract space. Several forms of space can come together only through an object of complex materiality. When Raymond Federman's writer tries to keep the past simple and to treat it as a fixed object, the "abject" voice arises to represent the suppressed materiality of the past. Likewise, when Jameson tries to keep the elements of a text or of social space simple and discrete, the materiality of these objects returns in the human body, which is both necessary to, and irreconcilable with, the other objects of social or textual space. To describe how the movement between several spaces demands that the objects within those spaces be materially complex, we can return to the term that my discussion of Derrida introduced—*worldliness*. Derrida described objects defined and structured by an interpreter as "worldly"—that is, they stand ambiguously between text and world and fluctuate between a concrete and a conceptual existence. We see a similar "worldliness" in the materially complex objects necessary to both Frank's spatial form theory and to Jameson's theory of cognitive mapping. In both cases, the mediator between world and interpretation—in Frank's case, between text and reader response, in Jameson's case, between real space and cognitive map—is an object with complex materiality.

The material complexity that Jameson refuses to acknowledge is precisely what makes the postmodern landscape fascinating to post-deconstructive critics. The objects of the postmodern landscape partially exist in the real world, but also are a product of cultural and media images. Such objects are, in other words, worldly, and thus the stuff of post-deconstructive narrative. McHale and Connor both criticize Jameson for failing to explain how postmodern objects resist the space-time compression brought about by contemporary production methods. McHale's critique of Jameson points specifically to the worldliness of the cultural objects that Jameson discusses—the fact that they are partially products of the interpretive goals that Jameson himself brings to them. McHale praises Jameson's willingness to "tell stories": "Rather than letting one's discourse be shaped—or deformed—by the desire to evade and deflect accusations of metanarrativity, better to try to tell as good a story as possible, one that makes the richest possible sense of the phenomenon in question and provokes the liveliest possible critical scrutiny, controversy, counter-proposals, and (why not?) counter stories" ("Anxiety" 31). Very much against Jameson's own arguments, McHale claims that Jameson creates the cultural objects that he "tells stories" about. Because these objects exist in the real world but are also defined and circumscribed by Jameson's interpretive text, they are "worldly." Jameson cannot admit the worldliness of these objects because he hopes to show that individual subjects negotiate a cultural or textual space comprised of shared elements. As long as the objects within this space are distinct and relatively self-present, individuals can recognize the possibilities of mapping or interpretation and share those with others. If we define these objects as "worldly" and partially themselves the product of interpretation, we no longer have a shared point from which mapping or transcoding will begin. Although we have seen that he does indeed rely on the complex materiality of the body, Jameson cannot discuss materiality directly without undermining the distinctness of the objects organized by cognitive mapping. Thus we can say that Jameson becomes caught up in the issues of post-deconstructive narrative despite himself. These problems are unavoidable because he starts from deconstructive questions objectivity and space, questions that force him to take extreme positions about these issues in order to counter the claims of writers like Baudrillard. Because he raises the issue of the "objectness" of these objects but refuses to consider their material complexity, this complexity returns to haunt his theory. Jameson thus shows the difficulty of willfully escaping the dynamics of post-deconstructive criticism.

The Open Landscape

The postmodern space that Jameson rejects is, we can say, deconstructive since it focuses primarily on the way in which these objects violate our expectations. This is not to say that this deconstructive understanding of the postmodern landscape cannot have positive consequences. One possible explanation of the appeal of the hyperreal objects that Baudrillard celebrates is that they draw attention back to a space and time that recent economic changes have suppressed. Baudrillard hints at how objects can make us aware of space and time when, in his book on seduction, he describes the power of a "superficial abyss": "The real is relinquished *by the very excess of its appearances*. The objects resemble themselves too much, this resemblance being like a second state; and by virtue of this *allegorical* resemblance, and of the diagonal lighting, they point to the irony of too much reality. Depth appears to have been turned inside out" (*Seduction* 63). In this passage, Baudrillard argues that postmodern objects can make us aware of the process by which space and time disappear. The contemporary fascination with objects then, might be a response to the gradual loss of space and time that Harvey described. If, to cite the Althusserian formulation of ideology that Jameson draws on so often, "[i]deology represents the imaginary relationship of individuals to their real conditions of existence" (162), we can see the fascination with postmodern objects and landscapes as a backhanded attempt to remind ourselves about the space and time that has disappeared in our "real conditions of existence."

One concrete example of where such a deconstructive landscape draws our attention back to space and time is the explosive popularity of the idea of *cyberspace*—a term that has far outpaced its original role in science fiction to take on a much larger cultural resonance. Indeed, Timothy Leary has claimed that in his novels about cyberspace, William Gibson "has produced nothing less than the underlying myth, the core legend, of the next stage of human evolution" (56; cited in Kellner 298). Whether Leary is right about the importance of cyberspace, his excitement about this concept is typical of American popular culture. Douglas Kellner has recently argued that "cyberpunk" writing, which exploits the concept of cyberspace, is a positive step beyond Baudrillard's hyperculture (319–23). Gibson's original definition of the term in *Neuromancer* makes it clear that *cyberspace* does indeed draw on the issues of objects and space that interest Baudrillard:

> The matrix has its roots in primitive arcade games . . . in early graphics programs and military experimentation with cranial jacks. . . . Cyberspace. A consensual hallucination experienced daily by billions of legitimate operators, in every nation, by children being taught mathematical concepts. . . . A graphic representation of data abstracted from the banks of every computer in the human system. Unthinkable complexity. Lines of light ranged in the nonspace of the mind, clusters and constellations of data. (51)

Gibson's cyberspace transforms an abstraction of "unthinkable complexity" into a more or less concrete object. During this act of creating an object, a larger network of space arises. Perhaps more than any other "spatial form" that we have discussed, cyberspace is "spatial" only in very metaphorical terms—a "place" where concepts of distance and location vanish. Cyberpunk writing explores space through the material body, focusing particularly on the body as it disappears into abstraction. In this passage, for example, Gibson emphasizes the clash between body and abstract cyberspace in the "cranial jack." This jack violates traditional assumptions about physical autonomy while revealing that our access to abstract cyberspace has very physical roots. McHale argues that cyberspace juxtaposes many "worlds" (*Constructing* 251), but we can say more precisely that Gibson is interested in the tension between cyberspace's realm of abstractions and the physical world that ultimately supports this realm. As an idea that has claimed a prominent place within the contemporary cultural consciousness, cyberspace embodies a concern for the tension between a (bodily) materiality and the abstract objects of computer representation. Cyberspace constructs a new kind of cultural space, but uses the tension between bodily materiality and abstraction to complicate this space. The fascination with the bodily basis of cyberspace transforms the abstract space of the "matrix" into at least two types of space, and implies complex links between them. In cyberspace we once again have a shared cultural locale, although one dependent entirely upon the contradictions of Baudrillard's postmodern landscape.

Neither Baudrillard's landscape or its cyberspace echo is post-deconstructive in the sense that I have defined it—that is, neither is a mode of recontextualizing textual conflicts in order to emphasize how its objects are available to other forms of articulation. By way of conclusion, let me provide a counterexample to the resistant or deconstructive images of postmodern space that we have described to this point. I would like to discuss a novel in which precisely the dynamics of post-deconstructive narrative provide the means by which a very different notion of the contemporary landscape is developed. Indeed, Janet Kauffman's little-known novel *The Body in Four Parts* approaches space in precisely the opposite terms that Jameson does, embracing spatial contradictions and material complexity. In the end, Kauffman develops the positive—and we could say, fully post-deconstructive—notion of social space that Jameson saw lacking in Baudrillard's hyperreal landscape. Kauffman's novel describes four siblings, each of whom represents a different physical element: water, earth, fire, and air. She is not subtle in creating these associations, but instead foregrounds their surrealism. Thus, Dorothea, who represents water, literally lives underwater—even though otherwise her character is psychologically realistic and interacts normally with other characters. The unnamed speaker represents earth; her brother Jean-Paul, whose hair burns continually, represents fire; their invisible brother Jack represents air. Although the narrator and her friend Margaretta remain the focus of the narrative throughout, they are involved with one particular sibling in each of the novel's four chapters. Margaretta is described as "amphibious" (35), and her no-nonsense approach to the world counterbalances the narrator's more philosophical and abstract interaction with her siblings: "Margaretta is body-in-process. Woman-at-work. Taxpaying American citizen, naked when she is naked" (36). The story itself opens with the easiest of the four elements to grasp—Dorothea, who represents water—and progresses toward the elusive, invisible brother Jack. The narrator and Margaretta's visits to each of the siblings are motivated by their search for a hidden well from which they hope to take watercress as a gift for Dorothea. In the end, as we will see, the discovery of the well unites the four siblings.

Kauffman works toward this unity primarily in spatial terms. In particular, *The Body in Four Parts* is a kind of "road novel" that moves between distinct locations (the homes of secondary characters met along the way) while describing the larger landscape in which they exist. As the narrator remarks, "Some rides, across open landscapes, on the turnpikes, suggest the layout of the whole planet. The horizon scrolls away, and you're aware that the road is a line, as visible as the Amazon, on a satellite photograph" (108). Kauffman often contrasts the whole landscape glimpsed in this passage to suburban subdivision. The narrator describes one character's house as the antithesis of subdivision: "If Lucy Del Laraine has interest in the comings and goings of the natural world, she could conduct some detailed studies here. Aunt Charlaine could guard the grounds—they could claim the place as an off-road refuge! A sign could read: This is not a Subdivision" (112–13). In the novel, subdivided spaces embody our routine blindness to "the comings and goings of the natural world"—everything that moves between individual locations. We cannot understand these natural connections if we accept the locations that conventional language and subdivision provide. Margaretta's no-nonsense approach to the world is somewhat guilty of accepting what is visible within conventional locations and not considering what is suppressed by those locations:

> She [Margaretta] says a camera should be mounted on a car—a cheap Horizon, I suppose—and run continuously. The car would just keep driving overland, then be ferried across water, in the hold of a ship, the camera still running down there—you'd see black for a while—that's what you'd watch, and then all the stops across Africa for gas, to buy food crossing borders, the camera would reel on and on. Across Egypt or the Sudan. Through the Middle East, no specials on the military or the oil, no specials on anything. On the concrete steps of a house, no trees around, you'd see three boys in shorts. You'd hear a voice shout, Where are the girls? Where are the rooted plants, the fish?
>
> "If you want to see the fish, fish not caught, you have to go underwater," I interject. (51)

Margaretta's camera cannot record what it cannot see—those things underwater. The nonpresent ("fish not caught") is part of the structure of what exists, but is unknowable so long as we insist on seeing distinct objects and locations. Kauffman's narrator remarks very early in the novel about Dorothea, "She *should* have the same last name as me, isn't that how naming works? Under the usual circumstances. On the usual plank floors" (4). The fact that the brothers and sisters do not seem to live in or even come from the same place (Jean-Paul's first language is, apparently, French) suggests that hidden relations exist between divided locations. Kauffman makes clear that her characters transcend individual locations when the narrator comments about subdivisions: "These are not, in the end, subdivisions. You can't subtract from a climate. They appear. They thrive. Dorothea underwater. Jean-Paul in flames. Jack in air" (11).

The search for the watercress, and thus the trajectory for the novel itself, embodies an appreciation of the material experience of everyday life. When the narrator and Margaretta decide to find the watercress for Dorothea, they describe the enjoyment of simple pleasures: "The trip to collect the plants was in fact an idea Margaretta cooked up, watching the blue hole in the ice: 'Go East, *mesdames* go East. Fuck holy grails,' she said, with her homegrown feminist finesse. 'You want these greens, okay. This is the opposite of conquest, Babe. No gold-encrusted shit. They ask, Ladies, what do you want? We say, A god-damned decent *salad*!'" (37). This passage suggests that Kauffman is worried that individuals have been severed from concrete experience by abstract values and goals. Kauffman's narrator states the problem of "elemental deprivation" explicitly:

> But it may be, in its essentials, a common place phenomenon: a body in numerous parts—Dorothea, Jean-Paul, Jack, and me—male, female, brother, sister, water, fire, air, you name it, walking around on the ground, all-in-one.
> I wouldn't call it a problem, but a resolution. Consider the possibilities. If a child can assemble sixteen or sixty selves, to survive the horrors attendant upon abuse, then I suppose four brothers and sisters are not too many, to survive—what would you call it?—*elemental* deprivation? Drastic loss of touch. The way we put on hats and keep away air. The way elements hide in the cells and we walk around, unaware. Even of oxygen, for instance. Blue air. Leaves and their component carbons, as everyday things. Sister and blood-brother leaves. Mud. Rock. The family before any other. (11)

Kauffman, it seems, has divided this family into four elements because she believes that individuals have lost touch with the material—they are "elementally deprived." Margaretta's call for a decent salad in the previous quotation rejects abstract values ("gold-encrusted shit") and instead embraces the earthy, the physical. Because she hopes to emphasize the importance of the material, Kauffman has chosen to make her speaker represent "earth"—the most mundane of these physical elements. As the narrator and Margaretta move through the novel, the watercress embodies those material things that have no abstract value—the watercress is "a nothing gift, for anybody but Dorothea" (31).

Kauffman treats abstraction with suspicion, but she believes that we can only understand matter by recognizing how language organizes and divides up the world. The best example of the importance of division in the novel is when Kauffman describes matter using four component elements. Kauffman jettisons contemporary scientific thinking about matter, and instead returns to the Greek theory (usually attributed to Empedocles but best known from Plato's *Timaeus*) that the material world is composed of fire, earth, water, and air. This ancient Greek theory depends much more on what today appear to be metaphors,[3] and assumes that the basic components of the world are evident in our experience and in the everyday concepts we use to describe the world. In embracing this theory, Kauffman rejects attempts to render matter less metaphorical and more abstract.[4] Kauffman may not be convinced that the world is actually composed of these four basic components, but this Greek theory provides a convenient way to emphasize that matter is divided—often in whimsical ways. In particular, the Greek theory treats matter as the unity of four different components that we recognize concretely in our everyday experience. Kauffman, likewise, believes that we understand matter only by dividing up the world into components and looking for where these familiar components unite. Thus, the quest for an appreciation of the material world, embodied in the watercress, leads the narrator and Margaretta through contact with each of the siblings, and ultimately to a kind of temporary unity when the watercress is found. Thus, the search for the material "subdivided" metaphorically into different elements and the attempt to understand the landscape without traditional locations resonate with each other. The search for the watercress, as a movement between distinct locations becomes a way of overcoming the division of the material.

Although she searches for the links between locations and the components of matter, Kauffman insists that understanding spatial and conceptual divisions is an important first step in seeing these unities. The narrator's opening description of Dorothea suggests how division helps characters to return to an "origin" that underlies individual locations: "She's shed her future, in a way, and gone under. She's linked herself to her origins, or you could say exploded herself, beyond everything, the way cataclysmic heat spits molecules off the body" (3). The usually unrecognized material nature of the world is exactly what holds individual locations together. The novel concludes with Jack, who represents air and consequently a matter that surrounds all things. "In the dark Jack assumes the spaces between the bodies of things, he fills in the blanks. In the dark, he is every shape, as a matter of fact, and the geese in the dark, after Jack has said his farewells, close their eyes and sleep on the water, and circle, and wake, and sleep again, and not one collides with another, there is no room there, or anywhere, for that to happen" (128). This passage suggests that all spaces are full even though we do not usually recognize the air that fills them. Air itself is Kauffman's principle example of matter that crosses media and spaces. The narrator asks about Dorothea's ability to breath underwater: "Has S. [i.e., Dorothea] learned to latch onto oxygen wherever she finds it, is that it? There is no struggle in the breathing, no struggle at all" (61). Oxygen exists where we have become blind to it. "Elemental deprivation," the problem that Kauffman's novel seeks to solve, describes just this subdivision-inspired blindness to matter:

> What I mean [by "elemental deprivation"] is: deprived of the elemental world—and who isn't, with a globe divided, the whole planet sectioned, roofed, cut and pasted—even its waters—what can a body do, if it *is* a body, but acknowledge, salvage, the elements in its own boundaries. . . . A part of the body, anyone's body, longs for a green, a blue, mud-enmired planet, with its own turnings and feedings and comings and goings. Something apart from the human. (12)

Kauffman divides the body in order to explore something "apart from the human" within the human. More specifically, we can say that Kauffman considers how the body shares in the materiality of the whole world. The body's materiality, for her, can only be recognized when it crosses the line between body and outside world, when it "longs for a green, a blue, mud-enmired planet."

Kauffman develops, then, a complex understanding of the contemporary landscape that insists on a tension between "mapped" locations and the sublime experience of the larger horizon. When the narrator and Margaretta eventually discover the well that contains watercress for Dorothea, Kauffman provides the fullest explanation of how individuals recognize materiality amid individual locations. The watercourse has been routed underground, and the narrator, as a figure of earth, can find it:

> What does Margaretta see—a blur? S. Jean-Paul and Jack, that's what I see. Myself. We spiral, we escalate—the fluid meltdown power of S., Jean-Paul's charged, blow-torch hair, Jack's invisibility, his whirlwind collisions and calms.
>
> To go underground, more problematic than diving underwater, there's nothing to do but call on the body in all its parts, fleshed, fisted, lathed, almost metallic—coppery with the tremendous turning. This is ferocity of will, not wish. It takes shape. The bullet body. (74)

All four siblings are unified at this moment of activity, as the narrator "call[s] on the body in all its parts" and creates a single object—the "bullet body." This scene suggests that the well is found because the elements represented by the narrator and her siblings come together in a particular location. What brings these elements together seems to be the narrator's willingness to act; as she says, "this is ferocity of will, not wish." The narrator's actions reveal matter in the unity of fire, earth, air, and water. Whatever insight the narrator gains into the matter within this location is only temporary: "Not an explosion, but a simple machine-cut, incisive, and fanned from my feet, pulled down with me, a crater, a sinkhole, closed back over, you'd never know a body had hit" (74). The narrator can reveal unities that exist between normally distinct elements and locations, but she also recognizes that she cannot permanently change the landscape or her understanding of it. In contrast to Margaretta, who believes that one can know a landscape simply by filming everything and making a permanent record, the narrator understands that any insight into a particular landscape is only temporary. The narrator makes the transience of insight clear, ironically, in her comment about Margaretta: "I am an admirer of Margaretta's exits. She never wants to leave where she is, but she also wants to be off to another place, attending to something else. There's a reluctance in her to say good-bye, then, and she drags it out. But she's headed towards the door, and when she's through it, that's it, her mind turns to the next thing" (115). We can recognize the continuity of a whole landscape because no place is self-contained; rather, every space is a jumping-off point for a journey toward the next location. We can understand a location only by acting within it, but those actions drive us on to the next location. Margaretta herself summarizes her attitude toward location: "That's it. Aimless. It's how I can stay in one place . . . and be far-flung" (117). The narrator and Margaretta's search for unity within a particular location drives them on to new places.

Kauffman's use of space in *The Body in Four Parts* shares a great deal with Jameson's theory of cognitive mapping, but the former is much more willing to embrace the instability of space. Jameson's theory, we will recall, asserted the role of the individual in negotiating social space. He hopes to show, we concluded in the previous section, that the individual acts within a stable total space both in understanding society (cognitive mapping) and in textual interpretation (allegorical transcoding). Kauffman's characters, likewise, act within locations to understand the matter beneath conceptual distinctions. Kauffman, however, does not start from a notion of total and stable space; her characters recognize that their awareness of continuity between spaces is only temporary. Like Federman's writer, who moves through an endlessly transforming textual space, Kauffman's characters travel from location to location with only a fleeting glimpse of some larger continuity between them. Because her characters are able to accept the transience of their insight and the instability of the spaces that they inhabit, Kauffman's notion of materiality is unconcerned with permanence and stability. Where Jameson insists on treating objects as discrete so that they support a stable total space, Kauffman embraces a materiality that is fluid and irreducible to individual objects or locations. Theorists of the material like Emmanuel Levinas and Samuel Weber, who I discussed in chapter 1, might disagree with Kauffman and argue that one cannot embrace materiality and give up the all-too-human hope of using external objects to stabilize one's sense of self. Nonetheless, Kauffman does provide us with a powerful example of how materiality spurs us on from one space to the next. Margaretta's quest for the watercress itself is thus both an attempt to grasp the material and, at the same time, a process of crossing many spaces. The narrator describes the watercress as a kind of road: "Floating greens, white-rooted in moving water—S. has made trips upstream every March to find it, and failed. We both recall a particular limestone spring in the East, thick with cress, dark-leaved, bank to bank, obscuring the stream flowing out. That may be the only past a body is able to retrace. A green waterway. One you can eat you way across" (31). In this passage, the watercress symbolizes the ability to cross spaces. Crossing spaces in *The Body in Four Parts* often involves embracing other material elements and accepting transformation; when the narrator finds the well, for example, she is temporarily transformed by her unity with her siblings into a "bullet body." Margaretta's "amphibiousness" embodies the positive value of being able to cross various spaces and media; she is described as having "a body adapted for floating across fresh or saltwater seas and then stepping onto land," and as a "body-in-process" (35–36). We have already seen that traveling through locations is the means by which characters gain insight into a whole landscape, but Kauffman makes this association of travel and insight particularly clear in Dorothea's story about people swallowed by a whale: "They were bodies within a body. And the more simply they saw themselves the more complexly they were linked to the whale, who swam them through oceans they could not remember or dream" (26). Dorothea implies that an individual can cross boundaries—here both the literal boundaries of oceans and the figurative boundaries between the real and the imagined—by being aware of a bodily materiality that passes through all locations. Because watercress embodies the crossings so important to recognizing materiality and avoiding "elemental depriva-tion," the narrator describes the watercress bridge as a "cure-all" for herself and Dorothea (37).

Kauffman's refusal *either* to return to a traditional notion of place or to wallow in the instability of the contemporary landscape makes her novel fully post-deconstructive in the sense that neither Jameson nor even cyberpunk fiction has achieved. Kauffman believes that accepting and exploring how metaphors divide and organize the world can lead us to recognize limitations in the locations, to grasp the materiality that crosses between them, and to move on to new spaces and new ways of articulating the world. Kauffman comments on the power of language near the end of the novel:

> It is the dream of the body—to know a place bodily and to say so. To take words into and out of itself. To have words assume bodily shape, *salaman-der* or *milk*, it doesn't matter. To inhabit a shore, a fabulous body of water, debris, insects drilled in the sand.
>
> Where in the world can the body say, I am in my element.
>
> The body strips to its flesh, and flame, and dives. When air gives out, and blues and greens simplify into dark, lips open the way lips open for kisses.
>
> But the body, more fully desirous, recalcitrant in the extreme, says, even there, No, this is not the world I dreamed of. This is not the world. (119)

Unlike Jameson, who denies the complexity of the material for the sake of a stable cultural space, Kauffman embraces material complexity as the point where world and language meet, and where language enters into new formulations. We live by dividing the world theoretically into spaces and locations, but our very actions in those locations drive us on to create new spaces by momentarily embracing the material world "with its own turnings and feedings, and comings and goings." These actions become the stuff of a positive type of narrative in the wake of deconstruction, a narrative that sees new potentials precisely in em-bracing these spatial contradictions.

chapter six

READING TIME

Temporality in the Worldly Text

We have seen that the appeal to narrative as an alternative form of textuality after deconstruction reveals a network of concerns that can be exploited by writers and critics to develop a more positive image of writing and interpretation. It should also be clear that these concerns can be expressed in different ways with different emphases. Where Raymond Federman's novel is concerned with the progression toward some object (the past), Janet Kauffman's novel moves much more fluidly across various spaces and through many media. Where Jacques Derrida seems principally concerned with the readerly "location" that the play of objects and materiality creates, writers like Ronald Sukenick and Federman keep their focus on the progression of the characters within the novel itself. It is clear that the dynamic relation between space, time, and materiality can be approached from very different perspectives with this broad post-deconstructive context. It is equally clear, I hope, that the term that best summarizes this network of qualities deployed in this context is *narrative*, which has seemed to so many critics as the concept that captures the ontological multiplicity of the represented objects and their mediation though textual form.

All of the writers that we have examined so far share, however, the tendency to see textual space against the backdrop of a more general temporality. Kauffman is perhaps the most explicit in treating space as a temporary construction subordinate to an ongoing intellectual and spatial movement, but all of the writers we have discussed emphasize the temporary quality of textual spaces. Are spaces unstable for these writers simply because texts are fundamentally temporal? In other words, can we produce a more stable and less contradictory poetics of narrative if we begin with time rather than space as its organizing element? Temporality is commonly privileged over space in many types of postmodern theory. Paul de Man's deconstructive allegory perhaps most clearly summarizes the positive power of temporality to figure disruption in contemporary thinking: "this relationship between signs necessarily contains a constitutive temporal element; it remains necessary, if there is to be allegory, that the allegorical sign refer to another sign that precedes it. The meaning constituted by the allegorical sign can then consist only in the *repetition* (in the Kierkegaardian sense of the term) of a previous sign with which it can never coincide, since it is of the essence of this previous sign to be pure anteriority" (*Blindness* 207). De Man's own "allegorical" readings are typical of the postmodern emphasis on the temporality of slippage and deferral.

In this chapter I would like to investigate whether temporality can provide a stable basis for a theory of post-deconstructive narrative. I will argue that temporal theories of textuality encounter many of the same problems that spatial theories do, but that we nonetheless can speak about an underlying textual temporality in certain limited ways. I would like to begin by examining briefly "reader response" theories of the literary text as time-based models of narrative. The problems that reader response theories encounter when they try to address broader issues of interpretation are well documented, and will provide an efficient way of discussing parallels between problems in time- and space-based textual theories. More importantly, however, this discussion will serve as a springboard for explaining the encounter between temporal and spatial aspects of the post-deconstructive text. Kauffman's *Body in Four Parts* describes the process of "crossing" conceptual spaces. The idea that this novel leaves us with is that moving between individual textual "sites" is more than a leap from temporary construction to temporary construction; instead, it appears to be a sustained effort to investigate and transform concepts. Can we apply Kauffman's idea of how an individual confronts concepts in everyday life to how we negotiate the concepts and objects of a text? Doing so will produce a theory of post-deconstructive narration that balances textual space and time, while nonetheless insisting that texts do "move" in hesitant, interrupted, but ultimately unceasing ways.

Theories of Reading Process

Reader-response criticism has embraced theoretical contradictions to a surprising degree. In a post-deconstructive context where feminists, Marxists, cultural critics, and poststructualists spar over issues of subjectivity, indeterminacy, and the construction of cultural space, reader-response criticism has gone its way largely untroubled by such broad theoretical issues. Reader response criticism still treats "response" as a predictable and coherent event, and still speaks about the "implied reader" as a more or less unified subjectivity. Some of these anachronisms arise from this criticism's tradition of producing interpretations of individual works—a task that forces critics to speak about "meaning," "response," and "intention" almost inevitably.[1] More importantly, reader response criticism has been numbed to such theoretical problems because of the contradictory interpretive task that it accepts. Kathleen McCormick has described what she calls "the fundamental paradox of reading theory": that such a theory attempts to describe in reading something that has a "strange, elusive quality" but in doing so tends to reduce this mystery to a formal, rigid structure that forecloses response (75). Reader response theory stages the rigidification of the text; in the name of the process of reading it produces claims about textual structures designed to control response. Such theories will be in different ways more subtle and more direct in how they encounter the theoretical problems which, as we saw in chapter 5, haunt spatial form theory. This encounter is more subtle because, unlike textual space, temporality seems to be a natural part of reading. It is more direct because the fundamental act of providing a *theory* for the process of reading transforms the act into an object and thus raises the issue of critics' purposes and methods of theorizing. Much more than spatial form theory, reader-response contradictions frame a desirable *narrative* practice—a method of telling stories about how texts work that seems to sidestep the problems of indeterminacy raised by deconstruction. Thus reader-response criticism is post-deconstructive at least in some weak sense: it is the one theoretical movement that has managed to incorporate deconstruction without losing a sense of the positive effects of texts and their interpretation. As we look for a response theory capable of fully admitting or exploiting these textual problems, we move toward a truly post-deconstructive theory and to an explanation of textual temporality.

Wolfgang Iser's theory of reading process is both the best-known and in certain ways most problematic treatment of textual temporality. For Iser, fictional texts invite and then invert reader expectations and "schema." Iser draws on the visual arts as his primary model:

> What is important for our purposes, however, is the fact that the correction [that we make when we realize the error of our expectations] violates a norm of expectation contained within the picture itself. In this way, the act of representation creates its own conditions of reception. It stimulates observation and sets to work the imagination of the observer, who is guided by the correction to the extent that he will try to discover the motive behind the change in the schema. (*Act* 91–92)

Literary works, according to Iser, lure the reader into adopting certain conventional expectations (which the work somehow "contains") and then violate them, encouraging the reader to rethink those expectations. At odds with the control that the literary text exerts over the reader in this quotation is Iser's assumption that the reader "concretizes" the text according to his or her own background. Concretization is an individualization of the text that nonetheless can be traced back to structures within the text:

> The fact that the reader's role can be fulfilled in different ways, according to historical or individual circumstances, is an indication that the structure of the text *allows* for different ways of fulfillment. Clearly, then, the process of fulfillment is always a selective one, and any one actualization can be judged against the background of the others potentially present in the textual structure of the reader's role. Each actualization therefore represents a selective realization of the implied reader, whose own structure provides a frame of reference within which individual responses to a text can be communicated to others. (37)

According to Iser, reading is a matter of following out a certain textual path, bridging "indeterminacies" within the text by providing details from one's own background. Iser seems to say two contradictory things. On the one hand, the text seems to control response, since it "violates a norm of expectation contained within the picture itself"; on the other hand, Iser wants to treat response as inherently personal and open to historical change and peculiarity, since he accused fellow phenomenologist Roman Ingarden of being "unable to accept the possibility that a work may be concretized in different, equally valid ways" (178). Stanley Fish has argued that this contradiction is part of "the attractiveness of Iser's theory":

> it seems able to accommodate emphases that have often been perceived as contradictory in the writings of other theorists. It is at once spatial—in that it conceives of the text as an object with a particular shape (the shape of the "designated instructions")—and temporal—in that the production of literary meaning is a process that the text only sets in motion, it is for the same reason a theory that can claim a measure of objectivity—its operations begin with something that is "given"—and yet at the same time it requires the subjective contribution of the reader who must do his individual part. ("Why" 3)

To understand why Iser falls into what appears to be a fairly straightforward contradiction, we might return to the inspiration for Iser's theory—Edmund Husserl's phenomenology and Ingarden's attempt to use that phenomenology to create an aesthetic theory of literature. Phenomenology has always sought to describe perception without fostering solipsism—that is, to explain how individual perceptions are shared among a group. It has explained this by claiming that perceptions are organized by common interpretational structures. According to Husserl, all objects are "intentional"—that is, they are produced by a consciousness "attending" to them, and actively (though not consciously) seeking to understand them *as* something: "In this manner, without exception, every conscious process is, in itself, consciousness *of* such and such" (*Cartesian* 33). Because we expect individual perceptions to coalesce into "something" with which we are already familiar, perception is prestructured. Because individual members of a community share an "ontology" of the types of objects that they expect to perceive, the objects that they do "see" will be recognizable by the whole group. In a sense, the whole process of perception for Husserl is circular: individuals are provided with an ontology that they use to interpret the world, and that is reinforced when they do manage to see the world through these terms. The objects of everyday perception do not appear abstract, however, since we are not normally aware of this process of interpretation. Husserl describes how individual perceptions seem to be one's own despite the fact that they depend on shared processes of perception in the following, rather difficult passage:

> Manifestly . . . the own-essenti[ality] belonging to me as ego comprises more than merely the [actualities] and potentialities of the stream of subjective [processes]. Just as it comprises the constitutive systems, *it comprises the constituted unities*—but with a certain *restriction*. That is to say: Where, and *so far as, the constituted unity is inseparable from the original constitution itself*, with the inseparableness that characterizes an immediate concrete ownness, not only the constitutive perceiving but also the perceived existent belongs to my concrete very-ownness. (103–4)

As Husserl argues here, the "constituted" nature of objects is reconcilable with its "immediate concrete ownness." This process is dependent on a culturally shared ontology, which organizes perceived phenomena into perceptions of an object understood the same way by all who share that ontology.

Ingarden was the first to apply Husserlian phenomenology to the fictional text in a systematic way, and his theory most clearly shows the problems of adapting Husserl's notion of "intentionality" to account for textual objects. Ingarden claims that the literary text offers an intentional object to our consciousness: "By a purely intentional objectivity we understand an objectivity that is in a figurative sense 'created' by an act of consciousness or by a manifold of acts or, finally, by a formation (e.g., a word meaning, a sentence) exclusively on the basis of an immanent, original, or only conferred intentionality and has, in the given objectivities, the source of its existence and its total essence" (117). Ingarden's theory parallels that of Husserl in a number of ways. Like Husserl's everyday objects, Ingarden's textual objects appear because they have a place within a mental ontology. Like Husserlian intentionality, Ingarden's literary intentionality is grounded in a general process of constituting objects that seem concrete rather than abstract. Yet, while Ingarden asserts that this process and the objects constituted are generalizable from reader to reader he lacks the sense of *exteriority* that Husserl has—the fact that the intentional process is directed toward the world outside of itself. When we read, we are not responding to perceptions so much as *creating* an idea of an object or character. Ingarden claims that the *real* cause of these acts is the author's intention for the work: "The concern, in effect, is not at all with the stream of experiences, i.e., with the *experiencing* of something, but with what these subjective experiences *refer to*, that is, with the *objects* of the author's thoughts and ideas" (16). Ingarden's use of authorial intention as the source of purely intentional literary objects severs his theory from Husserl's circular model of general yet concrete everyday perceived objects. Husserl's objects are concretely always exactly what we perceive; Ingarden's textual objects can be perceived only through a mediating structure of authorial intent. Rather than simply "seeing" a textual object as something, we must reconstruct the author's intentions before we know how to imagine this object. Ingarden explains how we recognize these intentions using the often-criticized notion of a level of metaphysical "schematized aspects": "We have indicated previously that represented objects can be exhibited by states of affairs but can never really attain intuitive apprehension through them, and that, in a literary work, still another special factor is needed to prepare the ground for the intuitive appearance of represented objectivities. This factor . . . is constituted by the aspects of represented objectivities" (255). According to Ingarden, the literary text contains "aspects" whose structure guides our perception of that text. These schematized aspects are supposed to provide a generalizing "skeleton" for the reader's constructive acts of imagination in the work: "what is in question here are not aspects that are experienced once and then lost for all time but certain *idealizations*, which are, so to speak, a *skeleton*, a *schemata*, of concrete, flowing, transitory aspects" (262). Ingarden argues that it is because these aspects are generally recognizable that the work is able to maintain an identity across all readings (364). Clearly Ingarden stumbles here, since it is difficult to imagine how a text can insert a structure within itself for its own perception. Mikel Dufrenne critiques Ingarden in exactly these terms, arguing that the claim that textual objects are produced through a schematic formation inserts an abstract process by which we decide how actually to perceive the text. "The very purpose of the doctrine of intentionality," remarks Dufrenne, "is to avoid this ruinous distinction, the pitfall of all psychologism" (208).

Iser inherits the problems in his theory of "concretization," then, from his sources in phenomenology. Because Ingarden's theory is "intentional" in the Husserlian sense, it must assume that reading is a process of perceiving certain textual objects; Ingarden is forced to admit, however, that how these objects are to be perceived depends on an abstract, reconstructed authorial intention. The same problem appears in Iser's writing, which argues both that textual objects are "concretized" according to individual perceptual dispositions and that the text controls perceptions so that the text has a uniformity of purpose across all readings. The status of textual objects appears to be the stumbling block of reader response theories, and as a result recent critics have simply avoided discussing the construction of textual objects altogether. Instead critics have developed a broader notion of response as a running reaction to the text as a whole. James Phelan, for example, claims that the meaning of a text arises out of its ability to introduce "instabilities" that drive the reader onward through the text looking for resolution:

> Progression, as I use the term, refers to a narrative as a dynamic event, one that must move, in both its telling and its reception, through time. In examining progression, then, we are concerned with how authors generate, sustain, develop, and resolve readers' interest in narrative. I postulate that such movement is given shape and direction by the way in which an author introduces, complicates and resolves (or fails to resolve) certain instabilities which are the developing focus of the authorial audience's interest in the narrative. (15)

For Phelan, reading is a temporal process of responding to problems within the narrative. His shift away from Iser's problematic language of schema and concretization jettisons the issue that troubles both him and Ingarden: how the text creates objects of perception both concrete and shareable. The most surprising part about this more recent reader response criticism is that it does end up presupposing a layer of concrete elements that are the base of the text. Fish's early essay, "Literature in the Reader," explains this shift in the concrete "bedrock" of interpretation to the reader:

> It [traditional interpretation] is a criticism that takes as its (self-restricted) area the physical dimensions of the artifact and within these dimensions it marks out beginnings, middles, and ends, discovers frequency distributions,

traces out patterns of imagery, diagrams strata of complexity (vertical of course), all without ever taking into account the relationship (if any) between its data and their affective force. Its question is what goes into the work rather than what does the work go into. It is "objective" in exactly the wrong way, because it determinedly ignores what is objectively true about the *activity* of reading. Analysis in terms of doings and happenings is on the other hand truly objective because it recognizes the fluidity, "the moving-ness," of the meaning experience and because it directs us to where the action is—the active and activating consciousness of the reader. (*Text* 44)

For Fish, reader-response criticism recognizes a different sort of objec-tivity in the text, not in the "physical dimensions of the artifact" but in the concrete reactions produced in the process of reading. By treating the text as leaving behind a trace of concrete reactions, Fish and Phelan both transform the temporality of reading into an object available to analysis. From this perspective, the problems of Iser's theory of con-structed concrete entities result from his desire to mix a reader-response theory with a more traditional belief in textual entities.[2] Phelan and Fish, conversely, sidestep this problem by treating the object of response theory as reader reactions in general, which in turn can be understood by examining the text that gives rise to these reactions.

The problems that reader response criticism encounters when it tries to explain the nature of textual objects repeats tensions we have seen in spatial form theories of narrative. As Matei Calinescu points out in *Rereading*, reader-response theories are haunted by what they can-not account for—the fact that these theories of how a text is "sup-posed" to affect readers on their first reading are always produced out of the holistic understanding of the work that results from many reread-ings. Calinescu argues that not only are first readings not critically ade-quate, they are also made up of partial rereadings of the work itself: "This double (first) reading is one in which two radically different kinds of attention and interest are involved (one diachronic, the other syn-chronic), and in which the 'normal' linear reading is already 'shadowed' by a sort of tentative rereading" (19). Calinescu goes on to argue that reader-response theory actually brings together several kinds of textual time: "a rereader might feel that a work with which he or she is already familiar is available to understanding not only as a past, remembered diachronic unfolding, but also as a present, synchronic structure. On closer inspection, however, such spatial metaphors ('landscape,' 'struc-ture') reveal their ultimate inadequacy. Rereading is less a matter of 'space' than of time, albeit a special time, a circular or quasi-mythical time" (18). Calinescu's argument describes a certain kind of blindness that we have already observed in spatial form theories. There I suggested that such theories inevitably group together several heterogeneous forms of space in order to account for the ontological multiplicity of the literary text. Calinescu claims that literary texts operate within several different types of time—most obviously, the literal time of reading and the structured time of the retrospective reading. Reader response criticism creates many forms of time for the same reason that spatial form theories describe several kinds of space; both try to produce a concrete "object" that they can interpret. This is particularly clear in Fish's work, where the progression of the reader through the work becomes transformed into a concrete trace that the critic can then analyze. Indeed, it is precisely because he lacks a theory of textual objects that Fish's theory has come under fire. Kathleen McCormick notes this lack in her discussion of why Fish is unable to explain dissonance between interpretations within an individual interpretive community: "Although a knowledge of certain rules is required to interpret a given object or action, it does not follow that once one knows the rules, one can then virtually ignore the characteristics of the object or action that allow it to be interpreted in a given way in the first place" (69). In particular, McCormick sees Fish's theory as lacking a consideration of the complexity of individual textual objects. Fish homogenizes the several "times" of reading to create a single object (the trace of reader reaction) whose ontological status is curiously simple and unproblematized.

Should we conclude that, because theories of reading process fall into similar rhetorical patterns, that we cannot speak about the reader's temporal movement through the text as especially fundamental? We should distinguish the unifying temporalities that critics like Phelan and Iser create from the problematic, hesitant time we saw in the work of Derrida and Kauffman. The latter two writers describe a broken and disunified movement through the text that seems to have the potential to become the foundation of a poetics of post-deconstructive textual construction. What causes these hesitations? What forces the text to slow its progression? Kauffman's idea that thinking involves crossing conceptual spaces suggests that spaces exist to make temporal movement possible even though they are antithetical to it. Derrida explains this claim more specifically when he describes the gramme as a *limit* that defines a site where the transformation of terms can be observed. In both cases, the limit stops temporal movement in order to construct a space, all the while making that space dependent on time and hence temporary. Likewise, Calinescu describes how rereading halts the movement of reading in order to construct a kind of space—a "synchronic structure"—which serves, paradoxically, to reveal the process of reading itself. Whether Calinescu is right in claiming that this space is really a kind of "quasi-mythical time" is less important than the fundamental confrontation that he defines: the moment at which the temporality of reading encounters some quality of the text (space) that both energizes that temporality and yet also requires rhetorical effort to explain it as another form of time. Calinescu's claim that this textual space is actually a kind of time makes sense in the context of his argument, since ultimately he continues to offer a kind of reader-response (and hence temporal) theory of narrative. We should recognize, however, that Calinescu works to define this quality of the text as "mythical time" even through it might also have been seen as a spatial element of the text. To generalize the rhetorical act that we can recognize in Calinescu, we could say that the temporality of reading eventually comes up against something that does not fit within it but that is necessary to it—an "other." This other aspect of the text initially appears to be spatial, if only because of its radical difference from the text's initial temporality. The opposite would appear to be true as well: that we could describe how textual space encounters something "other" to it that requires rhetorical effort to transform into another kind of space. Certainly this is the case of the nested spaces of Federman's novel, where we saw the initial space of the closet inserted into a narrative only to have the closet return as a spatial figure in the trunk: "they grabbed me and locked me in a box dragged me a hundred times over the earth in metaphorical disgrace" (8). In this passage, the closet's encounter with the temporality of narrative is transformed back into a kind of space (the trunk) that Federman is then able to keep as the symbolic center to his work. These encounters describe an ongoing *movement* of the text that does not allow any one of these forms to remain untroubled or complete. To be able to understand the moment that the temporality of reading confronts space—or, for that matter, the moment that spatial form confronts time—would be to describe a problematic, hesitant, but always ongoing temporality of the text. A text able to use such temporality would not merely be admitting the contradictions of literary time, but instead would be using those contradictions to compose a text. Indeed, the constant hesitation between time and its breaks embodies the dual textual problem posed by deconstruction: how texts can be both indeterminate and a totalizing system. The hesitant time of post-deconstructive writing is exactly this shift between a total horizon of temporal progression and the interruption and indetermination of that progression. In such broken, hesitant time, then, we have the fullest expression of post-deconstructive textuality.

A Poetics of the Hesitating Text

Our discussion of reader response theory suggests that we might define a particular kind of temporality inherent to the text so long as we do not ossify it into the totalizing forms of temporality that we saw in writers like Phelan and Fish. We should be able to describe what we might call the "arrhythmic temporality" of the post-deconstructive text—its penchant for hesitation, pauses, and spatial construction—using the model of *différance*, site, and readerly "location" that we developed in chapter 2. It is in Derrida's notion of the gramme that we find the clearest explanation of why the text's temporality constantly undergoes spatial "pauses." But Derrida's model also focuses narrowly on a single moment within the text, the moment at which a certain limit is constructed that allows us to recognize both the conflicts within a text and the critical "location" that we occupy. Indeed, for many critics the principle limitation of criticism claiming to be "located" is that it seems unable to describe a consistent ethical narrative that connects such individual sites of analysis. In chapter 1 we noted John McGowan's complaint about Edward W. Said's writing: "[Said] insists that 'there can be no neutrality or objectivity,' but adds in the next sentence that 'this is not to say that all positions are equal'; he goes on to discriminate among different positions on the basis of whether one is 'engaged openly on the side of justice and truth'" (167). "Local" criticism's inability to construct ethical narratives that organize individual sites of analysis arises out of its intense focus on the dynamics of individual textual "topoi." Derrida has made clear that our movement through a text cannot be a seamless progression, but McGowan nonetheless challenges us to explain how we move from one site to the next. This is precisely what critics are grasping for when they call for narrative after deconstruction, and what Derrida has struggled toward in his recent work on Karl Marx.

The challenge of explaining how we link together sites during the course of reading asks us to draw together all of the elements of post-deconstructive narrative that we have been considering thus far. The texts that we have discussed fall into one of two groups. On the one hand, we have seen fiction—like that of Kauffman, Federman, and Sukenick—where the construction of spaces and their disappearance is staged through the characters' struggles to negotiate space and time. On the other hand, we have seen critical writing like Derrida's theory of site and location that describes the interaction between text and reader. This latter approach to narrative and materiality places less emphasis on the temporal construction and deconstruction of spaces, and more on the structural relation between topos and critical location. If we are going to be able to speak about the process of moving through the text from site to site, we must find a way to bring together these two different ways of approaching textual dynamics. Doing so will mean describing the temporality of the text through the readerly locations that it creates and exploits. We can distinguish these two approaches to narrative temporality as, respectively, the novelistic and the critical, and I would like to suggest that their relation can be understood through the fiction of Kathy Acker. The meteoric rise of Acker's academic reputation testifies to how closely her literary concerns accord with post-deconstructive theory; she has also been praised for describing characters whose lives reflect the problems of poststructural theory. Acker's writing has not always managed to strike the balance the critics have recently praised; her writing changed from the "deconstructive" style of her fragmented work of the 1970s toward a more tenuously unified style in *In Memoriam to Identity* and *My Mother: Demonology*. The turning point for this development seems to be her novel *Empire of the Senseless*, which balances the novelistic and the critical treatments of the site and develops a full-fledged post-deconstructive narrative poetics. The resulting style of writing not only tells us a great deal about how we should think about the temporality of the text, but also provides us with a concrete example of how a writer can exploit the potential trajectories so many post-deconstructive writers have insisted on. As a result, my discussion of Acker will be more elaborate than that of any novelist I have treated thus far, but will also serve as a capstone explanation of the spatial and temporal tensions within texts.

Empire of the Senseless tells the story of Abhor and Thivai's problematic romance and its involvement in a consumer and technological "objectality." Like all of Acker's fiction, *Empire* draws on and rewrites past fiction. In this case, Acker's most important source is William Gibson's *Neuromancer*, which provides Acker with an example of a cybernetic romance, a relation between men and women mediated by technology and by the designs of multinational corporations to the point that their bodies themselves become constructs.[3] Acker has claimed that this novel's less fragmented style depends on a model for human society that rejects this techno-consumerism. Acker makes this connection between a social model and her recent style in an interview, in response to the question, "What is the new direction you've taken in *Empire*?": "The search for a myth to live by. The purpose is constructive rather than deconstructive as in *Don Quixote*. What I particularly like about *Empire of the Senseless* is [that] the characters are alive. For instance, in *Blood and Guts*, Janey Smith was a more cardboard figure. But I could sit down and have a meal with Abhor" (Friedman, "Conversation" 17). Acker concludes by remarking that, while the novel fails to provide readers with an image of a whole society freed from patriarchy and from its supporting taboos, it does offer a "myth" or model in the sailors—a group that defines itself by its eccentric and antisocial position. Robert Siegle describes the function of the sailors as follows:

> Bred in poverty, the sailor does not marry its binary opposite [the wealthy] as Nana did, but rather suspends the dialectic of wealth and privation with which the state of poverty encloses the individual's perception of social possibilities. To live in "material simplicity" means to displace commodities as the determining signifiers and to create the possibility for something other than "poverty of the heart." (114)

The sailors stand outside of consumerism and the power structures it supports. Critics have naturally focused their attention on the sailors, as Acker herself encourages us to. Acker has suggested, however, that myth interests her because it implies a fundamentally different relation between text and reader. Acker remarks in an interview with Sylvère Lotringer, "That's the way you feel in the mythical stories. You don't know quite why they act the way they act, and they don't care. . . . The reader doesn't own the character. There's a lot of power in narrative, not in story" (*Hannibal* 23). For Acker, the sailor myth leads to a new style of writing because it transforms the way in which the fictional text is represented. In this style Acker brings together the critical and fictional treatments of spatiotemporal conflicts; Acker explains both how readers encounter texts and how characters live through theoretical, textual conflicts on an everyday basis and in the process develop a rich understanding of post-deconstructive narrative.

Ownership is interwoven with conventional language use for Acker. Language conceals the problems in the conventional concept of individual identity. For Acker, identity is known by its continuity within time, yet individuals are trapped temporally, and hence are unable to glimpse this continuity. This problem is clear in Abhor's meditation on time: "Of course time cures everything. Human. It does because that time which will come, the future, is never present. Since everything will happen in the future: the present, me, was null" (113). For Acker, individual identity can be defined only through time in patterns of consistent actions, responses, and beliefs, thus locating coherent identity at some future point from which such patterns can be observed (hence "everything will happen in the future"). Individuals themselves, however, are trapped perceptually within the present and severed from this retrospective coherence (hence "the present, me, was null"). Because of the problems that time creates for identity, individuals are driven to define identity independently of the individual knowledge and perception problematized by time. Acker's early novels see idealized "images" as the transpersonal basis of knowledge. She suggests this in her first novel, *The Childlike Life of the Black Tarantula*, where she writes, "I call up images of myself, or just images. They are 'my' images and yet, they extend my knowledge. I usually hear that other people have the same images, and I know we are all connected" (*Childlike* 67). This passage suggests that identity is problematic only for those estranged from the "images" that society uses to cover over the fundamental gaps within identity. Acker's introspective, disenfranchised heroines are left without any such "images" or are forced to operate within artificial and "impossible" positions. As she writes in *Empire*, "I'm playing with *only* my blood and shit and death because mommy ordered me to be only whatever she desired, that is, to be not possible, but it isn't possible to be and be not possible" (51). As a result, Acker's female characters are painfully aware of the limitations in our current ways of bridging the gaps within identity.

Acker's more recent novels have moved away from a concern for "images," and have settled on language's apparent ability to reference distinct objects as an even more fundamental way of easing the problems of identity by providing seemingly transpersonal knowledge. At one point in *Empire*, Acker has a character make the seemingly nonsensical comment that "In French, 'flesh' is 'chair.' The flesh made real" (66). Flesh as an undefined physical substance becomes "real" (otherwise it is "intangible" [104]) only by being objectified by language into a single, easily namable thing that, like a chair, is taken for granted—mere furniture. Much as we have seen critics like Elizabeth Grosz do, Acker distinguishes here between the objects defined by language and a more amorphous, less conventionally meaningful materiality. This tension between defined objects and a more problematic, "painful" materiality is clear throughout Acker's writing. *Don Quixote*, for example, contrasts a comforting aesthetic detachment based on objectivity ("Each thing by itself was beautiful. Each thing had no meaning other than itself, or meant nothing" [190]) to the dangers of physical contact: "My physical sensations scare me because they confront me with a self when I have no self: sexual touching makes these physical sensations so fierce" (171). That this detached objectivity is specifically a product of language in *Empire* is clear in another scene. Speaking of a seller of "prosynthetic limbs and other works of art" (39) Acker writes that "His latest work-of-art, his newest find, find-and-keep so-to-speak, is a [human] head. . . . Despite the obvious value of this work of art, its humanity, not being a humanist, I advised Ratso to get rid of it" (40). Acker puns on the term *humanity*, playing off its use in art criticism (speaking of a work's "humanity") and its more literal meaning as being "of" a human. This passage slides from the latter to the former, from a concern for the physical origin of the part to an assertion of its artistic quality as an object. This shift suggests a general tendency to read back into the flesh the qualities associated with the person as an object—humanity. Language offers us the concepts of a *human* and of *humanity*—terms charged with political and social implications—and in the process ignores the ongoing, material relation of individual and world. Acker suggests that this is a calculated mistake that eases discontinuities within the world for those who occupy privileged positions within the society. As someone disenfranchised by the hegemony supported by language and its objects, Acker will seek to understand this painful materiality.

Although at times Acker seems to treat the materiality of "flesh" as a simple prelinguistic, pre-objectified substance, other passages suggest that she has a more complex understanding of this materiality that is commensurate with the model I have developed throughout this book. Indeed, Colleen Kennedy has criticized Siegle's reading of *Empire* on the grounds that he attributes to Acker a belief in prelinguistic materiality:

> In direct contradiction to Baudrillard, Siegle sees the culture's best writers as those able to distinguish between simulation and reality; what is real is what is tactile, what is painful, what reminds us of the body—the inscribed upon rather than the inscription. . . . Acker suggests, however, that the "blood" (accessible only as a metaphor) is no longer pure; the body cannot with any assurance be the untainted site of some reinscription of culture. (182)

Kennedy's critique of the naive belief in access to prelinguistic materiality is a valuable warning, but we must also recognize that Acker sees materiality as not simply unknowable, but as manifesting itself in the context of these inscriptions. In *Empire* Acker very clearly defines the physical as dependent on the mind: "Mentality is the mirror of physicality. The body is the mirror of the mind. A mirror image is not exactly the same as what is mirrored" (65). This passage suggests that, rather than taking the body (as flesh) as a prelinguistic base to be objectified and made meaningful by language, we should recognize that this materiality is at least in part a product of this process, this mirroring. Acker asks in *Don Quixote*, "Is there a split between mind and body, or rather between these two types of mentality?" (46–47), clearly implying that whatever materiality we might oppose to the objective is itself a mental product. More specifically, we can say that the material arises as a kind of trace left behind by one's relation to a (linguistically) defined object, a trace that reveals that object's constructed and artificial quality. Typically, Acker's heroines are most aware of their own physicality through their desire for some "other" (a romantic interest usually, but, more generally, something outside of the self that can only be under-stood as an object).[4] The first section of *Don Quixote*, for example, opens with the heroine "conceiv[ing] of the most insane idea that any woman can think of. Which is to love" (9), and ends with her "battered and bruised and couldn't rise out of her bed due to a severe infection" (15), of which she metaphorically "dies." Continually in Acker's writing, desire for some other leads not to the acceptance of objectivity, but to the recognition of the gap between material and object; as she writes in *Great Expectations*, "Desire makes the whole body-mind turn on itself and hate itself" (70). In this sense, Acker joins with the feminist writers discussed in chapter 1 who have sought to theorize bodily materiality in contrast to the traditional philosophical opposition between subject and object. There I quoted Grosz's use of Maurice Merleau-Ponty's notion of flesh as a particularly clear if somewhat limited model of materiality that undermines these traditional oppositions. Flesh, says Grosz, "is being's reversibility, its capacity to fold in on itself, a dual ori-entation inward and outward" (*Volatile* 100). In chapter 1 we saw that this concept of "flesh" is a model for a "corporeal feminism" that seeks to escape the belief that bodies and minds, and selves and others, are separate, a belief that she argues is responsible for a whole system of patriarchal values. Such a concept of flesh implies a greater interaction between individuals and the outside world by undermining the tradi-tional boundaries of the body: "Between feeling (the dimension of sub-jectivity) and being felt (the dimension of objectuality) is a gulf spanned by the indeterminate and reversible phenomenon of the being touched of the touching, the crossing over of what is touching to what is touched" (100). Acker shares with Grosz the attempt to complicate the body/mind and self/other oppositions, but sees this materiality as far more dependent on exterior objects to define it. For her, the mate-rial is not an alternative to this opposition between self and world, but is rather something produced out of the individual's desire for this objectlike "other." Much as we saw in Slavoj Žižek, Acker's concept of the material is always a retrospective construct, always partially men-tal—although it is a construct with the potential to critique the identity of mental and linguistic objects.

We have seen that narrative names a material ambiguity that can be exploited to negotiate textual problems raised by deconstruction; it is not surprising, then, that Acker's "mythical" narrative style emphasizes just such materially complex objects. Acker remarks on her interest in the material in an interview conducted shortly after the writing of *Empire:*

> The Western attitude towards the body in the twentieth century has to do
> with the fact that when reality (or the meanings associated with reality) is

up for grabs—which is one of the central problems ever since the end of the nineteenth century—then the body becomes the only thing you can return to. You can talk about sexuality as a social phenomenon, so that it's up for grabs; and you can talk about any intellectual thought and it will be "up for grabs" in the sense that anything can mean anything else and hence be completely perverted. You get to Baudrillard's black hole. But when you get to something called the actual *act* of sexuality, or the actual act of disease, there is a kind of undeniable materiality which *isn't* up for grabs. (McCaffery 93)

For Acker, materiality is not a fixed substance that we can recover, nor is it a prelinguistic state of the nonobjective. Rather, this "undeniable materiality" is an act—what I have described as a desirous moving toward an object that reveals the material. In developing a new style of writing, Acker must come to terms with the objectivity of the language she uses and find a way to reveal the material at work in the background of that act of creating textual objects. She makes the connection between her emphasis on materiality and her attempt to redefine the linguistic medium of fiction in a recent interview. To the question, "What is realism for you?" Acker responds, "It's the text. It's the body, it's the real body, which is language, the text. The actual words, that's what's real. Then there's the reality of the reader reading it . . . the reality of the writer writing it. . . . A sign is signifying something, but it also has its own aspects of sound, sight—its own materiality. It's always negotiating between its materiality and what it signifies" (Deaton 280). Acker's association of language with the body ("the real body, which is language") clearly suggests that her text not only references/creates specific fictional objects, but also emphasizes a materiality that runs counter to that objectivity. In the past, as Ellen G. Friedman suggests of *Don Quixote*, Acker has used her fragmented texts as a kind of self-consciously adopted irrationality to revolt against language and the conventional society it supports ("Now" 42). Because she recognizes that materiality appears in any language use, her directly confrontational style will no longer be appropriate. Acker's recent "mythical" style of writing, then, must find a way to harness the power of the materiality created by conventional linguistic reference in order to reveal the objectification at work in the literary text.

If Acker's writing more explicitly addresses the duality of object and materiality than any that we have seen before, she also strikes a better balance between the individual spaces that reading constructs and the larger temporality that ties them together. Acker's myth does rely primarily upon individual spatial locations. This is clear in the first description of the sailors, which comes from one of the sailors themselves:

This ship is our philanthropic association, our place of safety, our baby crib. Since they have enough dough to be our charity donors, all the people outside it, all the people outside us here, are our enemies. Since we live on this ship, we're orphans. Orphans are dumb and stupid. Since we're stupid, we don't know how to conduct ourselves in decent (monied) society and we kill people for no reason. (*Empire* 22)

Like most of the philosophical reasoning in Acker's novels, this statement is partially ironic. Nonetheless, it implies that being a sailor is a matter of self-consciously occupying a certain type of space. This space is naturally adversarial to mainstream society, but arises as a product of that society. Orphans in this sense are part of social reproduction, but fit nowhere within the traditional image of the family. They are literally the excess, and Acker's sailors rightly reverse the language of philanthropy to suggest that orphanages are ways to protect the hegemonic image of the complete and sufficient nuclear family. This space is not a simple marginality, a nomadic space outside the pale of society. Rather, by adopting the position of orphans, the sailors achieve a defined location that is conceptually necessary for the larger society—the place in which reproductive excess (kids without parents) is stored so it cannot disrupt the traditional image of the nuclear family. Acker is explicit in associating the critique of conventional society with the ability to occupy these contradictory conceptual places: "The realm of the outlaw has become redefined: today, the wild places which excite the most profound thinkers are conceptual" (140). Such spaces are not accepted as "real" since they have no place within conventional society, yet they can be traced back to specific social causes, thus taking on a peculiar specificity. Acker hints at the same sort of quasi existence when she describes the lives of prisoners as "imaginary, *imaginary* as in 'imaginary number,' not rationally possible" (148). Such objects are self-canceling, even though they have a logically necessary role within the system to which they can be traced. This helps to explain why Acker stresses that the sailors occupy negated locations. Several times Acker mentions that "no roses will grown on a sailor's grave" (117), and thus that sailor life is antithetical to the fixed, commemorative locations of traditional burial plots. Even more explicitly, Acker summarizes the sailor myth in their motto: "any place but here" (156). The sailors inhabit a nonplace with a temporary and self-negating but nonetheless real and precisely defined existence.

The connection between this peculiar space and the materiality that Acker hopes to recover still remains vague. As I have suggested, the sailors make sense only because they model a way of negotiating language and objects that is ultimately worked out most fully in Acker's own approach to writing. To explain this model, we must turn to the sailors' own form of representation: the tattoo. Interpreters have routinely granted tattooing a signal importance in the novel—as Acker encourages us to. Not only has Acker illustrated the novel with tattoo-like pictures, but the longest single scene in the novel is that in which Agone gets a tattoo, a scene that Acker herself has mentioned in interviews as the most positive in her career to that point (Friedman, "Conversation" 17). Agone goes to the tattooer looking for advice and to have his fortune told, but quickly finds his basic assumptions of individual choice and identity challenged by the tattooer and his art. Siegle sees the tattoo scene as a whole as raising the problem of identity for Agone:

> Agone is initially "caught between the rock of a false self-sufficiency," much like the illusory self that Thivai maintains, "and the rock of a need to go beyond his identity," as Abhor succeeds in doing. But he and the tattooer share first an uncertainty about their relationship and then, through that uncertainty and "insufficiency," what is for Agone "the first time in his life he began to feel something sexual"; that is, something sexual beyond the phallomorphic (and sadomasochistic) sense. Agone is taken beyond his traditionally male identity, one so formulaic and prescriptive that even he is alienated from it. (121–22)

This challenge to "traditionally male identity" initially involves homosexual desire, but more broadly means recognizing that individual identity is not "self-sufficient" and instead depends upon the interaction of self and other—what I just described as a painful materiality in contrast to a detached objectivity. Critics have recognized that the tattoo embodies this challenge to identity (according to Arthur Redding, for example, as a fetish that emphasizes the masochist's belief in the malleability of the body [294]) and have shown how it summarizes the goals of the sailors (imagination and freedom for Siegle [122]), but have largely failed to consider the implications of tattooing as a positive model of representation. Agone's male body is clearly an object that usually functions unproblematically—that is, without a trace of materiality—within hegemonic society and its representational systems. As a transformation of Agone's male body, the tattoo complicates a hegemonic object to produce a materiality essential to how Acker's female characters experience their bodies. As a form of representation, the tattoo undercuts the "objects to be owned" that Acker has associated with traditional stories, and instead reveals a materiality essential to her mythical style. It is appropriate, then, that Acker describes tattooing on the male rather than female body, since for her tattooing is a form of representation that has the power to reveal the material where it might otherwise go unnoticed. Attending to the process of tattooing, which Acker describes in great detail, reveals that the tattoo achieves a more material, less object-dependent form of representation by exploiting the same kind of conceptual space that we have associated with the sailors. In the tattoo Acker models a type of representation that is not inherently "female," not a kind of *écriture féminine*, but that rather redefines textual engagement in general to account for the materiality of which her female characters have been particularly aware.

Tattooing progresses in two stages—drawing the outline and filling in the colors. Critics have seen the tattoo as an attempt to undermine boundaries, "the epidermal borders between the internal and external" (Redding 295), but close analysis to the scene suggests that this distinction between outlining and coloring is important to the tattoo. Outlining defines a distinct space within which the act of coloring will then function:

> The tattooer began to fill in the outskirts of the drawing on the flesh that was the most sensitive.
> The far seas contained paradises. There, people lived harmoniously with themselves and their environment. Their writing was tattooing or marking directly on their own flesh.
> At the far edges of the ship's sails, the roses' petals turned into snakes. Medusa's hairs writhed through holes in the skulls of innocent humans and ate out their brains. There were the realms of danger. (138–39)

Acker associates the outlining of the tattoo with the historical origins of tattooing itself—particularly the tattoo's ability to represent the exotic, the "other" of European civilization. The second stage, the coloring of the tattoo, shifts to treat the tattoo as a produced object and to emphasize its materiality: "The first colour was red. The first colour was blood. The ship's sails were crimson. Blood makes the body move. Blood made the ship's body move. Blood changed the inhuman winds into human breath" (139). Whereas outlining is a temporal, historical process, filling in color emphasizes the products of the tattooing and how they resonate with the physical medium in which they appear. This two-part nature of the tattoo allows Acker to "narrate" the appearance of the tattoo as an object. That is, because she defines a space (through the outline), she can then watch the appearance of objects within that space and reveal their dependence on a materiality (the skin and blood) that supports and infuses them. That the tattoo attempts to recover a materiality normally hidden by the objective is clear in the anecdote with which Acker ends this scene. Having discussed the use of red and brown in the tattoo, Acker turns to blue:

The third colour was blue. The same substance was below and above the ship. It was inhuman. It was inimical to and separate from humans. Its colour was blue and its shape was that of a dragon. In the seventh century, a young warrior was carrying a jewel to her government on a ship. This jewel controlled the tides. The Dragon desired to steal the jewel. Just as he was about to grab her, to touch living human flesh, she slit open the skin between her left-side ribs and inserted the jewel into her hole. Since dragons will not touch dead flesh, her dead body was able to float until it and the jewel reached her land. (139–40)

Just as Acker has suggested that the female body is naturally more aware of the materiality behind social objects by virtue of its marginalization from these objects, she turns to a female warrior's awareness of the contradictions of materiality to explain how the material can be "saved" from the hoarding dragon of objectification. Acker treats the material as always moving toward an objectification that renders it meaningful within human society. The sea begins as meaninglessly material ("inimical to and separate from humans") but becomes anthropomorphized into the more meaningful and conventional figure of the dragon, which in turn is repelled by the material ("dead flesh"). This circular, even contradictory, story repeats the irony we have seen throughout. The material cannot be understood in and of itself, but appears only by moving toward the objective—as the meaningless sea becomes the discrete entity of the dragon. Like the female warrior, the tattoo saves the material by exploiting this movement. Just as the warrior hides the jewel within the cast-off dead flesh, so too does the tattoo exploit the materiality ignored by social objects. If, in real life, the material does not exist in quite so simple a sense before its transformation, this parable nonetheless embodies succinctly the representational strategy of the tattoo.

This tattoo embodies a problematic "solution" to Abhor's inability to live within a technological and patriarchal world, and brings together the two ways of describing the textual site that we have seen throughout this study. As a form of representation, the space of the tattoo becomes a stage upon which Acker narrates the coming-into-being of objects, thus suggesting the broader materiality out of which they arise. We just saw that Acker's heroines, by virtue of their marginalization by language and its social objects, are frequently aware of this materiality. In complicating and temporizing the seemingly simple object of Agone's male body, the tattoo provides a model for representation that draws attention to materiality for the less disenfranchised, and that makes the materiality obvious in the female body somewhat more meaningful through its necessary relationship to objectification. This space closely parallels that of the pirate ship, which similarly owed its existence to social and historical systems, and thus can be seen as a summary of the representational implications of the sailor myth. Like the ship, the tattoo's space is self-canceling. After all, once the outline is complete the process of coloring begins which, in turn, destroys that empty space for the sake of a produced image. The sailors use the self-consuming space of their motto ("any place but here") as a way to avoid getting caught up in consumerism and its dependence on objects to be owned; so too, the tattoo undermines unconscious acceptance of objects by continually pointing back, through the physical medium on which it is inscribed, to the tension between objectivity and materiality. Like Kauffman, Acker suggests that finding a way to negotiate representation is itself a way of living in the world; like Derrida, Acker approaches representation through the act of reading. At the end of the novel, Abhor escapes Thivai's attempt to turn her into a "great woman writer" (203), steals a motorcycle, and rides off calling for "discipline and anarchy" (221). Abhor remarks, "I didn't as yet know what I wanted. I now fully knew what I didn't want and what and whom I hated. That was something" (227). Her sense of freedom in the end appears to come out of analysis of representation. Her motorcycle ride is not a celebration of freedom in itself, but rather is an occasion for her to read and parody *The Highway Code* manual (213–22). Abhor's sense of freedom within the world is specifically an ability to read, critique, and rewrite the hegemonic narratives that she has been interpolated into. Indeed, Acker's call for "discipline and anarchy" echoes Derrida's sense that a close analysis of textual limitations reveals both a textual "play" (anarchy) and a system of precise structures (discipline). If she fails to see a positive basis for social arrangement, she has discovered during the course of the novel the lessons of the tattoo—how representation can be used against itself to produce new narratives.

One and Several Sites

As a temporary, conceptual space, the tattoo has much in common with the "sites" of critical inquiry that we discussed in chapter 2 and invoked at the outset of the previous section. The locale, Jean-François Lyotard suggests, is an intentionally delimited space in which a certain type of knowledge can be produced, with the cancellation of these conditions constantly hovering on the horizon. Theorists of the site have recognized that they cannot assume that such locations exist in any a priori way. Sites appear not independently of the representational systems that they help to reveal, but out of their very conflicts. Nonetheless, they retain a base in the real world as recognizable, concrete entities such as the body.[5] These entities have a peculiar concreteness only because of this clash of representational systems. Clearly, such entities exist in some sense before any discursive investment, but they only appear as "concrete" to the extent that they can be defined in contrast to the smooth functioning of linguistic and social systems. Acker makes the source of the concreteness of the site even more obvious in her own writing, recognizing that materiality appears only by staging the construction of objectivity. Having made clear how Acker's develops a post-deconstructive narrative poetics around the idea of textual materiality, I would like to conclude now by explaining the model she offers us of our temporal movement between sites and through the whole process of reading.

Acker develops an aspect of the site that we only hinted at briefly in chapter 2—that materiality is not simply a quality of such sites (the sense that they are "concrete"), but rather a product of them every bit as real and significant as the objects they define. Acker describes, in other words, how the ontological ambiguities of the representational site produce a material trace. This trace can be used to explain how readers move between sites. Acker's departure on this point from the Lyotard model of the site can perhaps best be approached through Acker's affinity for the writing of Gilles Deleuze and Felix Guattari. We should be circumspect in associating Acker with these thinkers; Acker, after all, notes that her reading in Deleuze and Guattari, like that in Michel Foucault and others, merely confirmed her original artistic impulses (*Hannibal* 10). Nonetheless, we can note a broad difference between the site as we have seen it in Lyotard and even in Derrida, and in the "rhizomatics" of Deleuze and Guattari. Both are concerned with the creation of temporary spaces of conflict and exchange. Deleuze and Guattari's use of such spaces is clear in their best-known concept, the "Body without Organs": "The BwO [Body without Organs] is not a scene, a place, or even a support upon which something comes to pass. . . . The BwO causes intensities to pass; it produces and distributes them in a *spatium* that is itself intensive, lacking extension. It is not space, nor is it in space; it is matter that occupies space to a given degree—to the degree corresponding to the intensities produced" (*Thousand* 153). For all its differences from the site as we have discussed it, this description of the Body without Organs relies on a space constituted purely by the temporal movement of forces across it, just as the site is normally understood to arise temporally out of contradictions. But much more than critics using the site that we have just considered, Deleuze and Guattari are concerned with how these spaces open up in new directions and give rise to "lines of flight." Glenn A. Harper describes the role of desire in Acker's writing in just these terms: "Desire, the only means of resistance or renewal in Acker's work, follows the subterranean paths of Deleuze and Guattari's rhizomes, undercutting any light-of-day, rationalized paths in creating a network with no priorities other than its own, circumventing any politicization of desire that would simply redirect it into new dichotomies" (49). Deleuze and Guattari make clear how such "subterranean" flights depart from the notion of a self-enclosed site elsewhere in discussing the Body without Organs: "Machines attach themselves to the body without organs as so many points of disjunction, between which an entire network of new syntheses is now woven" (*Anti-Oedipus* 12). Deleuze and Guattari's spaces always open outward, creating "new syntheses" that exceed any defined space. Like Deleuze and Guattari, Acker fights against any self-contained understanding of textual sites. Acker transforms the circumscribed and independent site that we see in Lyotard and others when she recognizes that the site produces a materiality not "contained" within it.[6] In developing this idea that materiality overruns the site, Acker begins to answer the question of how one moves temporally between one site and the next—how spaces arise, disappear, and reappear during the time of reading.

Acker's idea that materiality overflows individual sites depends on her understanding of the temporal interaction between reader and text. One of Acker's most commonly discussed comments on the relation between the text and its reader occurs early in *Empire*, as Abhor plans with Thivai:

> "I don't know who's backing him." Abhor turned around to face me. She must have woken up. "All I know is we call him 'boss' and he gets his orders. Like you and me."
> "Somebody knows something. Whoever he is, the knower, must be the big boss."
> "Look. . . . All I know is that we have to reach this construct. And her name's Kathy."
> "That's a nice name. Who is she?"
> "It doesn't mean anything." (34)

As critics have recognized, Acker rejects the humanist notion of the author as a stable origin of the text, and implies that her "authorship" is created out of the progression of the text itself (Sciolino 440). Acker suggests that, like the site, *Empire* moves toward a "construct" that ultimately has little to do with the work's real origin or effects ("It doesn't mean anything"). Acker makes this understanding of storytelling somewhat clearer in *My Mother*, where she associates narration with bodybuilding: "STORYTELLING METHOD: THE ACT OF BODYBUILD-

ING PRESUPPOSES THE ACT OF MOVING TOWARD THE BODY OR THAT WHICH IS SO MATERIAL THAT IT BECOMES IMMATERIAL" (110). Bodybuilding transforms the body into an object, but seems to make us more aware of materiality issues in the process. Given Acker's own interest in bodybuilding, and her own penchant for drawing connections between bodybuilding and her writing (see *Hannibal* 23), we should take this passage seriously as a statement of how she understands narrative. Acker suggests that the reader's movement through the novel is "material" in contrast with its objectlike end goal. This contrast is illuminated by her association of maps and desire in *My Mother*: "Maps are dreams: both describe desire, where you want to go, but never the reality of the destination" (37). Acker sees the map's failed reference to a destination as a more desirous, material relation with the text. That Acker's main characters are so often travelers (see Brennan), and that she associates herself with sailors only makes the connection between maps and her novels obvious. Indeed, Acker has associated mythical narrative with the attempt "to go into the space of wonder" (*Hannibal* 23) and thus, by implication, to pursue the desires contained within this space. Acker's narrative, then, sets into play desires that represent a materiality counter to the objectivity of the final product of the story. Like the tattoo, the novel creates a distinction between an exterior boundary and an interior materiality. A narrative can open up a space for desires only by virtue of its eventual reference to some "immaterial" object, some totality that the text creates as its goal. To return to Acker's interview comment about her desire to exploit the materiality of text, reader, and writer, we can see narrative as capable of balancing object of reference and material desires by virtue of the reader's position as *external* to the text. Only because the reader can view the text as an object—as a map with some eventual wholeness and reference—can the text open up a material play of desires en route to that object. More importantly, however, these desires move beyond the text itself. Indeed, Acker's novels refuse to stay within a single plot and constantly find themselves occupying other texts. In an interview conducted shortly after completing *Empire*, Acker notes that she appropriates texts not for parodic or structural purposes, but because they "describe the particular place I want to get to" (Friedman, "Conversation" 17). Given Acker's description of the novel as a kind of map, we can see these referenced, inserted, and rewritten texts as the product of just this sort of desirous relation to the developing text, a relation that spins off into other texts and overflows the final "construct" of the novel.

chapter seven

STRUGGLING
WITH OBJECTS

Respect for the Concrete

Perhaps more than any other contemporary theoretical movement, post-colonial criticism has made an issue of the "concrete," challenging us to recognize the complexity of the "concrete third-world subject" or the "concrete individual." These calls for attention to the concrete existence of individuals serve an essential rhetorical and practical purpose for post-colonial criticism by challenging readers to question Western narratives about colonized peoples. Although some critics have recognized the complexity of *the concrete* in this post-colonial context,[1] the term is often used uncritically. Arif Dirlik's discussion of generalizations about other cultures exemplifies the role that a presupposed "concrete" third-world subject plays in this criticism. Dirlik discusses the functioning of "culturalism" as a tool of hegemony that simplifies other cultures in a way that legitimizes certain rigid forms of social relations (398). He argues that we cannot fully jettison "culture as a question," but should instead challenge the premises of hegemonic culturalism by "bring[ing] out the historical complexities of these societies" (400–401). The goal of attending to historical complexity is certainly reasonable, echoing the traditional humanist goal of being "fair" to the objects (texts, cultures, and people) studied. Dirlik's admirable description of cultural complexity, however, depends on a rather simplistic notion of "the concrete." Defining hegemonic culture as "abstract[ing] culture from its social and political context" (424), Dirlik sets out the following goal:

> Abstractions are ideological not only because they represent "strategies of containment" in the definition of meaning, but because these strategies play a crucial role in the struggle for hegemony by suppressing alternative mean-

ings that challenge hegemony. Concepts reduced to abstractions, moreover, lose their temporality, and hence their ability to explain and to guide change. An authentically critical practice must take as a central task of social analysis the examination of the very concepts that make social analysis possible. . . . Only in this fashion, furthermore, is it possible to retain the concrete in the abstract, because the phenomena of life that concepts represent exist in the concrete not as isolated phenomena but as relationships. (426–27)

Dirlik's vilification of abstraction and championing of the concrete makes a certain intuitive sense, and it demands an overdue self-reflection by Western critics as they consider third-world texts and cultures. Chandra Talpade Mohanty's critique of how Western feminist scholarship's treatment of third-world women "discursively colonize[s] the material and historical heterogeneities of the lives of women in the third world, thereby producing/re-presenting a composite, singular 'Third World Woman'" (334), for example, uses the abstractness of past cultural analysis to expose the limitations of previous criticism.

Clearly this turn toward the concrete and away from the problems of deconstructive textuality is part of the post-deconstructive landscape. However, in contrast to Fredric Jameson's theory, which we noted was problematically both engaged with, and resistant to, deconstruction, these post-colonial writers seem antideconstructive in a more straightforward sense. That is, they simply deny that deconstruction has anything to say about this particular fact of culture and textuality. Although it is certainly untrue to say that these writers are acting as if deconstruction never existed—as we might say about popular, realistic novelists, for example—they do seem to be developing a theory of representation without beginning from the problems raised by deconstruction. Such theories and the interpretations that they develop will, we would expect, either reflect predeconstructive assumptions about textuality or reveal the kind of ambiguous, incompletely admitted engagement with deconstruction that we saw in Jameson. But can post-deconstructive writing respond to the challenges raised by these critics who valorize the concrete? What is the place of the concrete in the post-deconstructive textuality that is called "narrative"?

Problems of the Antihegemonic Concrete

Although it serves laudable goals, post-colonial criticism's call to "retain the concrete" can produce unintended rhetorical and theoretical consequences. Gayatri Chakravorty Spivak's well-known critique of

Gilles Deleuze and Michel Foucault's writing on liberation is the most forceful articulation of these consequences. Spivak discusses these two thinkers routinely used to buttress analyses like those of Dirlik and Mohanty,[2] focusing on the assumption that "intellectuals must attempt to disclose and know the discourse of society's Other" (272), that they must give voice to those people silenced by hegemony. Spivak particularly criticizes the claim that such intellectuals are attempting to understand concrete experience:

> The limits of this representationalist realism are reached with Deleuze: "reality is what actually happens in a factory, in a school, in barracks, in a prison, in a police station." This foreclosing of the necessity of the difficult task of counterhegemonic ideological production has not been salutary. It has helped positivist empiricism—the justifying foundation of advanced capitalist neocolonialism—to define its own arena as "concrete experience," "what actually happens." Indeed, the concrete experience that is the guarantor of the political appeal of prisoners, soldiers, and schoolchildren is disclosed through the concrete experience of the intellectual, the one who diagnoses the episteme. (274–75; citing Foucault, *Language* 212)

For Spivak, the construction of some third-world subject as "concrete" is itself a means of consolidating power for the first-world intellectual, allowing "the intellectuals . . . [to] become transparent in the relay race, for they merely report on the nonrepresented subject" (279). In calling for "defetishizing the concrete" (277), Spivak is clearly offering a critique of theorists like Dirlik and Mohanty. The terms in which Spivak formulates her critique should remind us a great deal of the concrete/conceptual tension that we discovered in Derrida's theory of textual "worldliness." Spivak argues that representation always functions in two different ways at the same time. In developing her explanation of the "micrological texture of power," Spivak suggests that

> one must move toward theories of ideology—of subject formations that micrologically and often erratically operate the interests that congeal the macrologies. Such theories cannot afford to overlook the category of representation in its two senses. They must note how the staging of the world in representation—its scene of writing, its *Darstellung*—dissimulates the choice of and need for "heroes," paternal proxies, agents of power—*Vertretung*. (279).

Spivak distinguishes between two forms of representation from Karl Marx's *Eighteenth Brumaire of Louis Bonaparte:* an object that serves a political function (as a "representative" official) and one that serves as an artificial or artistic "representation." In the latter case, Spivak is less interested in artworks than in the construction of fictional agents that embody economic processes: "the formation of a class is *artificial* and economic, and the economic agency or *interest* is impersonal because it is systematic and heterogeneous" (276). For Spivak, Foucault and Deleuze's belief that they can speak for the oppressed blurs the line between these types of representation. These forms of representation "are related, but running them together, especially in order to say that beyond both is where oppressed subjects speak, act, and know *for themselves*, leads to an essentialist, utopian politics" (276). This opposition echoes the tension that we noted between conceptual and concrete textual objects in Derrida's writing, especially in how Spivak destabilizes representation by questioning the "place" where oppressed subjects exist. In a representative relation, subjects are understood to be concrete outside of the abstract representational relation; in artistic representation, the subject remains abstract until given concrete, artistic embodiment. As Spivak makes clear, the "worldliness" of the third-world subject's paradoxical position within and outside of textuality is constructed by the Western critic's own interpretive location, even though critics refuse to acknowledge that location. By blurring the distinction between these two types of representation and not admitting the worldliness of the account of the third-world subject that they construct, critics suppress their own critical location and become "transparent."

We can go one step further and suggest that the textual worldliness that Spivak describes might be exploited to construct a post-deconstrutive narrative poetics that emphasizes the multiple ways in which its objects can be articulated. Indeed, Homi K. Bhabha's widely reprinted essay, "DissemiNation: Time, Narrative, and the Margins of the Modern Nation" uses a deconstructive concern for representational clashes to argue for the liberating potential of narrative. Spivak suggests that we recognize the third-world subject only in traces left by the momentary breaking down of hegemonic representations, and thus proposes a deconstructive critical practice of "systematic unlearning" (295), of critically examining imperialist representations of the East. In contrast, Bhabha claims that the kinds of representational conflicts that Spivak describes make nations multiple and heterogeneous: "The barred Nation *It/Self*, alienated from its eternal self-generation, becomes a liminal form of social representation, a space that is *internally* marked by cultural difference and the heterogeneous histories of contending peoples, antagonistic authorities, and tense cultural locations" (299). Bhabha describes representational clashes between the performative and the representational (what he calls "pedagogical") function of national narratives. Bhabha's discussion of this distinction is worth quoting at some length:

> The people are not simply historical events or parts of a patriotic body politic. They are also a complex rhetorical strategy of social reference where the claim to be representative provokes a crisis within the process of signification and discursive address. We then have a contested cultural territory where the people must be thought in a double-time; the people are the historical "objects" of a nationalist pedagogy, giving the discourse an authority that is based on the pregiven or constituted historical origin or event; the people are also the "subjects" of a process of signification that must erase any prior or original presence of the nation-people to demonstrate that prodigious, living principle of the people as that continual process by which the national life is redeemed and signified as a repeating and reproductive process. . . . In the production of the nation as narration there is a split between the continuist, accumulative temporality of the pedagogical, and the repetitious, recursive strategy of the performative. It is through this process of splitting that the conceptual ambivalence of modern society becomes the site of *writing the nation*. (297)

For Bhabha, narrative has two contradictory aspects. On the one hand, when functioning "pedagogically" narrative treats objects as permanent and concrete; on the other hand, when functioning "performatively" narrative treats textual objects as the means to achieving rhetorical goals. For Bhabha, national narratives are always marked by their need to negotiate this "conceptual ambivalence," and narratives that cannot admit this duality are likened to "the narcissistic wounded": "So long as a firm boundary is maintained between the territories, and the narcissistic wounded is contained, the aggressivity will be projected onto the Other or the Outside" (300). Denying this representational ambivalence is inherently "unhealthy" since it demands that we misunderstand the nation and its others; conversely, admitting this ambivalence is freeing. Bhabha asks, "But what if, as I have argued, the people are the articulation of a doubling of the national address, an ambivalent *movement* between the discourses of pedagogy and the performative?" and concludes, "The nation reveals, in its ambivalent and vacillating representation, the ethnography of its own historicity and opens up the possibility of other narratives of the people and their difference" (300). Bhabha agrees with Spivak that texts are inherently marked by representational tensions. Indeed, the opposition between the performative and the pedagogical dimensions of the text describe a kind of worldliness, a sense in which the text is both a real-world product (performance) and a textual construction (pedagogy). Bhabha departs from Spivak in his belief that these tensions can be admitted and used to open up a recognition of the multiplicity of any nation. Bhabha remarks, "Once the liminality of the nation-space is established, and its 'difference' is turned from the boundary 'outside' to its finitude 'within,' the threat of cultural difference is no longer a problem of 'other' people. It becomes a question of the otherness of the people-as-one" (301). Here we can see a fully post-deconstrutive narrative, since representational conflicts are being used to generate a style of writing that opens outward toward new forms of articulation.

Bhabha develops his theory of the liberatory potential within national narratives in just the way that we would expect from chapter 2: by turning to spatiotemporal clashes within the text's form. The problem with speaking about multiplicity within national narratives is that usually a "nation" describes a kind of totality, the unity of people within the country. Bhabha's theory of the openness of national narratives must therefore describe how a nation can, paradoxically, have many totalities. Bhabha emphasizes that narrative potentials arise not from representational lack (e.g., deferral, indeterminacy, and slippage) but from the fullness and multiplicity of culture: "Cultural difference must not be understood as the free play of polarities and pluralities in the homogeneous empty time of the national community. It addresses the jarring of meanings and values generated in between the variety and diversity associated with cultural plenitude; it represents the process of cultural interpretation formed in the perplexity of living, in the disjunctive, liminial space of national society that I have tried to trace" (312). What allows many totalities to come together is the space and time of the culture. Space and time can have many definitions, but each of these definitions implies a whole—the whole history, the whole nation, and so on. The multiplicity of space is clear in the act of telling: "The subject is graspable only in the passage between telling/told, between 'here' and 'somewhere else,' and in this double scene the very condition of cultural knowledge is the alienation of the subject" (301). Narration must construct a "here" that (pedagogically) describes the nation while at the same time performatively functioning across cultural spaces. These spaces seem complete in some ways, but at the same time depend on other spaces. Bhabha suggests that many spaces and times circulate through a culture:

> For the political unity of the nation consists in a continual displacement of its irredeemably plural modern space, bounded by different, even hostile nations, into a signifying space that is archaic and mythical, paradoxically representing the nation's modern territoriality, in the patriotic, atavistic temporality of Traditionalism. Quite simply, the difference of space returns as the Sameness of time, turning Territory into Tradition, turning the People

into One. The liminal point of this ideological displacement is the turning of the differentiated spatial boundary, the "outside," into the unified temporal territory of Tradition. (300)

Bounded space becomes signifying space when cultural time changes. We have seen a similar interrelation between space and time throughout this study. In spatial form theories, for example, we saw critics like W. J. T. Mitchell bring together several definitions of space in order to make sense of the ontological complexity of the literary text. In Kathy Acker's fiction, we saw how such spatiotemporal multiplicity can be exploited so that a text can suggest other possible ways of treating and developing its subject matter. Likewise, Bhabha deploys space and time in order to construct a complex notion of the openness of national narrative.

Although Spivak's and Bhabha's theories echo in different ways the conclusions that we have reached about narrative's negotiation of materiality, many critics have treated their claims with a great deal of skepticism. Critics commonly feel that Spivak's theory is too abstract, and that it fails to describe the victims of Western colonialism with sufficient emphasis and sympathy. Steven E. Cole writes, for example, "The problem is that the description of ideology seems not to offer any explanation of what aspects of the subject might stand outside the determinations of ideology, and thus serve as a candidate for what ideology has itself victimized" (62). Likewise, Benita Parry's claim that "Spivak's learned disquisitions issue from a theory assigning an absolute power to the hegemonic discourse in constituting and disarticulating the native" (34) implies that Spivak's theory of colonial discourse fails to empower the third-world subject. It is not surprising that critics have been put off by Spivak's deconstructionist reading of post-colonial discourse; we would expect critics to embrace Bhabha's upbeat, post-deconstructive understanding of post-colonial narrative more readily. Where Spivak suggests that we "recognize" the third-world subject only in traces left by the deconstruction of hegemonic discourse through "systematic unlearning," Bhabha suggests that representational ambivalences can be admitted and used to reveal the "possibility of other narratives of the people." Nonetheless, critics have found fault with Bhabha's theory of cultural multiplicity because it refuses to emphasize how the third-world subject has been victimized by Western representation. Abdul R. JanMohamed asks, "[T]he Europeans disrupted a material and discursive universe based on use-value and replaced it with one dominated by exchange-value. In this kind of context, what does it mean, in practice, to imply as Bhabha does that the native, whose entire economy and culture are destroyed, is somehow in 'possession' of 'colonial power'?" ("Economy" 60). JanMohamed claims that Bhabha's theoretical description of representation falters because it cannot describe the "concrete" experience of colonial exploitation.

What riles critics of Spivak and Bhabha is their unwillingness to speak about a concrete post-colonial subject in whose name critiques of hegemony function. But these critics are missing the value of the post-deconstructive narrative's complex engagement with the material and instead are hoping to return to an older style of writing and to a simpler understanding of the concrete. When Spivak and Bhabha describe the discursive construction of the post-colonial subject they seem to banish the very persons that critics struggle to be fair to. If there is no concrete subject who has been unfairly described by the West, these critics ask, what is the point then of critiquing those narratives? Although the use that critics like Dirlik and Mohanty make of the concrete post-colonial subject is theoretically simplistic, it does raise the issue of the goal of post-deconstructive criticism. What does post-colonial criticism strive to describe fairly? Regardless of the problems with the idea that objects are whole and concrete outside of discourse, can criticism really do without this belief to motivate its analysis?

Describing Whole Objects

We come to the question, then, of whether post-deconstrutive writing can be said to be describing a concrete object. When critics complain that Bhabha and Spivak banish the post-colonial subject, they ask indirectly what Western discourse is describing if it is not describing some entity that exists before colonial narrative. Is there a "something" before we describe it, a "something" whose concrete existence we can attempt to be fair to? Although this question raises very abstract issues about reference, we can focus on a much simpler and more pragmatic question in the context of post-colonial criticism, How do texts come together to describe a shared, real-world object? Discussing how the concept of the "third-world woman" has been deployed by Western feminists (to use Mohanty's example) obviously depends on finding many texts that refer to this entity. Linking texts together in order to analyze how a real-world object is being represented is the basis of cultural and social criticism, and the nature of these links has troubled deconstructive critics and driven them to explore narrative as a post-deconstructive textual model. We might recall from chapter 2 Nancy Fraser and Linda J. Nicholson's assertion that postmodern feminism "need forswear neither large historical narratives nor analyses of societal macrostructures" because "sexism has a long history and is deeply and pervasively embedded in contemporary societies" (34). This comment applies as well to post-colonial criticism, which similarly speaks about large Western "narratives" that run through many colonial texts. We can describe a narrative (sexism or Orientalism) only if we assume that all of these works refer to the same thing using similar terms and rhetorical maneuvers. In order to group together many texts to reveal rhetorical and ideological patterns, we must be able to assume that an entity exists independently of any one text. What is the relation between cross-textual narratives (sexism or Orientalism) and the "descriptions" of an extra-textual object (woman, man, or the Orient) by one particular text? A model that might prove useful in understanding this relation is the tension between narrative and description within individual literary works. Indeed, the difficulty of speaking about description within literature reflects many of the problems of a presupposed starting object for cultural criticism. At least since Shklovsky, narrative theory has been dominated by the fundamental distinction between events and how they are retold—story and plot. Not until Meir Sternberg's *Expositional Modes and Temporal Ordering in Fiction* did narrative theory in its contemporary sense address the tension between action and the description that surrounds it. Literary theory has difficulty understanding description because the latter steps out of the temporal continuity of the larger narrative. In coming to terms with description's place within a whole narrative, then, we provide a model for the relation between an individual text's "description" of an extra-textual object and the larger, cross-textual "narratives" in which that object reappears.

The *Yale French Studies* special issue entitled "Towards a Theory of Description" approaches texts from a loosely deconstructive perspective that provides the basis for the post-deconstructive narrative that we have been examining. Indeed, in placing issues of description in a deconstructive context, this collection allows us to explain how many texts come together to form cross-textual narratives without assuming that the entities around which these texts are organized are themselves unproblematic. Although this collection raises a variety of problems with past theories of narrative, one concern that many writers share is the place of description's stasis within the overall temporality of narrative. In one of the essays Michel Beaujour summarizes this issue: "The static scenes depicted are fictitiously and surreptitiously endowed with motion (usually in overt or implicit imitation of the poetry these pictorial scenes are supposed to *illustrate*). Static 'figures' spring into action: this effect is analogous to the animation of a motion-picture freeze shot" (33). We should not be surprised that these deconstructive critics focus on how space suppresses time, since we have seen throughout that spatiotemporal conflicts reveal the "worldliness" of criticism—how critical texts are constructed according to the critic's "location" and to the text's ontological slippage. Indeed, several of these critics conclude that when narrative temporality is suppressed for the sake of the static space of description, we become aware that description is a kind of rhetorical performance. Philippe Hamon, for example writes, "To describe is never to describe a reality, but to prove one's rhetorical know-how" ("Rhetorical" 6). Jeffrey Kittay suggests that the writer's rhetorical performance is a matter of creating a temporary space or surface that promises an insight into what is hidden:

> A surface is visible: it provides what can be seen. A surface may represent on itself one object which seems to partially hide another, but it never signals that *it* as surface, as representation, is hiding anything. It ultimately presents itself as a ground. It may suggest to the spectator a trip behind an object represented upon it, to see the other side of the object, but it does not invite the spectator behind *it;* in fact, it prohibits anyone who is a spectator of it from that particular *action*. The backdrop of a stage would be an example of this prohibition. Its purpose is ultimately that of a surface: for the purposes of the play, it cannot itself have a back. As many figures as it may have upon it, it is a ground not to be penetrated or reversed. It closes off the possibility of a trip behind it. It blocks perceptual possibilities. It is a limit. (228)

Description, according to Kittay, must be taken as a temporary construction which, while at odds with the work as a whole, serves to encapsulate the structure and message of that larger work. In description, Kittay and Beaujour both see an element that is problematically integrated into the narrative action, which pulls the reader out of the perspective of an "implied reader," and that draws attention to the act of writing and reading.[3] In doing so, these theorists suggest, description reveals a degree of "activity" and "turn[s] into micro-narratives" (Beaujour 33). Description creates a second kind of temporality (the narrative of the author's own rhetorical performance) inside a space that is itself placed within the larger narrative of the text. This characterization of description echoes how we have treated spatial moments within the overall temporality of a text throughout this study. According to Jacques Derrida, the "topos" temporarily suspends the movement of the text when it constructs a gramme that refers to movement as a kind of *limit*—a word that Kittay also uses to describe this space. Likewise Acker's fiction moves unevenly through a number of textual sites, pausing at these moments to reveal its own representational acts, but ultimately resuming the narrative movement. Like Derrida and Acker, these theorists of description insist that spatiotemporal conflicts reveal the "constructedness" of the text.

Although these description theories seem merely to repeat the discussion of spatiotemporal negotiations that has run throughout this study, these theories also suggest that the descriptive site becomes meaningful because of its eventual integration back into a larger narrative. More than any of the critics that contribute to this collection, Beaujour explains how description helps to interpret the larger narrative in which it appears. According to Beaujour, description at its extreme is a kind of allegory that embodies the larger concerns of the novel and makes them available to interpretation:

> Descriptions of *places* and *figures* (of backgrounds and images in the somewhat theatrical metaphor of rhetorical mnemonics) are particularly abundant in texts which purport to conceal spiritual meanings within "visible," earthly events and scenes. Those texts we call *allegories*. To make sure that the meaning is definitely encoded while remaining to some extent hidden, such texts have to be scrupulous in the depiction of places and figures, leaving no meaningful feature or attribute unspecified. The world of allegory is framed by literary devices that are predominantly descriptive (the *Vision* and the *Dream*), and this world is filled with wonderful beings which must not simply be named or *mentioned*, as if they were familiar creatures: they have therefore to be described, especially since their only reason for appearing in the dream or vision is to carry a message, part at least of whose signifier is their own appearance (the rest being, of course, what they say and do). Allegorical creatures, therefore, will be as completely interpretable as the meaning of allegory demands. (34)

Although this passage describes allegory specifically, its conclusions apply to how all texts make their creatures and places meaningful. Beaujour's focus on how allegory summarizes the larger concerns of the novel helps to correct Kittay's emphasis on description's *separation* from the rest of the narrative. As Beaujour makes clear, a description can only be "read" when it is balanced against the larger narrative in which it appears. Indeed, Beaujour claims that description is "Janus-like" and "demands to be read as an *allegory* and a *metamorphosis*" (58)—that is, as reflecting but also transforming the concerns of the larger narrative. If writers like Kittay have emphasized the latter, let us not forget that a descriptive "site" is able to transform the larger narrative only by referring back to it. Indeed, there is a sense in which description is merely the point at which two narratives come together and reflect on each other. We might recall Beaujour's suggestion that description has a tendency to "turn into micro-narratives" (33) which are being "performed" by a writer. Rather than simply a break in the larger narrative, description can be seen as the point where different narrative trajectories touch: the text's primary narrative and the "story" of the writer's own act of constructing the text.

Like all deconstruction, these theories of description are very abstract and universalized; nonetheless they do provide a model for thinking about the place of individual textual "descriptions" in relation to a whole, extra-textual object that post-deconstructive narrative can use. Description theory begins with the problem of reference: description, remarks Kittay, "is a trip that always has an 'about-ness' to it, the *de-* of the description" (229). Writers like Kittay and Beaujour explain this referentiality by recognizing that description both uses and transforms its place within a larger context. Likewise, we can say, a text that "describes" a real-world object (e.g., "third-world woman") both constructs it in specific ways and at the same time depends on its place within the world to bring it into contact with other texts and thus to make that construction meaningful. The extra-textual existence of an object described does not mean that texts have direct access to this object and do not need to negotiate its materiality through spatiotemporal conflicts. The comparison to description theory is particularly valuable because it allows us to think about this extra-textual object of reference as always already involved in other narratives. Even though we must presuppose the existence of some object that description treats, presupposing such an object forces us to connect this description to a larger context of other narratives. The same, we can say, is true of cultural criticism: in assuming that criticism must presuppose some real-world object (however problematic that idea is), we define a way in which one text connects to others that talk about that object. These conclusions about the necessary referentiality of description suggest that critics like Dirlik and Mohanty who designate a concrete post-colonial subject as the goal of any narrative or critical act may not be theoretically naive so much as they are aware of the critically necessarily belief in some real-world object.

The idea that texts connect to others by presupposing some whole, extra-textual object that they seek to describe suggests that such wholes actually help post-deconstructive texts to open up to new lines of textual development and other narrative articulations. I would like to explore how description opens toward other articulations by turning to Steve Katz's short story, "Parcel of Wrists," which is part of his collection *Moving Parts*. In his acknowledgments, Katz refers to *Moving Parts* as a novel, even though the stories themselves treat seemingly unrelated characters and represent very different types of stories.[4] They are, however, obviously intended to form a whole entity whose "moving parts" allow this entity to act in unconventional ways. "Parcel of Wrists" is a surrealistic story about a man, Steve, who receives a package of forty-three human wrists. He plants each wrist in a pot and leaves his apartment in search of the person who sent the package from Irondale, Tennessee. Steve discovers that no such place exists. When he returns home he discovers that the wrists have sprouted and, with his increasingly obsessive care, the plants bloom and produce a crop of various body parts—a different part from each plant. Steve alienates his remaining friends by trying to give these parts to them, and becomes at the end of the story a benefactor of body parts for those few people who bother to seek him out. Like the collection to which it belongs, "Parcel of Wrists" describes how we can divide off elements of a whole, transform them, and reintegrate them into the whole in a way that transforms the narratives in which this whole object operates. Like theories of description, then, Katz's story suggests that presupposing some whole object allows a text's "description" to be integrated back into other narratives.

"Parcel of Wrists" is a travel story. The person who sends the wrists to Steve is "C. Routs," a name that clearly suggests that the trip to find this person will result in nothing more than "seeing the route" of the travel. The trip jolts Steve out of his characteristic belief in distinct and stable locations and forces him to accept a much more fluid notion of space. Several times Steve describes the wrists as a "detour my life had taken" (3) and suggests that going on a trip to "see the route" is a break from his past. Steve implies his past belief in distinct locations in the opening scene of the story: "I am often prone to distractions. I sometimes read twenty books at a time. I leave them at different locations in my apartment so that I have something to read wherever I pause" (4). Steve's plants, conversely, undermine distinct locations, since they project colors "nowhere visible," and move "as if there is something they want to hold back from the world of men" (29). But it is Steve's trip to find Routs that most clearly demands a different understanding of place:

> His accent made me realize I was in the South. I hadn't been thinking about going south, what that meant. The map in the bus station showed Tennessee to be just north of Mississippi, Alabama, and Georgia; what most New Yorkers assume is enemy territory. There was no Irondale, Tennessee, on the map. I didn't know what my next move would be. Generous hospitality and sheer brutality were the two polarities I had stored among my Northern preconceptions of the South. I wanted to make no friends and intimidate no one: utter neutrality was my goal. (6)

Steve's journey will demand that he think about space in terms other than those of distinct locations. He must be "neutral," give up his belief in the difference between these two places, and come to understand a place that does not exist literally. Katz quotes a Johnny Paycheck song about "Heartbreak, Tennessee" (7); this blending of a state of mind and a place describes how his protagonist must reject distinct locations and come to understand more transient and fluid spaces.

Katz's challenge to the idea that locations are distinct and separate is part of his larger interest in the problems of thinking about the world as systematic and organized by the interrelation of static individual entities. When Steve takes off to "see the route" of his journey, he is weaned away from an understanding of location based on a distinct, stable, and systemic place. Katz makes clear how the journey works against the systematic understanding of place only at the end of the story:

> I sometimes try to put my finger on the one problem that caused this life that I have, to all intents and purposes, lived, to take the peculiar turn it did at a certain point. I think it's that I never really trusted the United States Post Office. I didn't really believe in it. If I had I would have done what I should have done in the first place when I received my parcel of wrists in the morning mail. Without thinking about it I should have wrapped it up again and shipped it back to C. Routs in Irondale, Tennessee, where it came from. (36).

Katz implies that the postal system fails *as a system* capable of functioning repetitiously and unchangingly. Where in the past Steve believed in distinct and stable locations, the wrists and the trip that results suggest that places do not stay the same and fit together into some sort of systematic whole. The problems of thinking about space and objects in systematic, atemporal terms run throughout the novel. One of Steve's stopping points in his trip to Irondale is a commune in which he works to restore an old sawmill. This sawmill comes to embody the problems of thinking about objects as distinct entities. Steve describes the first log that he cuts with the newly repaired machine:

> All the wheels in the room start to turn. I throw another lever and without a hum the sawblade picks up momentum. I feed the small log into it by hand. There is no sound as the blade easily rips the wood. It is like drawing a line across a sheet of paper, as if the blade were inking the separation of the wood into halves. They fall apart. I shut off the blade and generator. The two halves are perfect, shining as if they had been minutely sanded. They looked like two surfaces of polished stone. There is no sawdust left on the table. (14)

This passage questions where distinct, seemingly stable objects come from when it describes the two objects produced seamlessly out of one.

The starting point of the story is the existence of the forty-three wrists, "prepared so neatly, without a trace of torn flesh, that it occurred to me they might never have been attached to hand or forearm" (3). So too the sawmill's objects are cut off from any sense of temporality or origin: the two halves of the log appear perfect without any trace of their severing. The route, conversely, is about indistinctness, movement, and fluidity. Katz's story as a whole, then, attempts to reconcile our belief in stable objects with our recognition that objects have origins and do change.

Katz is interested in temporality and in the origins of objects and places, but he explains the way in which objects change over time in a very surprising way—by describing how they are marked and circumscribed within certain contexts. In the sawmill, rather than showing how the blade actually cuts the log, he describes the blade as marking it, "as if the blade were inking the separation of the wood into halves." The production of the two pieces of wood is not itself represented; instead, Katz only describes the marking of the object. Changes in this object are expressed indirectly by the temporality of marking. A much more important but also more complex example of this indirect means of describing changes in objects is Katz's own use of the number forty-three in his story. Forty-three is the number of the wrists in the box, and thus the number of body parts that he ends up with once those wrists sprout into fruit-producing bushes. Equally importantly, however, it is also the number of the route that he follows in trying to find Irondale—a parallel that associates the parts with the route, the product with a process.[5] Clearly, this process does not produce the wrists literally. But the cut of the saw suggests a similar causal ambiguity: the saw seems merely to mark the log rather than cutting it. Likewise, the forty-three of the route of Steve's own trip merely "marks out" a time during which the wrists will change and grow. Katz's oddly indirect way of talking about change suggests that we have a difficult time thinking directly about the origin and transformation of objects. Steve's own belief in distinct locations at the beginning of the novel implies that we usually think about the world in terms of stability and differentiation. The fluidity of movement or change seems to be naturally difficult to understand. Only when the context for an object changes do we see it in new ways. Katz marks objects literally (in the sawmill) or figuratively (in the trip), recontextualizing and thus transforming them.

The principle objects that are transformed in "Parcel of Wrists" are the forty-three body parts that Steve grows during his trip. The result of the redefinition of body parts that Katz effects through this story is seen when Steve returns to his normal life and attempts to insert these new parts into his relations with his friends. When Steve returns to New

York he discovers that his friend Michael has been mugged. Michael has lost one eye and can no longer control the movements of the other. Steve, naturally, takes a bag of eyes from his harvest when he visits him in the hospital. He holds an eye out to Michael to show him what he has brought:

> At this point something very unexpected happens. At first I don't know it's happening, but then I realize that my arm is moving, without my intending it; indeed, if I wanted to I couldn't do it. The arm was moving in perfect synchronization with what I imagine to be the random motion of Michael's injured eye. I am following it. It isn't difficult. I can feel in my fingertips the eye I have brought making minute adjustments of angle and focus. Then I suddenly perceive, or begin to understand that I am beginning to see through the palm of my hand. (32)

The eye that Katz brings with him redefines sight for the two men, and creates a fundamentally new way for the men to interact with and to "see" each other. Indeed, all of Steve's harvest seems to have the power to open up new ways of acting by redefining the "moving parts" of the body. Katz makes this most clear when Steve offers lips to his girlfriend. The conversation begins by thematizing the issue of potential: "Steve . . . I wish I knew where our relationship was going" (33). Shortly after this, Katz makes the connection between potential and the parts offered to her explicit:

> I have always been obsessed with watching Linda's mouth. It is her most expressive feature. It tends, in fact, to telegraph her feelings, to demonstrate them on such a level of exaggeration, so much sadness weighing down the lips, so much passion in their pucker, that when I was in a more intimate position not of watching her, but of being a subject of love, I would find myself hurtling off on long blind journeys of guilt or hormones just from noticing her mouth. (33–34)

The lips, and by implication all of Steve's produce, open up a range of potential actions on which he "hurtles off." The body parts are pivotal points whose transformation during the story redefines the whole bodies on which they appear. This story, after all, is named for wrists—a body part that connects hand and arm but is also able to bend and twist in many directions.

Katz's story suggests that new potential narrative trajectories arise when individual elements, which have been marked and redefined, are integrated back into a whole object. Throughout, marks are layered on top of a larger object, in the process redefining some part while maintaining its reference to a whole. It is for this reason that the body parts that Steve offers to others seem to have a particularly superficial status: "I slipped one of my hands out of hers, and took from my inside jacket pocket a large billfold and picked from it one of the lovelier sets of lips I had gleaned from my tree. I leaned forward and attached them to her mouth" (34). Such markings allow parts of this whole object to be redefined, and allow that object to spin off in new directions. I just suggested that description theory creates a second temporality within the text; descriptions move around an object, but then return to the larger narrative in which these descriptions occur. Katz likewise uses the "route" of Steve's trip to open up a second narrative within the larger story of Steve's life—it is, as we already noted, "a detour [his] life had taken." Katz makes clear that this second narrative, this "detour," only becomes meaningful and is able to open up new potential actions when it is reintegrated into a whole object and narrative—in Steve's case, back into his relations with friends. Like Beaujour, Katz suggests that description is a detour that becomes meaningful when it rejoins a larger narrative. This reference back to a whole object and to a larger narrative is evident in Acker's fiction as well. Acker used the metaphor of bodybuilding to describe the tension between a spatial "detour" and a reference to a larger narrative. Bodybuilding focuses on parts of the body—individual muscles—even though those muscles are part of a whole whose image and strength depend on the integration of all body parts. We should not assume that this total body is somehow the "real" object and that individual markings (separate parts in Katz, separate muscles in Acker) are merely momentary pauses; Acker in particular shows how individuals and bodies are constructed by language. Let us think about these descriptive moments as the transition between several kinds of narrative circulating within a single text, and through which that text is able to open outward toward new types of development. Thus, we see in both Katz and Acker the creation of a descriptive "site" that transforms the larger narrative (the lives of Steve and Abhor, respectively) when that description transforms how we think about the bodies of the characters in that larger narrative. So too, we can say that any text's description of an object (third-world woman or the Orient) only becomes meaningful when it is understood as an extra-textual object that serves as the touchstone for many texts. Even though both Katz and Acker recognize that there can be no simple concrete "thing" in the world, both recognize that post-deconstructive narrative will need to reference such an object if its constituent narratives are to be joined together and descriptions made meaningful.

We can see this post-deconstructive narrative style appearing in some post-colonial criticism. Edward W. Said's writing provides a useful complement to the very theoretical claims of Spivak and Bhabha. Said himself has explicitly written against Spivak's pessimistic understanding of colonial subjectivity; as a whole Said seems more explicitly concerned with opening up new potential narratives within imperialist texts.[6] The theoretical concept in *Culture and Imperialism* most relevant to our discussion of narrative potential is "counterpunctual reading" that attempts to "open it [the colonialist text] out both to what went into it and to what its author excluded" (67). This call for counterpunctual reading is based on Said's belief that a text is not a simple or direct representation of a world; it is, rather, a heterogeneous mixture of unifying and disunifying elements as the text admits and denies parts of colonial life: "What we have in *Heart of Darkness* [for example]—a work of immense influence, having provoked many readings and images—is a politicized, ideologically saturated Africa which to some intents and purposes was the imperialized place, with those many interests and ideas furiously at work in it, not just a photographic literary 'reflection' of it" (67). Although much of Said's writing is concerned with the task of criticizing Western narratives, late in *Culture and Imperialism* he considers to what extent authors can construct narratives that open outward toward new narrative potentials. He asks, "if European theory and Western Marxism as cultural co-efficients of liberation haven't in the main proved themselves to be reliable allies in the resistance to imperialism—on the contrary, one may suspect that they are part of the same invidious 'universalism' that connected culture with imperialism for centuries—how has the liberationist anti-imperialism tried to break this shackling unity?" (278–79). Said posits a peculiar method for constructing texts: "an investment neither in new authorities, doctrines, and encoded orthodoxies, nor in established institutions and causes, but in a particular sort of nomad, migratory, and anti-narrative energy" (279). Said describes this antinarrative quality that works against a hegemonic, imperialist vision of the East specifically as a "contrapunctual, non-narrative turn" (281) that appears within larger narratives. Discussing C. L. R. James's *Black Jacobins*, he starts by asking, "[h]ow can a non- or post-imperial history be written that is not naively utopian or hopelessly pessimistic, given the continuing embroiled actuality of domination in the Third World?" (280). The solution that Said finds in James's novel is a digression to discuss Aimé Césaire's *Cahier d'un retour au pays natal*, a digression that offers a vision of other narrative possibilities: "By moving so unexpectedly from Césaire to Eliot's 'Dry Salvages,' verses by a poet who, one might think, belongs to a totally different sphere, James rides the poetic force of Césaire's 'truth unto itself' as a vehicle for crossing over from the provincialism of one

strand of history into an apprehension of other histories, all of them animated by and articulated in an 'impossible union'" (281). Narrative can
open up to "apprehension of other histories" when it gives way to a
description capable of being at odds with the whole narrative:

> Neither an abstract, packaged theory, nor a disheartening collection of nar-
> ratable facts, this moment in James's book embodies (and does not merely
> represent or deliver) the energies of anti-imperialist liberation. I doubt that
> anyone can take from it some repeatable doctrine, reusable theory, or mem-
> orable story, much less the bureaucracy of a future state. One might per-
> haps say that it is the history and politics of imperialism, of slavery, con-
> quest, and domination freed by poetry, for a vision bearing on, if not
> delivering, true liberation. Insofar as it can be approximated in other begin-
> nings then, like *The Black Jacobins*, it is a part of what in human history can
> move us from the history of domination toward the actuality of liberation.
> This movement resists the already charted and controlled narrative lanes
> and skirts the systems of theory, doctrine, and orthodoxy. (281)

For Said, narrative can "be approximated in other beginnings" and
move away from the unifying narratives of imperialism. This openness
is not an effect of the whole of the text, but is rather the result of
moments, pivots that suggest new lines of development that cannot
become a "packaged theory." Nor, as Said states directly, can these pivots simply be the moments of concreteness that we saw Dirlik
describe—not "narratable facts." As this quotation has suggested, these
pivotal moments inherently work against narrative development; they
are, like Katz's wrists, points where the narrative can create a secondary narrative that has the potential to transform the larger narrative in
which it exists.

Although Said's writing emphasizes descriptive breaks within the
text, in more concrete examples we can see how he relies on a notion
of some whole "object" that provides the basis for new narrative trajectories. Said's discussion of Edward William Lane's *Account of the
Manners and Customs of the Modern Egyptians* makes the importance
of some extra-textual whole clear. Along with the writings of François
de Chateaubriand, Lane's account became one of the standard guides to
the Orient for European travelers and, as Said notes, provides so strong
a model for the Orient that "gifted pilgrims like [Gérard] Nerval and
[Gustave] Flaubert preferred Lane's descriptions to what their eyes and
minds showed them immediately" (177). The key to Lane's narrative
method is the appearance of objectivity: "What matters is that the
report seem accurate, general, and dispassionate, that the English
reader be convinced that Lane was never infected with heresy or apos-

tasy, and finally, that Lane's text cancel the human context of its subject matter in favor of its scientific validity" (161). For Said, this need to be objective is deeply rooted in the way in which Lane makes the Orient meaningful. For Lane's readers, only a timeless, universal individual can serve as the West's intermediary in the Orient:

> He writes about himself as the observer of scenes that follow the major divisions in the human lifetime: his model is the narrative pattern, as it is in *Tom Jones* with the hero's birth, adventures, marriage, and implied death. Only in Lane's text the narrative voice is ageless; his subject, however, the modern Egyptian, goes through the individual life-cycle. This reversal, by which a solitary individual endows himself with timeless faculties and imposes on a society and people a personal life-span, is but the first of several operations regulating what might have been the mere narration of travels in foreign parts, turning an artless text into an encyclopedia of exotic display and a playground for Orientalist scrutiny. (161)

The objectivity that drives Lane's description of the Orient becomes problematic precisely because of the "visibility" that it presupposes to be its goal. Said argues that Lane's attempt to present a complete and objective encyclopedia of the Orient rests upon the larger goal of making the Egyptian "totally visible," and that this visibility is what ultimately makes his narrative problematic: "What prevents narrative order, at the same time that narrative order is the dominating fiction of Lane's text, is sheer, overpowering, monumental description. Lane's objective is to make Egypt and the Egyptians totally visible, to keep nothing hidden from his reader, to deliver the Egyptians without depth, in swollen detail" (162). In doing so, however, Lane continually finds himself confronted by the need to become involved in the very life from which his objectivity seeks to distance him. While "Lane's capacity to rein in his profuse subject matter with an unyielding bridle of discipline and detachment depends on his cold distance from Egyptian life and Egyptian productivity" (162), he ultimately must marry in order to complete his exemplary life: "*his* story cannot continue, he seems to be saying, so long as he does not enter the intimacy of domestic life, and so he drops from sight as a candidate for it" (163). To put this conflict into more general terms, we could describe a fundamental conflict between Lane's narrative and descriptive functions. Lane must narrate his life as exemplary; likewise, however, that narration is undermined because his description of the Orient depends on maintaining his distance. Lane actually tells two stories: his life as an exemplary Egyptian, and his task as an objective cataloger of the Orient. He functions as the pivot between several kinds of narrative in much the same way that we have seen in descriptive theory and in Katz's story. Thus, the very textual dynamics of Lane's task destabilize his account and draw our attention to how he has constructed his text. Recognizing these tensions within Lane's text therefore allows readers and critics to make the leap back to the larger narrative and to pursue it in new ways—to consider how Lane's exemplary life might have been pursued without concern for descriptive objectivity. We can make this leap because we assume that some concrete entity exists that Lane has struggled to define—the individual Egyptian subject. Is this subject a "concrete" entity upon which discursive constructions reveal themselves to be inadequate? Certainly not, since we have seen that the source of Lane's narrative contradictions arise from tensions within the nature of textuality itself. We can say, instead, that this subject is a relay within the many possible narratives that surround Lane's text. This subject can function as a relay when we assume that it exists as an extra-textual entity with which critics will struggle. Even if the stability of this object is constantly drawn into question by narrative convolutions, this assumption is essential to our ability to envision new directions for narrative development.

chapter eight

NARRATIVE AND POST-DECONSTRUCTIVE ETHICS

Ethics after Deconstruction

One of the nagging issues in contemporary literary and cultural criticism after deconstruction is how the ubiquity of discourse that structuralism and poststructuralism describe affects our understanding of other people. Contemporary literary theory has been dominated largely by a model of social identity perhaps most clearly embodied in Michel Foucault's early to middle period, where social institutions and discourse construct an episteme that seems to interpellate individuals in a suffocatingly totalizing way. When Foucault defines his "archaeological" method as the analysis of *savoir,* "that is, in a domain in which the subject is necessarily situated and dependent, and can never figure as titular" (*Archaeology* 183) he explains how individuals are "placed" through discourse. Contemporary theorists have felt that they need either to accept this model of social identity fully or to reject it out of hand in favor of a more traditional understanding of identity and social space. Thus, John McGowan surveys poststructuralism and concludes with a call for a very traditional understanding of a subject's place within social space: "[w]hat we need instead [of poststructuralism] is an account of the self's inevitable immersion in the social that also explains how selves can experience themselves as integral agents capable of dissenting from or choosing alternative paths among the options social situations present" (211). This study has developed a theory of textual objects in a post-deconstructive context that refuses to grant them either simple extra-textual existence or complete linguistic construction. Would it be possible to take these conclusions about post-deconstructive textuality and apply them to ethics? I have, of course, no intention of beginning this discussion from ethical theory in general—which would be well beyond the scope of a concluding chapter of this sort. Instead, I would like to describe specifically how the understanding of textuality developed in this study might offer the grounds for responding to the ethical problems raised by deconstruction. If deconstruction has undermined traditional definitions of ethical action by suggesting that such ethics and our interaction with others is always already subject to textual instabilities, might not post-deconstructive theories of textuality offer a new way to think about the relation between ethics and representation?

The problems of ethics in a post-deconstructive context are clear in Alan Dunn's critique of Jean-François Lyotard, which was discussed briefly in chapter 1. Lyotard, it will be recalled, claims that ethics can be formulated in a more open-ended way through the notion of the "differend." "The differend," writes Lyotard, "is the unstable state and instant of language wherein something which must be able to be put into phrases cannot yet be. . . . The state is signaled by what one ordinarily calls a feeling: 'one cannot find the words,' etc." (*Differend* 13). Lyotard claims that we must attend to such feelings and search for the moments at which aporia within argumentation make us aware of how justice and legal discourse are constructed. This claim that we should attend to "feelings" has come under fire from a number of sources,[1] but Dunn articulates the problems with this claim particularly clearly:

> [T]he differend's very immunity from the language of adjudication threatens to reduce it to mere tautology, to a programmatic discontent with systems simply because they are systems. According to the logic of the differend, there is no way of analyzing the evils of hegemony, of explaining why notions of a cognitive totality must necessarily be harmful, nor can we learn anything about the differend from its historical contexts, since the differend is produced by a pure contingency that is devoid of cause or historical determination. . . .
>
> Most generally, Lyotard fails to reconcile his insistence that the differend is the product of a purely linguistic incommensurability that cannot be referred to any prior structures of consciousness or intention with his claim that the differend is shaped by struggle, frustration, and suffering. (197)

Dunn implies that any deconstructive belief that all knowledge is contingent will be at odds with the ethical recognition of suffering and struggle. Although Dunn's critique is valid and insightful, the criteria that he establishes for what we might call a "poststructuralist ethics" are too stringent. Indeed, one might partially defend Lyotard by suggesting that Dunn's critique is based merely upon the reassertion of the very legal discourse that Lyotard has set out to critique. If, as Dunn has suggested, Lyotard's claim that we simply "know" something to be unjust is too simplistic, we will also get nowhere if we follow Dunn and demand that a new ethics be cast from the same mold as the old.[2]

Since the theory of objectivity and materiality that I have developed speaks about the relation between subjective interpreter and objective outside world, extrapolating this discussion to the relation between individuals is reasonable. Some of the groundwork for this extrapolation is done when we note that Gilles Deleuze, who provided an important model for the movement between sites in chapter 4, has developed a theory of interpersonal ethics based on a "mechanical" model of sites and materiality.[3] Elizabeth Grosz describes what Deleuze (with Felix Guattari) promises to bring to ethical theory:

> In the wake of Spinoza's understanding of ethics, ethics is conceived of as the capacity for action and passion, activity and passivity; good and bad refer to the ability to increase or decrease one's capacities and strengths and abilities. Given the vast and necessary interrelation and mutual affectivity and effectivity of all beings on all others . . . the question of ethics is raised whenever the question of a being's, or an assemblage's, capacities and abilities are raised. Unlike Levinasian ethics, which is still modeled on a subject-to-subject, self-to-other, relation, the relation of a being respected in its autonomy from the other, as a necessarily independent autonomous being—the culmination and final flowering of a phenomenological notion of the subject—Deleuze and Guattari in no way privilege the human, autonomous, sovereign subject; the independent other; or the bounds of communication and representation between them. ("Thousand" 196–97)

What Grosz sees in Deleuze's work is an ethics that attempts to escape the "self-to-other" relation that is the basis of traditional ethics. Grosz's understanding of Deleuzian ethics depends on the latter's book on Spinoza. Deleuze finds within Benedict de Spinoza's writing a theory of social acts based on individuals joining with rather than confronting each other. Deleuze explains this idea of a body "doing what it can": "Everyone seeks, soul and body, what is useful or good for them. If someone happens to encounter a body that can combine with his own in a favorable relation, he tries to unite with it. When someone encounters a body whose relation is incompatible with his own, a body that affects him with sadness, he does all in his power to ward off the sadness or destroy the body, that is, to impose on the parts of that body some new relation that accords with his own nature" (*Expressionism* 257–58). In theorizing the relation between individuals in terms of power and combination, Deleuze neither claims that social interaction interpellates individuals into epistemological pigeonholes nor falls back on a traditional theory of essentialist identity. Instead, Deleuze develops a notion of conjunction based on the idea that one's own "essence" depends on combining with others. Thus, Deleuze concludes that social interaction is always the exercise of a "power" that expresses one's essence: "existence, whether possible or necessary, is itself power; *power is identical to essence itself*" (89).[4] In contrast to our usual way of understanding power as a quality independent of whether and how it is exercised, Deleuze defines power (and the personal "essence" that it reflects) as dependent on the kinds of "conjunctions" that one is able to enter into and through which one is able to exercise this power. Deleuze insists that "conjunctions" express some personal essence, but also suggests that this essence depends on the kinds of conjunctions available to it. Deleuze thus strives to balance personal essence and social context in defining identity.

The balance that Deleuze strikes between personal essence and conjunction in Spinoza echoes the much more familiar theory of production in *Anti-Oedipus*, which helps to clarify the rationale behind this seemingly paradoxical definition of personal identity. This work, along with its sequel, *A Thousand Plateaus*, offers a "mechanical" model of individuals and their bodies. For Deleuze and Guattari, the body can be connected to the outside world in mechanical ways in order to function productively: "Something is produced: the effects of a machine, not mere metaphors" (*Anti-Oedipus* 2). Deleuze and Guattari provide the following examples of bodily machines at the outset of *Anti-Oedipus:* "The breast is a machine that produces milk, and the mouth is a machine coupled to it. The mouth of the anorexic wavers between several functions: its possessor uncertain as to whether it is an eating-machine, an anal machine, a talking-machine, or a breathing-machine" (1). Such couplings between the body and the outside world are productive in an especially broad sense, since what is produced can be as abstract as the Oedipal triangle (3). This production always presupposes another machine that consumes it; indeed, Deleuze and Guattari write that "everything is production, since the recording processes are immediately consumed, immediately consummated, and these consumptions directly reproduced" (4). Production in this sense is also another way of speaking about the machines themselves, since conjunction between machines serves to produce other machines, and vice versa. The inherent connection between machines and production in his work with Guattari explains why conjunction is so important to personal essence in Deleuze's book on Spinoza. We see in *Anti-Oedipus* that the production of a "machine" is immediately consumed; in some sense the consumption creates the machine as much as the converse.

Likewise, in his book on Spinoza Deleuze suggests that essence is as much created out of its expression as actions serve to express a preexistent essence. According to Deleuze, Spinoza posits a three-part structure of expression—"We everywhere confront the necessity of distinguishing three terms: substance which expresses itself, the attribute which expresses, and the essence which is expressed" (27). As this definition suggests, essence (what is expressed) and substance (what expresses itself) are not identical; the substance that strives to express itself is not the same as the "content" of the attribute in which this expression occurs. In other words, the original cause (substance) cannot be recognized in the manifestation that gives it shape. Instead, the entire process of "expression," like the process of "production" in *Anti-Oedipus*, creates elements in order to complete the route of expression, elements that did not exist originally.

Deleuze uses the concept of expression in order to argue that one's essence is bound up with what one finds in others. Because we cannot assume that essence preexists its interactions, it is partially created out of the conjunctions that it is able to enter into—it is, as Deleuze says, "virtual." The fact that one's essence is virtual does not mean, however, that it is merely an accidental product of one's circumstances. Deleuze's early work on Henri Bergson confronts the Hegelian theory that differentiation occurs by bringing one object into connection with another external to it; he argues that the Hegelian dialectic always leaves the difference between thesis and antithesis "accidental" in the sense that it is contingent on the two elements that happen to be brought together. In contrast, when he describes one's relations to another as virtual, Deleuze implies that these relations are inherently related to the essence of those individuals. Michael Hardt summarizes this claim well:

> [J]ust as Deleuze charges that external mediation implies an accidental relation, he also refuses a dialectics of contradictions the power of real synthesis: The "combining" and "joining" of abstract terms cannot have a real, concrete result. To these two attacks we can add the charge that the very terms that Hegel uses are imprecise. For this argument Deleuze invokes Plato and his metaphor of the good cook who takes care to make his cuts in the right place according to the articulations of reality. What Hegelian terminology lacks is close attention to the specificity and singularity of real being; Hegel appears as a careless dialectical butcher when compared to Plato's fine talents. (12)

Deleuze's idea of the virtual characterizes one's "essence" as contingent on one's place within the social world without conceding that this essence is simply an accident. Rather, one's possible conjunctions always form a system of virtual actions that define one's essence.

Although virtuality is crucial to Deleuze's study of Spinoza, he describes it most explicitly in *Bergsonism:*

> What is the nature of this one and simple Virtual? How is it that, as early as *Time and Free Will*, then in *Matter and Memory*, Bergson's philosophy should have attributed such importance to the idea of virtuality at the very moment when it was challenging the category of possibility? It is because the "virtual" can be distinguished from the "possible" from at least two points of view. From a certain point of view, in fact, the possible is the opposite of the real, it is opposed to the real; but, in a quite different opposition, the virtual is opposed to the actual. We must take this terminology seriously: The possible has no reality (although it may have an actuality); conversely, the virtual is not actual, but *as such possesses a reality.* (96)

The virtual in this passage is real in a way that the possible is not—it is part of how reality is constructed and has an effect on our understanding of our actual circumstances. Clearly, in claiming that the virtual is part of reality Deleuze argues for a radically open-ended understanding of everyday life. Deleuze's Spinoza sees existence as constantly engaged in the act of expression. This active understanding of being is crucial to making sense of Deleuze's claim that existence is power: "the distinction between power and act, on the level of modes, disappears in favor of two equally actual powers, that of acting, and that of suffering action, which vary inversely one to the other, but whose sum is both constant and constantly effective. . . . It remains that a mode, in any case, has no power that is not actual: it is at each moment all that it can be, its power is its essence" (*Expressionism* 93). Thus, Deleuze is able to claim that interpersonal interaction both reveals and creates a virtual essence. Deleuze, then, seems to strike a balance between conventional ways of understanding personal identity as inherent in the individual, and deconstructive claims that identity is subject to a play of *différance* and to discursive interpellation.

Deleuze's observations about essence and virtuality have much in common with the materially complex objects that are staged in post-deconstructive narrative. To appreciate how Deleuze's virtual objects are materially complex, we must return to *Anti-Oedipus* and to the notion of production. Deleuze and Guattari claim that individuals always resist production at the same time that they participate in it. Associating the mechanical connection between individual and outside world with bodily organs, they claim that individuals struggle to create a "Body without Organs" (BwO): "In order to resist organ-machines, the body without organs represents its smooth, slippery, opaque, taut surface as a barrier" (9). Although Deleuze and Guattari treat the Body without Organs as characteristic of the schizophrenic, they also suggest that such "antiproduction" is inherent to the individual's productive relations to the outside world and "perpetually reinserted into the process of production" (8). Although the nature of antiproduction and the Body without Organs is complex and much debated, we can note one basic quality that is particularly relevant to our discussion of interpersonal ethics and materiality. The antiproduction that forms the Body without Organs arises from the urge to create a plane more fundamental than any mechanical connection to the outside world. In *A Thousand Plateaus*, Deleuze and Guattari conclude that the Body without Organs is the construction of a kind of spatial precondition for desire:

> Something will happen. Something is already happening. But what comes to pass on the BwO is not exactly the same as how you make yourself one. However, one is included in the other. Hence the two phases set forth in the preceding letter. *Why two clearly distinguished phases*, when the same thing is done in both cases. . . . One phase is for the fabrication of the BwO, the other to make something circulate on it or pass across it. (152)

The Body without Organs is constructed as a kind of site across which desire can travel, "the *field of immanence* of desire, the *plane of consistency* specific to desire (154). This *"plane of consistency"* in turn can become the basis of a new series of mechanical connections. Thus, Deleuze and Guattari remark, "We come to the gradual realization that the BwO is not at all the opposite of the organs. The organs are not its enemies. The enemy is the organism. The BwO is opposed not to the organs but to that organization of the organs called the organism" (158). The Body without Organs, Deleuze and Guattari suggest, is the attempt to create a new, less unified ground for one's mechanical interaction with the outside world. This ground takes the form of a materiality distinct from the specific external objects with which one enters into productive and desirous relations. Deleuze and Guattari describe the Body without Organs as a kind of brute matter that serves as an impersonal precondition for the movement of desire: "It is not a space, nor is it in space; it is matter that occupies space to a given degree—to the degree corresponding to the intensities produced" (153). What they seem to have in mind is that matter, like the Body without Organs, is a constructed precondition for more mechanical relations with external objects. This "matter" obviously does not exist in any simple way, but is rather created out of our need to understand what existed before we entered into mechanical relations with the outside world.

Deleuze's claim that matter is actually a constructed precondition of our relation to the outside world echoes the notion of materiality that I have just developed. In chapter 2, I have defined materiality as a general post-deconstructive concern, and suggested that it could take its place as a textual figure in certain kinds of recent textual construction. Deleuze certainly seems to share at least the broader concern with materiality as a philosophical problem. The materiality issues that arise point back to how we have worked to create stable and defined objects, even though materiality also seems to be a precondition of those objects. We can see a similar understanding of matter as a produced precondition in Deleuze's work. The point at which Deleuze and Guattari explain their understanding of matter most directly is their discussion of the distinction between form and substance. Using their fundamental distinction between the molar (the aggregate of distinct elements) and molecular (the flexible joining of intensities and flows),[5] they write,

> Double articulation is so extremely variable that we cannot begin with a general model, only a relatively simple case. The first articulation chooses or deducts, from unstable particle-flows, metastable molecular or quasi-molecular units *(substances)* upon which it imposes a statistical order of connections and successions *(forms)*. The second articulation establishes functional, compact, stable structures *(forms)*, and constructs the molar compounds in which these structures are simultaneously actualized *(substances)*. . . .
>
> It is clear that the distinction between the two articulations is not between substances and forms. Substances are nothing other than formed matters. Forms imply a code, modes of coding and decoding. Substances as formed matters refer to territorialities and degrees of territorialization and deterritorialization. But each articulation has a code *and* a territoriality; therefore each possess both form and substance. (40–41)

Deleuze and Guattari suggest that substance and form presuppose each other. We should be careful to avoid associating matter directly with substance. Substance is what form seems to give shape to; it appears as the seeming precondition of form. In some irretrievable sense, matter actually exists before form; once form appears, any attempt to reconstruct the prior state merely reveals substance and not matter. Like the distinction between substance and essence in Deleuze's work on Spinoza, matter and substance in *A Thousand Plateaus* designate two different, although easily confused, concepts. Deleuze and Guattari clarify this distinction later in the book:

> It seems to us that Husserl brought thought to the decisive step forward when he discovered a region of *vague and material* essences (in other words, essences that are vagabond, anexact and yet rigorous), distinguishing them from fixed, metric and formal, essences. We have seen that these vague essences are as distinct from formed things as they are from formal

essences. They constitute fuzzy aggregates. They relate to a *corporeality* (materiality) that is not to be confused either with an intelligible, formal essentiality or a sensible, formed and perceived thinghood. (407)

This distinction between matter and substance embodies all the paradoxes of the virtual that we have seen in Deleuze's writing. Our interactions with the world, all our attempts to give shape to the world, construct forms and the substance that appears to fill those. Matter itself always remains a precondition that can never be related logically to form.

In much the same way that post-deconstructive narrative does, Deleuze's theory of interpersonal relations depends on a complex notion of materiality. Deleuze describes, we can say, a notion of interpersonal interaction based on the idea that bodies are materially complex, and that they are created and shaped by the interaction between self and other. Indeed, he shares with the feminists we examined in chapter 1 an interest in the "corporeal" nature of interpersonal relations.[6] At the very outset of this study we saw in the idea of materiality a complicity between subject and object that promised to rework metaphysics' traditional subordination of objective world to subjective knower. Deleuze seems to describe just such a materially complex interaction between subject and object; the object is always entangled with the subject because it contains the virtual expressions of the subject's power. As we have seen, the act of "expression" produces something that was never simply present in the subject before the act, even through it seems to be the precondition for that expression. In Deleuze's Spinoza book, this "something" is the essence formed from substance; in his work with Guattari, it is the substance formed from matter. Because of the way in which expression produces something not part of the original act, the relations between individuals are always unstable and transient. In chapter 1 we have likewise seen Weber argue that the subject works to create something (an object) whose difference from a seemingly earlier condition (materiality) destabilizes that object. Furthermore, Deleuze describes interpersonal relations using the spatiotemporal tensions that this study has drawn on throughout, most obviously in how the Body without Organs defines a "plane of consistency" that allows the temporal movement of "intensities." Although he is obviously not concerned with textuality itself, Deleuze repeats much of the textual theory that I have developed in this book by emphasizing the tension between object and materiality and its appearance within a spatial context.

Imagining how Deleuze's claims about the ongoing, virtual relation between subject and object translate to practical issues of how we think about others reveals some problems in an ethics based on material complexity. Rosi Braidotti offers the following upbeat summary of Deleuze's affirmative ethics:

> The notion of rhizome is Deleuze's leading figuration: it points to a redefinition of the activity of philosophy as the quest for new images of thought, better suited to a nomadic, disjunctive self. One of these figurations is the notion of an idea as a line of intensity, marking a certain degree or variation in intensity. An idea is an active state of very high intensity, which opens up hitherto unsuspected possibilities of life and action. For Deleuze, ideas are events, lines that point human thought toward new horizons. An idea is that which carries the affirmative power of life to a higher degree. The force of this notion is that it finally puts a stop to the traditional search for ideas or lines that are "just" (in theory and politics alike). For if ideas are projectiles launched into time they can be neither "just" nor "false." ("Toward" 165)

Although Braidotti's description only touches on ethics tangentially toward the end of this passage, her understanding of Deleuze's thought as open and affirmative certainly resonates with the reading of Spinoza's ethics that we have previously discussed. Braidotti calls for a certain kind of "nomadic" subjectivity open toward "new ideas" as the basis of a new post-deconstructive ethics. Braidotti understands Deleuze to share Jean-François Lyotard's attempt to construct ethics after the renunciation of the notions of the "just" and "false." Braidotti's Deleuze is, however, open to the same charge that Allen Dunn made against Lyotard: that this notion of thought and affirmation makes no sense without some implied (traditional) structure of judgment. Although it appeals to multiplicity, Braidotti's "nomadic subject" (see Braidotti's book of the same name) is in many ways a very traditional consciousness concerned with "having" ideas and exploring his or her potential. Braidotti's traditionalization of Deleuze seems to be a natural part of her attempt to bring his model of being and power to bear on the traditional ethical concern for individuals and human potential—indeed, the privilege granted to the term *potential* in much of the post-colonial criticism that we considered in chapter 7 probably takes some of its force from the operation of traditional humanist resonances within it. We cannot, however, base a post-deconstructive ethics on such assumptions. Deleuze finds Spinoza's theory of expression interesting because it implies the construction of individual essence out of a mechanical, even antihumanist process of expression. Hardt describes Deleuze's project as an attempt to create a "materialist ontology" that is free from the primacy of thought: "Any privilege of the intellect . . . would subvert the ontological structure of the system, so that not only matter but also being itself would somehow be dependent on thought. Deleuze finds it necessary, then, to combat an idealist account of being not only in order to valorize the material world, but more importantly to preserve the coherence of the ontological perspective" (74). Braidotti's understanding of Deleuze's ethics is unsatisfactory because it retains a traditional image of subjectivity and thought.

Despite the problematic nature of her reading of Deleuze, Braidotti raises an important issue in any theory that we develop of interpersonal ethics. Although Deleuze describes how we can think about one's materially complex involvement with another, do we need to retain some notion of a concrete individual that exists as a whole despite whatever material complications that we recognize? Deleuze's affirmative notions of combination and virtuality do not appear to take the other individual seriously as a distinct entity whose desires may not be reconcilable with the conjunctions that one hopes to enter into. Simply suggesting that one should "respect the wishes" of the other is simplistic, since Deleuze draws into question the access that we have to another's "wishes," where wishes come from, and what it would mean to treat another person "respectfully." Nonetheless, we need not entirely accept the terms of Deleuze's materialist model of the relation between self and other. Indeed, in chapter 7 we saw that criticism needed to presuppose a whole object that it could discuss, despite the problems that the theory of materiality raised. We must walk a fine line between Deleuze's fluid understanding of interpersonal materiality and Braidotti's willingness to recuperate traditional notions of subjectivity uncritically. How can we treat other individuals as concrete wholes despite their ultimately complex materiality?

The Ruins of the Other

In chapter 7 I concluded that the concrete whole object was a necessary presupposition for post-deconstrutive criticism because of the necessity of bringing together many texts in order to analyze a broad cultural "narrative." Precisely what is missing in Deleuze's account, we can say, is the narrative that balances such material concerns and an appeal to a concrete object. As I have suggested throughout this study, narrative names the condition of textually after deconstruction in a way that allows that textuality to be exploited for the positive end of revealing other ways in which a textual object can be articulated. What is missing in Deleuze's writing on ethics is precisely a belief that individuals locked within social relations are also engaged in some form of textuality. At first this lack seems quite obvious and necessary, since ethics seems to describe real-world relationships and thus to be extra-textual. Nonetheless, there is a long tradition of placing textuality and particularly narrative at the core of understanding ethical action. Writing about the formation of the self through narrative, Anthony Paul Kerby writes,

> Values arise in the drama of our life, especially in the choices this life involves. It should be understandable, then, why dramatization is the form of expression most adequate to the direct disclosure of human action in its social and moral significance, and hence for disclosing individuals in their characteristic (and valorized) traits and identities: as villainous, heroic, vain, humble, and so on. (55)

If Kerby is right in suggesting that we establish value and hence evaluate ethical choices through narrative, then we must ask how Deleuze's theory of the material complexity of social relations would be transformed with more attention given to representation—indeed, narrative—in this process. To fill in this gap, I would like to turn to a novel that seeks to reclaim a notion of a "whole person" from an understanding of subjectivity as fragmented and ultimately unstable. Clarence Major's *Reflex and Bone Structure* is one of the most melancholy novels of the American metafictional movement, a novel concerned both with the freedom and the loss that comes along with a deconstructive understanding of individuals and their relations. More importantly, Major gives us a rare example of how we can think about our continuing relation to an individual despite the complexities of the material. He suggests that individuals always fragment and transform through our interaction with them, but that we nonetheless can construct narratives whose reference back to a whole inspires a sense of ethical responsibility. The result is a novel that applies Deleuze's abstract theory of "virtual" relations to more pragmatic contexts while somewhat challenging the fluidity of Deleuzian interaction between individuals.

The novel tells the story of Cora Hull, a Greenwich Village actress, particularly focusing on her romantic/sexual entanglements and eventual murder. Cora is first and foremost a character, however, and chief among her romantic pursuers is the author himself. The story focuses on Cora's encounters with her husband Canada, the undescribed and uncharacterized author, and the much more shadowy figure of Dale, who the author himself describes as lacking character (42) and who appears to embody elements of the author himself.[7] Where the novel departs from the modernist tradition of "unreliable narration" is the fact that the author who functions as part of this romantic triangle is not merely a narrator, but is instead very clearly in control of (parts of) the plot itself. Early in the novel Major describes a scene between Cora and the author:

> Cora has a high ass and big shapely legs. She's wearing her jacquard tapestry textured white print dress now. Having just changed. Carefree elegance. Chocolate ice cream.
>
> My elbows on the dressing table begin to ache.
>
> And someone opens the door. It's Dale who stands there, mouth open, watching us. I erase him. He's still on stage. In his glory. Cutting another notch into the totem pole of his career.
>
> Dale opens the door again and this time he enters. (20)

Clearly Major has characterized his author as in many ways petty, jealous of his characters, and as often as not, willing to treat Cora as a sexual object to be possessed. Because of this pettiness, this author is often driven to unmake events within the novel. Yet, as the end of this passage suggests, he does not have the power to reconfigure the relations between his characters fundamentally, and often his interventions are merely momentary interruptions.

Cora is murdered early in the novel, and much of the plot concerns the attempts by Canada and the author to come to terms with her death. Cora's death is part of the novel's larger concern for fragmentation in our understanding of others. Major echoes Donald Barthelme and notes that "Fragments can be all we have" (17), but later describes his attempts to understand his characters in nonfragmentary ways: "I try not to see in segments. Cora is a whole. Canada is a whole. Dale attempts to be whole. He is whole regardless of my inability to see him whole. Like the others he is living tissue" (123). The novel's nostalgia for a time before Cora's death is also nostalgia for a time without fragmentation. The author is, however, unable to escape from fragmentation—"I find everything I touch falling to pieces, and the pieces themselves continue to break into smaller and smaller segments" (50)—and the novel's final line describes fragmentation: "With my bare hands I break the phone. Canada is still talking to me through the pieces. I throw them on the floor and kick them" (145). Fragmentation arises from the fact that knowledge objectifies people. Major writes,

> Cora. She has sap.
>
> A tree. You can rub your saliva into its gray wood. Watch it turn purple. Then blue. And possibly even pink. Wood is often as pink as pussy. Still it remains essentially untouched. It is only when you begin to approach it technologically, as an object, a thing of utilitarian possibilities, that it falls to pieces. (16)

Major distinguishes between treating a person as an object and attempting to understand that person in a way that maintains his or her complexity and mystery. The novel appears to search for ways of achieving the latter, but also seems to be aware that the author's use of Cora as a character is essentially objectifying. Throughout the novel this objectification is associated with the process of repetition. After suggesting that spoken language is less objectifying ("When he read the words, speaking them to himself, they came closer to being the items themselves than the scribble—since the scribble itself had already achieved an entity, a concreteness, an independence" [43]), the novel associates the repeated use of a word with "breaking" it: "Say it a number of times. Watch what happens. The idea begins to break" (51). Such repetition appears to go hand in glove with the utilitarian use of an object.

Major seeks to challenge objectifying ways of knowing. His interest in complicating knowledge is clearest in how he insists on placing characters within space. Cora's name, after all, implies a hollow, hidden space—Hull. Major is not subtle in drawing out these spatial connotations: "Canada tries too hard sometimes. He tries to crack into Cora. Burst into Cora. Open Cora with his sledgehammer. But I weave *around* the stern cathedrals in her holy city, her very pure spirit" (2). Cora, likewise, is described as approaching the author and Canada "at [their] edges" (53). For Major, space complicates our definitions of individuals by emphasizing their continuity with the surrounding environment. Twice the author asks the same sort of question about the boundary line between self and world: "The space around me: who does it belong to" (17); "*What is my skin?* How do I live in it?" (87). Within the novel, spatiality is equivalent to material complexity. Whereas Cora is spatially complex ("Things fit into her" [119]), the much more abstract Dale is described as irreconcilable to space: "Here I am touching the words that touch his face and hands. They do not fit into the blank space that is Dale" (144). We should not, however, simply assume that abstraction is antithetical to material complexity. On the one hand, Major associates abstraction with fragmentation when he constructs a story of Cora from "known variables":

> You're ice skating in Canada. Your name is Cora. Your story is based on known variables. You want to be a successful actress but your agent—your agent?—yes, your agent, the author, tells you you are only an extrapolation. Your toilet training and intellectual experience are not in order. You need to clean up your act.
>
> You're figure skating near the border. You're arrested for being too fragmented. (92)

In this passage, Major associates an abstract "extrapolation" with the utilitarian understanding of characters as objects, an understanding that leads to the fragmentation for which the character is arrested at the end of this passage. On the other hand, Major suggests that one of Cora's principle strengths is her ability to believe in the abstract, in theoretical possibilities. Major writes, "She still believes in electronic scanners. I can testify to that! She believed in a lot of things and shit that people hadn't gotten around to even thinking about" (33), and shortly after remarks, "The *idea* of a person, from her point of view, was sacred" (33). How theoretical possibilities aid or hinder a complex understanding of others is one of the most important but paradoxical issues in *Reflex and Bone Structure*.

Surprisingly, Major associates theoretical possibilities and the body. Major brings these two ideas together perhaps most clearly in his discussion of pregnancy. Midway through the novel, pregnancy is described as a theoretical condition: "There is one thing that bugs Cora: the theory that she *can* be a mother. She has no real proof" (71). This idea is picked up a short time later by Canada: "Maybe, Cora, you've always been pregnant. Maybe all women are, from their beginning to forever, pregnant" (81). Canada's comment associates the theoretical possibility of the earlier passage with the specific physiological characteristics of Cora as a woman—the fact, we can suppose, that in possessing the ability to give birth to a child, she is already "pregnant" in the sense of owning such a potential. Thus, surprisingly, the theoretical is intimately connected to physical complexity. When individual objects are spatially and physically simple they can easily be treated as distinct and cut off from potential; when their physical complexity is recognized, they can open up onto new possible forms and encounters. Certainly the novel itself places a great deal of emphasis on articulating other possible narratives out of its constituent objects and characters. The following scene is typical of much of the novel's fantastic creation of potential scenes and events out of concrete objects. The author is surprised by Canada, who takes a gun from the kitchen drawer, and threatens him:

> Here I go into the gun manufacturing business. I have the boy working for me. Cora is the business manager. Just the thing for her. Dale runs the warehouse. Canada is the salesman, travels everywhere. When sales are down we all cry together. When the business is up we party. Throw big parties. Dance and get drunk. Stay up all night. We're secure. We're even advertised in *Field & Stream*.
>
> Late at night, I drive one of my own delivery trucks. I deliver thousands of pistols to Cora's apartment. Hide them all in the kitchen drawer. (9)

Scenes like this arise out of the actual objects that appear, and suggest alternative ways in which the narrative can be articulated and developed. As this passage makes clear, however, the objects that concern much of Major's alternative narratives are not particularly physically complex. Nowhere in this passage, for example, does Major suggest that the gun shares Cora's spatial complexity. Indeed, we come up against a fundamental paradox in this novel: despite their physical complexity, the characters often seem to be treated like objects; despite their utilitarian purposes, objects such as the gun appear to open up potential narratives. Major describes such potentials late in the novel: "Changes. Nothing seems to stop changing; things slide or bump into other things" (136). The idea that change occurs when "things" bump into each other is the opposite of the body's openness to potential that we just saw. On the one hand, we have the claim that all potentials arise out of objects; on the other hand, potential seems to arise only by recognizing a spatial complexity and refusing to treat objects as discrete.

This paradox is the key to Major's novel, and the point at which his interests most closely touch on Deleuzian ethical theory. Major summarizes this paradox as follows: "In one sense Cora has to wait for me to tell her what to do, what to think. She hasn't changed and, yet, she changes all the time, right under my fingertip" (107). The conflict in this passage is obvious: Cora is both an object constructed according to a purpose and, at the same time, something open to new articulations. Were Cora described simply as a body unable to be understood, or as open to new articulations by virtue of a physicality that refused to be defined, we might make sense of Major's novel as a more traditional call for recognition of the physical; in associating this potential nonetheless with distinct objects, Major confounds us. It is here that Deleuze's understanding of materiality in personal relations can illuminate the novel, as Major explains the idea of whole persons in post-deconstructive ethics. We will recall Deleuze's idea that individuals already contain virtual conjunctions within their essential "structure"; individuals express themselves through external actions that are also in some sense implicit within the structure of the individuals involved. Deleuze's idea that individuals interact not accidentally, but because of the "essence" of each and how it is able to manifest itself in these conjunctions is quite similar to the paradoxical transformations that we see in Major's novel. Interaction and transformation in *Reflex and Bone Structure* arise externally (things bumping up against each other) and internally (the spatial structure of Cora). The balance between internal structure and external confrontation also appears to be part of what Major has in mind in his title for the novel, *Reflex and Bone Structure*. The novel itself is about the reactions that result from character interaction, but it defines these reactions through an internal "bone structure." That this reaction does not simply reveal some internal truth is clear in the novel's one reference to actual bone structures: "Cora has an X-ray of her own brain, one of her heart, one of her vagina, I mean her womb; she also has a set of X-rays showing her bone structure. She has these things framed and they hang in the living room. Though other people do, she herself hardly notices them anymore" (104). As this passage suggests, internal structure interests characters, but it cannot serve as an ongoing gloss; as Deleuze might suggest, internal structure is crucial to external "conjunctions" but is constantly changing. This fundamental paradox between internal and external sources for one's "essence" helps to explain the ubiquity of fragmentation in Major's novel. If the process of differentiation and change is based upon internal structures, it nonetheless manifests itself as a series of objects external to each other. Thus, an individual is continuously subjected to various differentiations that reflect different personal "essences," thus fragmenting him or her into many selves.

This image of fragmentation is essential to the complex materiality of objects understood by post-deconstructive narrative, and is the hallmark of the ethics implied by Major. Adam Zachary Newton sees in Levinas an alternative to traditional ways of thinking about ethics, and uses the interaction between subject and object that I discussed in chapter 1 to describe an ethics of the "binding claim excised by a concrete and singular other" (12). Newton suggests a fundamental affinity between this ethical claim and narrative itself: "narrative situations create an immediacy and force, framing relations of provocation, call, and response that bind narrator and listener, author and character, or reader and text" (13). It should be clear from my discussion, however, that Major is thinking about narrative in ethics not as another instance of the responsibility of self to other, but as a way to understand the inevitable loss of that concrete other.[8] It might be easy to see in Major's description of Cora as fragmented an acceptance of a valueless deconstruction that sees no meaning as stable. Yet, the novel is profoundly concerned with Cora's meaning. Indeed, the author attempts to construct a positive meaning for Cora, rather than focusing on her fragmentation: "I'm a detective trying to solve a murder. No, not a murder. It's a life" (32). Major suggests that one understands a whole individual (a life) in retrospect, and out of a certain homage to the fragmented person. The homage to the lost person that Major embraces helps to make the process of fragmentation meaningful. Major's characters, we can say, attempt to reconstruct a kind of *narrative* of fragmentation through which they can understand Cora. These fragmented subjects echo Walter Benjamin's description of allegorical art as a kind of "ruin" that points beyond itself back to the beauty that has decayed. Both describe an object whose fragmentation embodies its history and keeps our attention on the present ruin and the past whole entity. Benjamin writes, "In the ruin history has physically merged into the setting. And in this guise history does not assume the form of the process of an eternal life so much as that of irresistible decay. Allegory thereby declares itself to be beyond beauty. Allegories are, in the realm of thoughts, what ruins are in the realm of things" (177–78). Both Benjamin's ruins and Major's fragmented characters draw our attention to the history contained within decay, and both describe an attraction "beyond beauty" that compels others to understand that process of decay. Major's "ruined" characters call us to give meaning to their lives, and in the process suggest the outline of a post-deconstructive ethics. Major discovers the importance of presupposing a whole subject before fragmentation for exactly the same reason that post-colonial criticism makes reference to whole, extra-textual entities. Both Major's novel and this criticism see in the whole object an opportunity to make discursive slippages and conflicts meaningful. Major's characters never achieve a fixed and universalizable system of interpersonal relations, but in retrospect they attempt to understand Cora and the nature of their relations to her. These relations are filtered through what we might see as traditional ethical dicta—that the characters attempt to understand her in a full, whole way and that they make amends for the way in which they have contributed to fragmentation and manipulation—but they nonetheless refuse to grant to Cora or themselves self-consciousness of their actions. Rather, the characters are left with a degree of guilt and fondness which, we sense, will always be mixed and recognized after the fact.

Major's novel and the Deleuzian reading of it that I have offered here in some ways merely repeat the conclusions of the previous section. Individuals interact by recognizing a complex materiality in others, and by following out the virtual relations that result. Nonetheless, Major also challenges us to recognize that others do exist apart from how they enter into "conjunctions" with us—even if we can never understand them in terms other than these conjunctions. Major suggests that any attempt to understand fragmentation will always be temporal and retrospective, a kind of narrative constructed to create ethical responsibility. Equally important, Major suggests that thinking about ethics after deconstruction cannot be done except as a kind of textuality, by taking narrative into account. Only in narrative do we find a way of using the philosophical paradoxes that deconstruction raises in a productive way through the figure of materiality.

Conclusions

Major's novel embodies the complex textuality that I have associated throughout this study with writing after deconstruction. It is an understanding of writing that accepts practically everything that we associate with deconstruction—the loss of subjectivity, the inadequacy of representation, and the slippage of meaning within language. At the same time, Major's novel struggles constantly not to allow these negatives to become the whole story. No work that we have considered better conveys the mixture of loss, anxiety, stubbornness, and hope that characterizes the emotional atmosphere of writing after deconstruction.

What Major articulates in response to this atmosphere is what we have seen over and over through this book: narrative. Major finds a value in narrating the story of the loss of Cora, not as a simple remembrance or as a way to fix her identity, but precisely as a productive enactment of the deconstructive contradictions that surround her. This is not an image of narration that conforms to the naive belief in traditional ethical responsibility that I identified with some critics of deconstruction and postmodernism in chapter 1. For those critics, the only possible response to deconstruction seems to be a return to insistently "local" writing, with a recognizable author taking responsibility for his or her writing, and endowing the whole with moral force. Throughout this study we have seen that narrative does bring with it a certain ethical power when it responds to deconstruction, but that the nature of that relation and power is considerably more complex than these critics suggested. Post-deconstructive narrative does indeed respond to an object or text from a very specific local "site," but in doing so it merely opens the text up to new articulations and to new forms of critique. We have no better example of how narrative responds to these contradictions than the title of Major's novel: *Reflex and Bone Structure*. Major discovers in the nature of the characters and situations themselves—their "bone structure"—the seeds of new articulations and new responses or "reflexes" in regard to them. The movement that we see here from object, to material complexity, to new articulation is a dynamic that has run throughout post-deconstructive criticism and fiction.

This dynamic is both a new way of thinking about writing and itself a rearticulation of deconstruction. Like Major's response to Cora, critics find in deconstruction the seeds of a new critical method that may or may not have been there all along. Narrative is both a rearticulation and a transformation of deconstruction, both "bone structure" and "reflex." It is precisely this complex temporal and textual relationship that is the condition of narrative after deconstruction.

notes

—◆—

Preface

1. See in particular Paul de Man's "Rhetoric of Temporality" (*Blindness* 187–228).

2. See Vincent B. Leitch's discussion of Derrida's midcareer interest in the "assault on the institution of style" (25–37).

Chapter 1. The Narrative Turn

1. On narrative in the "linguistic turn" see Richard T. Vann.

2. See Janice Carlisle for a helpful overview of the emergence of *narrative* as a concept in contemporary criticism, especially as coupled to *culture* as a way to talk about traditional appeals to coherence and control.

3. In this sense, this project is not an attempt to revisit narrative concepts in the light of deconstruction. Such a task has been handled well in books by Andrew Gibson (*Towards*) and Mark Currie. Instead, this book examines narrative as a broad theoretical model for thinking about writing and criticism.

4. On the importance of narrative's poles of enunciation in language games, see Alex Segal.

5. Bill Readings describes a similar tension between mutually necessary but heterogeneous discursive systems in Jean-François Lyotard's first major work, *Discours, figure:*

> In insisting that through reference language encounters "the depth of the visible," Lyotard does not argue against de Saussure that things have a real pre-linguistic meaning. Rather, the capacity of language to point, to refer, to

indicate, is not itself a matter of meaning. Pointing, the referential or indicative function, is both necessary to and disruptive of signification. That is to say, it is *figural*. Reference does not introduce language to a reality that cannot be signified; rather reference and deixis as linguistic functions of pointing cannot be reduced to signification because they introduce to the functioning of language a difference which cannot be reduced to oppositionality. (14; citing Lyotard, *Discours* 27)

6. On this shift as applied specifically to issues of plot, see Ruth Ronen ("Paradigm").

Chapter 2. Deconstruction and the Worldly Text

1. On the importance of such spatial language, see Kathleen M. Kirby.

2. Often the claim that deconstruction has no relation to, or interest in, the outside world is based on a misinterpretation of Jacques Derrida's famous claim that there is nothing outside of the text (*il n'y a pas de hors-texte*). For a discussion of this misreading and the context of Derrida's comment, see Jeffrey T. Nealon (57).

3. Gregory Ulmer's emphasis on Derridian allegory appears explicitly in "The Object of Post-Criticism."

4. In *The Use of Pleasure*, for example, Michel Foucault describes how individuals participate in discursive structures to "transform themselves, to change themselves in their singular being, and to make their life into an *oeuvre* that carries certain aesthetic values and meets certain stylistic criteria" (10–11). This image of individuals participating within the construction of being has offered many critics an alternative to Foucault's earlier theory of power's "inscription" of individual bodies.

5. Actually, one might argue that the same is true of Foucault's later work. Gilles Deleuze argues that Foucault's idea of space undergoes a fundamental change: "For a long time Foucault thought of the outside as being an ultimate spatiality that was deeper than time; but in his late works he offers the possibility once more of putting time on the outside as being time, conditioned by the fold" (*Foucault* 108). Deleuze's theory of the "folding" of space in Foucault's last work echoes the spatial multiplicity that I have described in Derrida.

6. In fact, at one point in *Specters*, Derrida mentions "Ousia and Grammē" as an essay that examines the temporality of "spectralizing" and the creation of the "'non-sensuous' thing" (155).

Chapter 3. The Search for Form in American Postmodern Fiction

1. Raymond Federman, for example, notes, "A friend of mine once described my books to me in a letter as long tenor sax solos. The language of my novels just goes on and on, improvising as it goes along, hitting wrong notes all the time—but, after all, jazz also built itself on a system of wrong chords that the player stumbles upon and then builds from" (LeClair and McCaffery 131). Reed discusses jazz in his interview with John O'Brien (Bellamy 131).

2. Typical of the degree to which American postmodernist writers embrace such principles is Ronald Sukenick's interview comments about character: "What's happening actually is that I'm making up my character. I mean, I'm really a very amorphous individual, as a matter of fact. That's a true admission—that I'm an amorphous individual. And what happens when I write is that I'm making myself up. . . . I really believe that we have an enormous need to dissolve our character structures" (Bellamy 61). Here, clearly Sukenick both offers a critique of our usual ways of thinking about character and subjectivity, but subordinates that critique to the positive goal of *creating* a self through writing.

3. For a more recent articulation of postmodernism that continues to follow the pattern laid down by Linda Hutcheon, see Joseph Francese.

4. A number of critics have recently argued that defining the term *postmodernism* usually involves constructing an earlier period (modernism) in a very interested and limited way. For a summary of this argument and the ways in which postmodernism has been defined, see John Frow. Much the same thing seems to occur in the distinction between reflexive and historical postmodernism, where the former is delimited (often by accusing it of being a version of late *modernism*) in order to explain the meaning and relevance of the latter.

5. The idea of defining narrative after deconstruction through self-reflexive contemporary runs counter to trends within recent criticism, which has tended to associate Hutcheon's historical strain of postmodernism with the "narrative turn." See Jay Clayton.

6. Joseph Frank writes, "For Lessing . . . aesthetic form is not an external arrangement provided by a set of traditional rules. Rather, it is the relation between the sensuous nature of the art medium and the conditions of human perception" (9).

7. See, for example, Sukenick, "The Underground Rears Its Ugly Head."

8. For examples of how this issue of "unwriting" appears in Sukenick's critical essays, see the notion of "Degenerative Prose" in Sukenick's "Narrative Thinking v. Conglomerate Culture" essay, and of "unwriting" directly in the essay of the same name.

Chapter 4. A General or Limited Narrative Theory?

1. Paul de Man's *Allegories of Reading* is typical of much deconstructive criticism when it suggests that some works are more rigorous and hence more appropriate for deconstruction: "The deconstruction is not something we have added to the text but it constituted the text in the first place. A literary text simultaneously asserts and denies the authority of its own rhetorical model, and by reading the text as we did we are only trying to come closer to being as rigorous a reader as the author had to be in order to write the sentence in the first place" (17).

2. Raymond Federman's novel is not paginated and has text only on every other page (the other pages are taken up by drawings of boxes made up of simple lines that are added, one per page, across the course of the narrative). For convenience I will refer to the first page of text as "1" and number only the pages on which text appears.

3. Although Wayne C. Booth does note the limitations of the term *point of view* (149), and certainly does introduce issues that cannot be reduced to this spatial distance (e.g., the scene and summary distinction [154]), his most enduring contribution has been to foreground the issue of the "perspective" of telling and the relations between author and narrator as crucial to aesthetic response in reading.

4. Booth does address the temporality of fiction in discussing issues such as the "ordering of intensities" of the reader's emotional involvement (60–64), but the temporality of the literary work has been most fully exploited by "reader response" narratologists who have followed up and extended Booth's insights. Such temporal theories will be discussed in chapter 6.

5. Actually, Michael Spencer defines two problems: the one noted here of the position of form inside or outside of the text, and "following on from this . . . it seems to have occurred to nobody before W. J. T. Mitchell that there might be several kinds of spatial form" (187). The issue of multiple types of spatial form will be taken up directly in the next section.

Chapter 5. Resisting Post-Deconstructive Space

1. In his otherwise scathing attack on Jean Baudrillard, Christopher Norris remarks, "Now one could hardly deny that Baudrillard's diagnosis does have a bearing on our present situation in the 'advanced' Western democracies. That is to say, it speaks directly to a widespread sense that we are living in a world of pervasive unreality, a world where perceptions are increasingly shaped by mass-media imagery, political rhetoric and techniques of wholesale disinformation that substitute for any kind of reasoned public debate" (*What's* 171).

2. We should note that David Harvey's model refuses to grant primacy to space in Baudrillard's sense. Harvey's concern for the lessening of distance in production and consumption (e.g., the internationalization of available products in everyday supermarkets) implies that postmodernity suppresses space as well as time.

3. Empedocles formulates the combination and separation of these four elements, for example, in terms of love and hate: "And these never cease their continuous exchange, sometimes uniting under the influence of Love so that all become One, at other times again each moving apart through the hostile force of Hate" (Empedocles fragment, cited in Sambursky 17).

4. The urge to describe matter through abstractions is almost as old as the idea of matter itself; Aristotle, for example, distinguishes material elements from the forms toward which they "incline": "Surely, the form cannot tend towards itself, for it does not come short of itself; and a contrary cannot tend to it, for contraries are mutually destructive. But as the female or the ugly inclines to the male or to the beautiful (albeit not essentially but incidentally), so what [naturally] tends to a form is matter" (22). For Aristotle, matter merely fills up forms, which themselves are what we recognize within the world. In associating her principle characters with fire, earth, air, and water, Janet Kauffman, conversely, treats matter as manifesting itself in various ways that we can recognize directly within the world.

Chapter 6. Reading Time

1. See Terry Beers's claim that reader response criticism is often dependent for its practical interpretive methods on inherited New Critical assumptions.

2. Note, however, Wolfgang Iser's response to Stanley Fish's critique

in *Diacritics*, where Iser appears to shift ground and emphasize the text's individual words as the starting point of analysis ("Talk" 85), rather than speaking about textual entities.

3. On Kathy Acker's reworking of William Gibson, see Brian McHale (*Constructing* 233–36).

4. Typical is a comment in *Don Quixote:* "I want you. . . . I don't want just another affair, fantasy. All that romance, cause the mind always changes its thoughts, is peripheral. I want something beyond. I want you" (134). Passages such as this clearly suggest that the romantic strivings of Acker's characters ultimately rest upon the larger philosophical problem of the gap between self and other.

5. Such sites need not be tied to the body. In chapter 2 I quoted Elspeth Probyn, who describes the home as such a site: "the concept of 'locale' will be used to designate a place that is the setting for a particular event. I take this 'place' as both a discursive and nondiscursive arrangement which holds a gendered event, the home being the most obvious example" ("Travels" 178).

6. The recent work by Probyn and others has begun to formulate sites in such open-ended terms. See Probyn, "Queer Belongings." I would like to thank Kate Cummings for drawing my attention to this more open-ended, Deleuzoguattarian model of the site in Probyn's recent work.

Chapter 7. Struggling with Objects

1. See, for example, Rey Chow's excellent discussion of materiality and ethics in Gayatri Chakravorty Spivak and Slavoj Žižek.

2. Chandra Talpade Mohanty herself uses Michel Foucault to analyze the kind of "abstraction" at work in Western feminist discourse (350). Abdul R. JanMohamed's "Humanism and Minority Literature" is probably the best example of how Gilles Deleuze's work on "minor literature" is used to define an antihegemonic approach to third-world literatures.

3. Also see Philippe Hamon's discussion of architecture within French realist literature, which he suggests is a point at which the artificiality of literary construction becomes obvious: "it is as if the artifice of literature (an articulated semiotic ensemble that produces meaning) possessed a structural complicity or deep preestablished homology with that very thing whose existence in reality is *already* artificial: namely the building (an articulated semiotic ensemble that produces space)" (*Expositions* 6).

4. The first story in the collection by Steve Katz, "Female Skin," is about writing a story; the second, "Parcel of Wrists," is a somewhat

more traditional but uncanny story told without explicit metafictional reference; the third story, "Trip," is more traditionally autobiographical, and the final story, "43," is primarily collage.

5. This is even more explicit in the story that follows "Parcel of Wrists" in *Moving Parts*. In this story, "Trip," Katz rewrites the trip in "Parcel of Wrists" from an apparently nonfictional perspective, and emphasizes in particular the reappearance of the number forty-three throughout the trip. See also the fourth and final story in the novel, titled "43," which discusses directly the author's interest in this number.

6. Although perhaps somewhat disingenuous, Edward W. Said remarks in his afterword to *Orientalism*, "among American and British academics of a decidedly rigorous and unyielding stripe, *Orientalism*, and indeed all of my other work, has come in for disapproving attacks because of its 'residual' humanism, its theoretical inconsistencies, its insufficient, perhaps even sentimental, treatment of agency. I am glad that it has!" (339).

Chapter 8. Narrative and Post-Deconstructive Ethics

1. Theodore R. Schatzki criticizes Jean-François Lyotard in these terms:

> Lyotard's notion that wrongs are signaled by feelings is both too broad and too narrow. It is too broad because people have and share feelings for many reasons, including spite, envy, and ignorance, and at least some feelings presumably also have physiological causes. So feelings, including those we have difficulty expressing, do not always signal hegemony and oppression. His notion is too narrow, on the other hand, because wrongs emanating from hegemony and oppression are not always signaled by feelings, for example, when the people suffering them are not aware of the hegemony and oppression at work. (58)

2. This reaction to poststructuralist thought is common. See, for example, John M. Ellis's critique of deconstruction as failing to provide a logic that will function as an alternative to logocentrism (41), a critique that merely reinscribes deconstruction into the demands of traditional logical thought.

3. Note in this section that I will treat Gilles Deleuze as the source for most of my discussion of interpersonal relations, even though much of the work I will draw on was done in partnership with Félix Guattari. Clearly, distinguishing between the contributions of each to Deleuzoguattarian thought is beyond the scope of this section. I choose to emphasize Deleuze as the source for this chapter because his individual

philosophical work on Benedict de Spinoza and Henri Bergson are the starting points for this ethics.

4. Although Deleuze's reading of Spinoza may seem to call for a vulgar Nietzscheanism of the will to power, the complex dependence of self and other that Deleuze describes changes how we must think of power in this context. Michael Hardt explains this distinction in discussing Deleuze's book on Friedrich Nietzsche: "The entire discussion of power has little to do with strength or capacity, but with the relation between essence and manifestation, between power and what it can do. What Nietzsche contributes to this discourse on power is an evaluation—he judges the power internal to its manifestation as noble" (36).

5. Deleuze and Félix Guattari describe this distinction in *A Thousand Plateaus:*

> [W]e distinguish between arborescent multiplicities and rhizomatic multiplicities. Between macro- and micromultiplicities. On the one hand, multiplicities that are extensive, divisible, and molar; unifiable, totalizable, organizable; conscious or preconscious—and on the other hand, libidinal, unconscious, molecular, intensive multiplicities composed of particles that do not divide without changing in nature, and distances that do not vary without entering another multiplicity and that constantly construct and dismantle themselves in the course of their communications, as they cross over into each other at, beyond, or before a certain threshold. The elements of this second kind of multiplicity are particles; their relations are distances; their movements are Brownian; their quantities are intensities, differences in intensity. (33)

6. We should note, of course, that a number of critics that I have quoted in chapter 1 themselves draw on Deleuze's work. In particular, see Elizabeth Grosz's discussion of Deleuze's notion of "becoming woman" and "desiring machines" (*Volatile* 160–83).

7. Clarence Major describes Dale, for example, as a constructor of plots: "I cannot help him if he refuses to focus. How can I be blamed for his lack of seriousness. And it isn't that he doesn't talk to me. He talks too much to me, really, and he plots to much, has too many secrets, leaves nothing in the open. Whatever it was about him that attracted Cora shall always remain a mystery to me" (42).

8. See also Andrew Gibson, who likewise describes Levinas as a way to link narrative and ethics through "participation" (*Postmodernity* 31). To his credit, Newton recognizes the loss associated with this ethics: "'getting' someone else's story is also a way of losing the person as 'real,' as 'what he is'; it is a way of appropriating or allegorizing that endangers both intimacy and ethical duty" (19). Major makes clear that this loss is precisely what makes ethics narrative.

works cited

Abish, Walter. "The Writer-to-Be: An Impression of Living." *Substance* 27 (1980): 101–14.

Acker, Kathy. *The Childlike Life of the Black Tarantula by the Black Tarantula. Portrait of an Eye: Three Novels.* New York: Pantheon, 1992. 1–90.

———. *Don Quixote: Which Was a Dream.* New York: Grove, 1986.

———. *Empire of the Senseless.* New York: Grove, 1988.

———. *Great Expectations.* New York: Grove, 1982.

———. *Hannibal Lecter, My Father.* New York: Semiotext(e), 1991.

———. *In Memoriam to Identity.* New York: Grove, 1990.

———. *My Mother: Demonology.* New York: Grove, 1993.

Althusser, Louis. *Lenin and Philosophy and Other Essays.* Trans. Ben Brewster. New York: Monthly Review Press, 1971.

Aristotle. *Aristotle's Physics.* Trans. Richard Hope. Lincoln: University of Nebraska Press, 1961.

Auster, Paul. *Art of Hunger: Essays, Prefaces, Interviews and The Red Notebook.* New York: Penguin, 1993.

Baudrillard, Jean. *America.* Trans. Chris Turner. London: Verso, 1988.

———. *Seduction.* Trans. Brian Singer. New York: St. Martin's, 1990.

———. *Selected Writings.* Ed. Mark Poster. Stanford: Stanford University Press, 1988.

Beaujour, Michel. "Some Paradoxes of Description." *Yale French Studies* 61 (1981): 27–59.

Beers, Terry. "Reading Reading Constraints: Conventions, Schemata, and Literary Interpretation." *Diacritics* 18.4 (1988): 82–93.

Bellamy, Joe David. *The New Fiction: Interviews with Innovative American Writers.* Urbana: University of Illinois Press, 1974.

Benhabib, Seyla. "Feminism and Postmodernism." *Feminist Contentions: A Philosophical Exchange.* Eds. Seyla Benhabib et al. New York: Routledge, 1995. 17–34.

———. "Epistemologies of Postmodernism: A Rejoinder to Jean-François Lyotard." Nicholson 107–30.

Benjamin, Walter. *The Origin of German Tragic Drama.* Trans. John Osborne. London: Verso, 1977.

Bhabha, Homi K. "DisseemiNation: Time, Narrative, and the Margins of the Modern Nation." Bhabha 291–22.

———, ed. *Nation and Narration.* New York: Routledge, 1990.

Booth, Wayne C. *The Rhetoric of Fiction.* 2d ed. Chicago: University of Chicago Press, 1983.

Bordo, Susan. "Feminism, Postmodernism, and Gender-Scepticism." Nicholson 133–56.

Boundas, Constantin V. and Dorothea Olkowski, eds. *Gilles Deleuze and the Theater of Philosophy.* New York: Routledge, 1994.

Braidotti, Rosi. *Nomadic Subjects: Embodiment and Sexual Difference in Contemporary Feminist Theory.* New York: Columbia University Press, 1994.

———. "Toward a New Nomadism: Feminist Deleuzian Tracks; or, Metaphysics and Metabolism." Boundas and Olkowski 159–86.

Brennan, Karen. "The Geography of Enunciation: Hysterical Pastiche in Kathy Acker's Fiction." *Boundary* 2.21 (1994): 243–68.

Butler, Judith. *Bodies that Matter: On the Discursive Limits of "Sex."* New York: Routledge, 1993.

Calinescu, Matei. *Rereading.* New Haven: Yale University Press, 1993.

Caramello, Charles. *Silverless Mirrors: Book, Self & Postmodern American Fiction.* Tallahassee: Florida State University Press, 1983.

Carlisle, Janice. Introduction. Carlisle and Schwarz 1–12.

Carlisle, Janice and Daniel R. Schwarz, eds. *Narrative and Culture.* Athens: University of Georgia Press, 1994.

Chow, Rey. "Ethics after Idealism." *Diacritics* 23.1 (1993): 3–22.

Clayton, Jay. "The Narrative Turn in Minority Fiction." Carlisle and Schwarz 58–76.

Cole, Steven E. "The Scrutable Subject: Davidson, Literary Theory, and the Claims of Knowledge." *Literary Theory after Davidson.* Ed. Reed Way Dasenbrock. University Park: Pennsylvania State University Press, 1993. 59–91.

Connor, Steven. *Postmodernist Culture: An Introduction to Theories of the Contemporary.* London: Basil Blackwell, 1989.

Cornis-Pope, Marcel. "Narrative (Dis)articulation and the *Voice in the Closet* Complex in Raymond Federman's Fictions." *Critique* 29 (1988): 77–93.

———. "Narrative Innovation and Cultural Rewriting: The Pynchon-Morrison-Sukenick Connection." Carlisle and Schwarz 216–37.

Currie, Mark. *Postmodern Narrative Theory.* New York: St. Martin's, 1998.

Davenport, Guy. *Every Force Evolves a Form.* San Francisco: North Point Press, 1987.

de Certeau, Michel. *The Practice of Everyday Life.* Trans. Steven Rendall. Berkeley: University of California Press, 1984.

de Lauretis, Teresa. "Feminist Studies/Critical Studies: Issues, Terms, and Contexts." *Feminist Studies/Critical Studies.* Ed. Teresa de Lauretis. Bloomington: Indiana University Press, 1986. 1–19.

de Man, Paul. *Allegories of Reading: Figural Language in Rousseau, Nietzsche, Rilke, and Proust.* New Haven: Yale University Press, 1979.

———. *Blindness and Insight: Essays in the Rhetoric of Contemporary Criticism.* 2d ed. rev. Minneapolis: University of Minnesota Press, 1983.

Deaton, Rebecca. Interview with Kathy Acker. *Textual Practice* 6 (1992): 271–82.

Deleuze, Gilles. *Bergsonism.* Trans. Hugh Tomlinson and Barbara Habberjam. New York: Zone Books, 1991.

———. *Expressionism in Philosophy: Spinoza.* Trans. Martin Joughin. New York: Zone Books, 1990.

———. *Foucault.* Trans. Seán Hand. Minneapolis: University of Minnesota Press, 1988.

Deleuze, Gilles and Félix Guattari. *Anti-Oedipus: Capitalism and Schizophrenia.* Trans. Robert Hurley, Mark Seem, and Helen R. Lane. Minneapolis: University of Minnesota Press, 1983.

———. *A Thousand Plateaus: Capitalism and Schizophrenia.* Trans. Brian Massumi. Minneapolis: University of Minnesota Press, 1987.

Derrida, Jacques. *Archive Fever: A Freudian Impression.* Trans. Eric Prenowitz. Chicago: University of Chicago Press, 1996.

———. *La Dissémination.* Paris: Éditions du Seuil, 1972.

———. *Dissemination.* Trans. Barbara Johnson. Chicago: University of Chicago Press, 1981.

———. *L'écriture et la différance.* Paris: Éditions du Seuil, 1967.

———. *Edmund Husserl's "Origin of Geometry": An Introduction.* Trans. John P. Leavey. Lincoln: University of Nebraska Press, 1978.

———. *Margins of Philosophy.* Trans. Alan Bass. Chicago: University of Chicago Press, 1982.

———. *Of Grammatology.* Trans. Gayatri Chakrovorty Spivak. Baltimore: Johns Hopkins University Press, 1976.

———. *The Other Heading: Reflections on Today's Europe.* Trans. Pascale-Anne Brault and Michael B. Naas. Bloomington: Indiana University Press, 1992.

———. *Positions.* Trans. Alan Bass. Chicago: University of Chicago Press, 1981.

———. *Specters of Marx: The State of Debt, the Work of Mourning, and the New International.* Trans. Peggy Kamuf. New York: Routledge, 1994.

———. *Speech and Phenomena and Other Essays on Husserl's Theory of Signs.* Trans. David B. Allison. Evanston, IL: Northwestern University Press, 1973.

———. *Writing and Difference.* Trans. Alan Bass. Chicago: University of Chicago Press, 1978.

Dillon, M. C. *Merleau-Ponty's Ontology.* Bloomington: Indiana University Press, 1988.

Diprose, Rosalyn. *The Bodies of Women: Ethics, Embodiment and Sexual Difference.* New York: Routledge, 1994.

Dirlik, Arif. "Culturalism as Hegemonic Ideology and Liberating Practice." *The Nature and Context of Minority Discourse.* Eds. Abdul R. JanMohamed and David Lloyd. New York: Oxford University Press, 1990. 394–431.

Dowling, David. "Raymond Federman's America: Take it or Leave It." *Contemporary Literature* 30 (1989): 348–69.

Dufrenne, Mikel. *The Phenomenology of Aesthetic Experience.* Trans. Edward S. Casey. Evanston, IL: Northwestern University Press, 1973.

Dunn, Allen. "A Tyranny of Justice: The Ethics of Lyotard's Differend." *Boundary* 2.20 (1993): 192–220.

During, Simon. "Literature—Nationalism's Other? The Case for Revision." Bhabha 138–53.

Eagelton, Terry. *Literary Theory: An Introduction.* Oxford: Basil Blackwell, 1983.

Ellis, John M. *Against Deconstruction.* Princeton: Princeton University Press, 1989.

Federman, Raymond. "Surfiction—Four Propositions in Form of an Introduction." *Surfiction: Fiction Now . . . and Tomorrow.* Ed. Raymond Federman. Chicago: Swallow, 1975. 5–15.

———. *The Voice in the Closet.* Madison, WI: Station Hill Press, 1979.

Fish, Stanley. *Is There a Text in This Class? The Authority of Interpretive Communities.* Cambridge: Harvard University Press, 1980.

———. "Why No One's Afraid of Wolfgang Iser." *Diacritics* 11.1 (1981): 2–13.

Flax, Jane. "Postmodernism and Gender Relations in Feminist Theory." Nicholson 39–62.

Foucault, Michel. *The Archaeology of Knowledge and The Discourse on Language.* Trans. A. M. Sheridan Smith. New York: Pantheon, 1972.

————. *Discipline and Punish: The Birth of the Prison*. Trans. Alan Sheridan. New York: Vintage, 1979.

————. *Language, Counter-Memory, Practice: Selected Essays and Interviews*. Trans. Donald F. Bouchard and Sherry Simon. Ithaca, NY: Cornell University Press, 1977.

————. *The Use of Pleasure*. Trans. Robert Hurley. New York: Vintage, 1990.

Francese, Joseph. *Narrating Postmodern Time and Space*. Albany: State University of New York Press, 1997.

Frank, Joseph. *The Idea of Spatial Form*. New Brunswick: Rutgers University Press, 1991.

Fraser, Nancy and Linda J. Nicholson. "Social Criticism without Philosophy: An Encounter between Feminism and Postmodernism." Nicholson 19–38.

Friedman, Ellen G. "A Conversation with Kathy Acker." *Review of Contemporary Fiction* 9.3 (1989): 12–22.

————. "'Now Eat Your Mind': An Introduction to the Works of Kathy Acker." *Review of Contemporary Fiction* 9.3 (1989): 37–49.

Frow, John. *Time and Commodity Culture: Essays in Cultural Theory and Postmodernity*. Oxford: Clarendon Press, 1997.

Frye, Nothrop. *Anatomy of Criticism: Four Essays*. Princeton: Princeton University Press, 1957.

Gasché, Rodolphe. *The Tain of the Mirror: Derrida and the Philosophy of Reflection*. Cambridge: Harvard University Press, 1986.

Gass, William H. *Fiction and the Figures of Life*. Boston: David R. Godine, 1979.

————. *The World Within the Word*. Boston: David R. Godine, 1978.

Gelley, Alexander. "Metonymy, Schematism, and the Space of Literature." *New Literary History* 11 (1980): 469–87.

Genette, Gérard. *Figures II*. Paris: Éditions du Seuil, 1969.

————. *Narrative Discourse: An Essay in Method*. Trans. Jane E. Lewin. Ithaca, NY: Cornell University Press, 1980.

Gibson, Andrew. *Postmodernity, Ethics and the Novel: From Leavis to Levinas*. London: Routledge, 1999.

————. *Towards a Postmodern Theory of Narrative*. Edinburgh, Scotland: Edinburgh University Press, 1996.

Gibson, William. *Neuromancer*. New York: Ace Books, 1984.

Grosz, Elizabeth. "A Thousand Tiny Sexes: Feminism and Rhizomatics." Boundas and Olkowski 187–210.

————. *Volatile Bodies: Towards a Corporeal Feminism*. Bloomington: Indiana University Press, 1994.

Gullón, Ricardo. "On Space in the Novel." *Critical Inquiry* 2 (1975): 11–28.

Haraway, Donna J. *Simians, Cyborgs, and Women: The Reinvention of Nature.* New York: Routledge, 1991.

Hamon, Philippe. *Expositions: Literature and Architecture in Nineteenth-Century France.* Trans. Katia Sainson-Frank and Lisa Maguire. Berkeley: University of California Press, 1992.

———. "Rhetorical Status of the Descriptive." *Yale French Studies* 61 (1981): 1–26.

Hardt, Michael. *Gilles Deleuze: An Apprenticeship in Philosophy.* Minneapolis: University of Minnesota Press, 1993.

Harper, Glenn A. "The Subversive Power of Sexual Difference in the Work of Kathy Acker." *Sub-Stance* 54 (1987): 44–56.

Harvey, David. *The Condition of Postmodernity: An Enquiry into the Origins of Cultural Change.* Cambridge, MA: Blackwell, 1989.

Hayles, N. Katherine. "Postmodern Parataxis: Embodied Texts, Weightless Information." *American Literary History* 2.3 (1990): 394–421.

Husserl, Edmund. *Cartesian Meditations: An Introduction to Phenomenology.* Trans. Dorion Cairns. Dordrecht, Netherlands: Martinus Nijhoff, 1960.

———. *Ideas: General Introduction to Pure Phenomenology.* Trans. W. R. Boyce Gibson. New York: Collier, 1962.

Hutcheon, Linda. *A Poetics of Postmodernism: History, Theory, Fiction.* New York: Routledge, 1988.

Ingarden, Roman. *The Literary Work of Art: An Investigation on the Borderlines of Ontology, Logic, and Theory of Literature.* Trans. George G. Grabowicz. Evanston, IL: Northwestern University Press, 1973.

Iser, Wolfgang. *The Act of Reading: A Theory of Aesthetic Response.* Baltimore: Johns Hopkins University Press, 1978.

———. "Talk Like Whales." *Diacritics* 11.3 (1981): 82–87.

Jameson, Fredric. *The Political Unconscious: Narrative as a Socially Symbolic Act.* Ithaca, NY: Cornell University Press, 1981.

———. *Postmodernism, or, The Cultural Logic of Late Capitalism.* Durham: Duke University Press, 1992.

JanMohamed, Abdul R. "Humanism and Minority Literature: Toward a Definition of Counter-Hegemonic Discourse." *Boundary* 2 12.3 and 13.1 (1984): 281–299.

———. "The Economy of Manichean Allegory: The Function of Racial Difference in Colonialist Literature." *Critical Inquiry* 12 (1985): 59–87.

Jay, Paul. "Bridging the Gap: The Position of Politics in Deconstruction." *Cultural Critique* 22 (1992): 47–74.

Johnson, Barbara. *The Critical Difference: Essays in the Contemporary Rhetoric of Reading.* Baltimore: Johns Hopkins University Press, 1980.

Johnson, Galen A. and Michael B. Smith, eds. *Ontology and Alterity in Merleau-Ponty*. Evanston, IL: Northwestern University Press, 1990.

Jones, LeRoi. Introduction. *The Moderns: An Anthology of New Writing in America*. Ed. LeRoi Jones. New York: Corinth Books, 1963. ix–xvi.

Katz, Steve. *Moving Parts*. New York: Fiction Collective, 1977.

Kauffman, Janet. *The Body in Four Parts*. St. Paul, MN: Graywolf Press, 1993.

Kellner, Douglas. *Media Culture: Cultural Studies, Identity and Politics between the Modern and the Postmodern*. New York: Routledge, 1995.

Kennedy, Colleen. "Simulating Sex and Imagining Mothers." *American Literary History* 4.1 (1992): 165–85.

Kerby, Anthony Paul. *Narrative and the Self*. Bloomington: Indiana University Press, 1991.

Kermode, Frank. "A Reply to Joseph Frank." *Critical Inquiry* 4 (1978): 579–88.

———. *The Sense of an Ending: Studies in the Theory of Fiction*. New York: Oxford University Press, 1967.

Kirby, Kathleen M. "Thinking through the Boundary: The Politics of Location, Subjects and Space." Boundary 2.20 (1993): 173–189.

Kittay, Jeffrey. "Descriptive Limits." *Yale French Studies* 61 (1981): 225–243.

Kripke, Saul A. *Naming and Necessity*. Cambridge: Harvard University Press, 1980.

Kristeva, Julia. *Powers of Horror: An Essay on Abjection*. Trans. Leon S. Roudiez. New York: Columbia University Press, 1982.

Langer, Susanne K. *Feeling and Form: A Theory of Art*. New York: Scribner's, 1953.

Leary, Timothy. "Quark of the Decade." *Mondo* 2000.7 (1990): 53–56.

LeClair, Tom and Larry McCaffery. *Anything Can Happen: Interviews with Contemporary American Novelists*. Urbana: Illinois University Press, 1983.

Leitch, Vincent B. *Postmodernism—Local Effects, Global Flows*. Albany: State University of New York Press, 1996.

Levinas, Emmanuel. "Intersubjectivity: Notes on Merleau-Ponty." Johnson and Smith 55–60.

———. "Sensibility." Johnson and Smith 60–66.

Lindsay, Cecile. "Experiments in Postmodern Dialogue." *Diacritics* 14.3 (1984): 52–62.

Lyotard, Jean-François. *The Differend: Phrases in Dispute*. Trans. Georges Van Den Abbeele. Minneapolis: University of Minnesota Press, 1988.

————. *Discours, figure*. Paris: Klincksieck, 1971.

————. *The Postmodern Condition: A Report on Knowledge*. Trans. Geoff Bennington and Brian Massumi. Minneapolis: University of Minnesota Press, 1984.

Major, Clarence. "A Meditation: Space and Time in Bamism." *Representation and Performance in Postmodern Fiction*. Ed. Maurice Couturier. Proceedings of the Nice Conference on Postmodern Fiction, 1982. 163–77.

————. *Reflex and Bone Structure*. New York: Fiction Collective, 1975.

Merleau-Ponty, Maurice. *The Visible and the Invisible*. Trans. Alphonso Lingis. Evanston, IL: Northwestern University Press, 1968.

McCaffery, Larry. "An Interview with Kathy Acker." *Mississippi Review* 20.1–2 (1991): 83–97.

McCormick, Kathleen. "Swimming Upstream with Stanley Fish." *Journal of Aesthetics and Art Criticism* 44 (1985): 67–76.

McGowan, John. *Postmodernism and Its Critics*. Ithaca, NY: Cornell University Press, 1991.

McHale, Brian. *Constructing Postmodernism*. New York: Routledge, 1992.

————. "Postmodernism, or the Anxiety of Master Narratives." *Diacritics* 22.1 (1992): 17–33.

————. *Postmodernist Fiction*. New York: Methuen, 1987.

Mitchell, W. J. T. "Spatial Form in Literature: Toward a General Theory." *Critical Inquiry* 6 (1980): 539–67.

————. *Iconology: Image, Text, Ideology*. Chicago: University of Chicago Press, 1986.

Mohanty, Chandra Talpade. "Under Western Eyes: Feminist Scholarship and Colonial Discourses." *Boundary* 2 12.3 and 13.1 (1984): 333–58.

Nealon, Jeffrey T. *Double Reading: Postmodernism after Deconstruction*. Ithaca, NY: Cornell University Press, 1993.

Newton, Adam Zachary. *Narrative Ethics*. Cambridge: Harvard University Press, 1995.

Nichols, Peter. "Divergences: Modernism, Postmodernism, Jameson and Lyotard." *Critical Quarterly* 33.3 (1991): 1–18.

Nicholson, Linda J., ed. *Feminism/Postmodernism*. New York: Routledge, 1990.

Norris, Christopher. *The Contest of Faculties: Philosophy and Theory after Deconstruction*. New York: Methuen, 1985.

————. *What's Wrong with Postmodernism*. Baltimore: Johns Hopkins University Press, 1990.

O'Brien, John. "An Interview with Gilbert Sorrentino." *Review of Contemporary Fiction* 1.1 (1981): 5–27.

Parry, Benita. "Problems in Current Theories of Colonial Discourse." *Oxford Literary Review* 9.1–2 (1987): 27–58.

Pavel, Thomas G. *Fictional Worlds*. Cambridge: Harvard University Press, 1986.

Phelan, James. *Reading People, Reading Plots: Character, Progression, and the Interpretation of Narrative*. Chicago: University of Chicago Press, 1989.

Poirier, Richard. *A World Elsewhere: The Place of Style in American Literature*. New York: Oxford University Press, 1966.

Probyn, Elspeth. "Queer Belongings: The Politics of Departure." *Sexy Bodies: The Strange Carnalities of Feminism*. Eds. Elizabeth Grosz and Elspeth Probyn. London: Routledge, 1995. 1–18.

———. "Travels in the Postmodern: Making Sense of the Local." Nicholson 176–189.

Propp, Vladimir. *Morphology of the Folktale*. Trans. Louis A. Wagner. Austin: University of Texas Press, 1968.

Rand, Richard, ed. *Futures: Of Jacques Derrida*. Stanford, CA: Stanford University Press, 2001.

Readings, Bill. *Introducing Lyotard: Art and Politics*. New York: Routledge, 1991.

Redding, Arthur F. "Bruises, Roses: Masochism and the Writing of Kathy Acker." *Contemporary Literature* 35 (1994): 281–304.

Ronen, Ruth. "Paradigm Shift in Plot Models: An Outline of the History of Narratology." *Poetics Today* 11 (1990): 817–42.

———. "Space in Fiction." *Poetics Today* 7 (1986): 421–38.

Rorty, Richard. "Habermas and Lyotard on Postmodernity." *Zeitgeist in Babel: The Postmodernist Controversy*. Ed. Ingeborg Hoesterey. Bloomington: Indiana University Press, 1991. 84–97.

Ross, Andrew. Introduction. Ross vii–xviii.

———, ed. *Universal Abandon?: The Politics of Postmodernism*. Minneapolis: University of Minnesota Press, 1988.

Said, Edward W. *Culture and Imperialism*. New York: Vintage, 1993.

———. *Orientalism*. New York: Vintage, 1994.

———. *The World, the Text, and the Critic*. Cambridge: Harvard University Press, 1983.

Sambursky, Samuel. *The Physical World of the Greeks*. Trans. Merton Dagut. Princeton: Princeton University Press, 1987.

Schatzki, Theodore R. "Theory at Bay: Foucault, Lyotard, and Politics of the Local." *Postmodern Contentions: Epochs, Politics, Space*. Eds. John Paul Jones III et al. New York: Guilford Press, 1993. 39–64.

Sciolino, Martina. "Kathy Acker and the Postmodern Subject of Feminism." *College English* 52 (1990): 437–45.

Segal, Alex. "Language Games and Justice." *Textual Practice* 6 (1992): 210–24.

Siegle, Robert. *Suburban Ambush: Downtown Writing and the Fiction of Insurgency.* Baltimore: Johns Hopkins University Press, 1989.

Soja, Edward W. *Postmodern Geographies: The Reassertion of Space in Critical Social Theory.* London: Verso, 1989.

———. *Thirdspace: Journeys to Los Angeles and Other Real-and-Imagined Places.* Malden, MA: Blackwell, 1996.

Spencer, Michael. "Spatial Form and Postmodernism." *Poetics Today* 5 (1984): 182–95.

Spivak, Gayatri Chakravorty. "Can the Subaltern Speak?" *Marxism and the Interpretation of Culture.* Eds. Cary Nelson and Lawrence Grossberg. Urbana: University of Illinois Press, 1988. 271–313.

Stephanson, Anders. "Regarding Postmodernism—A Conversation with Fredric Jameson." Ross 3–30.

Sternberg, Meir. *Expositional Modes and Temporal Ordering in Fiction.* Baltimore: Johns Hopkins University Press, 1978.

Sukenick, Ronald. *Blown Away.* Los Angeles: Sun and Moon, 1986.

———. *In Form: Digressions on the Act of Fiction.* Carbondale: Southern Illinois University Press, 1985.

———. "Narrative Thinking v. Conglomerate Culture." *Critical Quarterly* 37.4 (1995): 27–33.

———. "The Underground Rears Its Ugly Head." *American Book Review* 16.1 (1994): 1.

———. "Unwriting." *American Book Review* 13.5 (1991): 4.

Ulmer, Gregory. *Applied Grammatology: Post(e)-Pedagogy from Jacques Derrida to Joseph Beuys.* Baltimore: Johns Hopkins University Press, 1985.

———. "The Object of Post-Criticism." *The Anti-Aesthetic: Essays on Postmodern Culture.* Ed. Hal Foster. Port Townsend, WA: Bay Press, 1983. 83–110.

Vann, Richard T. "Turning Linguistic: History and Theory and History and Theory, 1960–1975." *A New Philosophy of History.* Eds. Frank Ankersmit and Hans Kellner. Chicago: University of Chicago Press, 1995. 40–69.

Vidan, Ivo. "Time Sequence in Spatial Fiction." *Spatial Form in Narrative.* Eds. Jeffrey R. Smitten and Ann Daghistany. Ithaca, NY: Cornell University Press, 1981. 131–57.

Weber, Samuel. "Objectivity Otherwise." *Objectivity and Its Other.* Eds. Wolfgang Natter et al. New York: Guilford Press, 1995. 33–47.

Weedon, Chris. *Feminist Practice & Poststructuralist Theory.* Oxford: Blackwell, 1987.

White, Hayden. *The Content of the Form: Narrative Discourse and Historical Representation.* Baltimore: Johns Hopkins University Press, 1987.

———. *Tropics of Discourse: Essays in Cultural Criticism.* Baltimore: Johns Hopkins University Press, 1978.

Žižek, Slavoj. *The Sublime Object of Ideology.* London: Verso, 1989.

Zoran, Gabriel. "Towards a Theory of Space in Narrative." *Poetics Today* 5 (1984): 309–35.

index